*To Thomas Corrigan Doyle, for fixing the plug onto
that first record-player and setting me on my way*

Contents

Introduction

The first time I met and interviewed Paul McCartney, unsettlingly, he kept on stealing distracted glances at his watch.

It's tough enough to consider the fact that you're interviewing the most famous musician on the planet, someone who was being interrogated by other writers before you were even born, but it's more disconcerting to realise that you're failing to engage a former Beatle and, as the old song goes, stop his mind from wandering.

The date was Monday, 15 May 2006, and the location was a photographer's studio in Kentish Town, north London, where McCartney was having his picture taken by his similarly mooneyed daughter Mary for one of a series of *Q* covers to mark the magazine's twentieth anniversary. I was there to talk to him about his experiences of the twenty years gone, their events and innovations.

During our half-hour-long conversation, I managed to keep him on-subject long enough to discuss everything from his eyewitness account of the immediate aftermath of 9/11 (parked on the tarmac at JFK Airport in a commercial jet that was suddenly going nowhere) to the fact that he couldn't really get with the iPod since headphones reminded him of work and being in the studio. He then revealed the surprising holes in his knowledge of Beatles history.

'I'm the world's worst analyst of me,' he reasoned brightly. 'Beatles fans can tell you exactly what was going on in the 1960s, and I kinda go, Oh yeah, that's right. I know *Sgt. Pepper* was 1967. I know that much.'

In many ways, he proved as affable, laidback and hey-whatever as I'd imagined he might be. When I'd arrived, he'd instantly seemed to warm to the fact that his interviewer for the day was Scottish (having of course enjoyed a decades-long relationship with the country and its people), had hung around the studio's buffet table urging me, with typical bonhomie, to try the caramelised vegetables. Yet his head was clearly elsewhere and a heavy air of *something* hung over him.

Only when he briefly mentioned his second wife, Heather Mills, saying her first name almost under his breath, in admitting that she hadn't quite taken to his penchant for the odd spliff ('She's violently against it'), did I get an inkling that the rumours might be true that the pair's marriage was in deep trouble. The previous day, one of the tabloids had run papped shots of Paul mooching around alone on a break in France. Two days after our conversation, his publicist made the announcement that the pair were to split.

Having done a fair bit of this interviewing thing, I hadn't taken his semi-detached state that day as some kind of failure on my part, and it was now clear what had been weighing on his mind. But it made me determined to try to hold his full attention, to ask and say the things that other writers might not dare, if and when we should meet again. Printed encounters with Paul McCartney in recent years had tended to be fairly stiff affairs, with many journalists – entirely reasonably, since I'd suffered from a touch of nerves myself – too intimidated to ask him much beyond the ho-hum or draw him into a spot of lively banter, or even just try to have a good old laugh with him.

Next time, I thought.

The next time arrived sixteen months later, when I was given the opportunity to meet him in his lair, two floors above the reception of 1 Soho Square, at the offices of MPL, McCartney Productions Limited. This is Paul's comfort zone, the room where he most often chooses to be interviewed – the dark, wood-panelled Art Deco den having been the centre of his operation since 1975. In this environment he instantly seemed more relaxed, more focused, very much in control and virtually unflappable, even when it came to broaching some of the more difficult times in his life.

Outside his office door there was an air of brisk business being done by his staff, of meetings being arranged and schedules being plotted. It is no coincidence, you felt, that this man is a multi-millionaire.

Inside, McCartney, settling on a sofa, was surrounded by Willem de Kooning originals and backlit by his neon-piped Wurlitzer jukebox, which contained the old rock'n'roll 45s that were his sacred texts as a teenager. As we talked, he made his way through a cheese and pickle sandwich, a spare triangle of which he repeatedly offered to me during the interview. He seemed to be disappointed that I wasn't really keen on it. 'Go on,' he urged me, for the third time. I gave in and took a bite.

'So this'll be vegetarian cheese, then?' I wondered aloud.

'It's just cheese,' shrugged the famed animal-rights campaigner, missing the point that I was surprised he wasn't plumping for the rennet-free variety.

Up close, McCartney had worn pretty well, given the sheer intensity of his past. Only a wrinkling around the lips and his slightly sunken cheeks gave away his age, with his hair more expertly dyed now than the plum shades of his fifties when – being nothing if not a homemade guy – you suspected he was doing it himself. His hazel eyes flashed with a greenish tinge when caught in a certain light. He appeared trim but moaned that he had a bit of a gut on him.

'You haven't got a belly on you,' I said.

'I'm sucking it in, 'cause there's a journalist here,' he grinned. His cheeks swelled when he laughed, and the years fell from his face, returning the impish Beatle of old.

Most people, from the Beatles films and his countless TV interviews, have some idea of how Paul McCartney talks. Face to face, however, his tone is more earthy, more Scouse, his speech peppered with lovingly delivered swear-words.

But interviewing McCartney is a bit like panning for gold. He can be as slippery as a politician, expertly ducking a question and sometimes making you return to it three times before he tackles it head-on. At other points, he begins to drift into old anecdotes that you've heard or read him relate dozens of times. In these moments, you're forced to interject to try to steer him gently back towards less familiar terrain.

Sometimes, particularly when he digresses, you feel as if he's growing a bit bored, either by the question or his response to it, and he says 'anyway', quite definitely, urging you to move on. Other times, you suspect this is a handy defence mechanism when he is finding the line of questioning too intrusive.

Being a seasoned interviewee, he is well practised in the art of talking a lot while giving very little away. John Lennon once sniffily complimented his former bandmate on being 'a good PR man . . . about the best in the world'. There remains a fair amount of truth in this, and, ultimately, it forces you to push McCartney harder to get beneath his usual surface spiel. You know you're getting somewhere when he emits an almost exasperated sigh and says, 'Look, to be *honest*.'

At the same time, perhaps because he is surrounded by reverence most of the time, he seems to relish repartee, to enjoy measured mickey-taking. He is, of course, a man few ever dare to say no to, never mind lightly take the piss out of. But it's clear that he loves getting back in touch with the rougher, former working-class Macca, who is never too far away.

On this occasion, with a second meeting scheduled for six days later and in the same location, we were due to talk about the 1970s, an often tumultuous and uncertain time for McCartney. During our chat he began to open up more and more, offering a carefully controlled honesty about his trials during the period: the emotional crash he'd suffered after the collapse of The Beatles; the brutal public bickering that went on between himself and Lennon; the vilification of Linda by press and fans alike; the troubled benign dictatorship of Wings, a band which seemed to suffer from a messy, revolving-door membership policy.

'You could never force musicians to do stuff,' he stressed, 'but you'd *suggest* strongly.'

'I imagine you can be quite . . . *persuasive* in your arguments,' I said.

'There were some arguments,' he conceded. 'But there were arguments in The Beatles too. It's unpleasant. But it's actually quite a good thing.'

'Was it tough finding musicians who weren't overawed to be working with "Paul McCartney, ex-Beatle?"' I wondered.

'I don't blame 'em,' he replied, deadpan. '*I'm* overawed by me, Tom. It's true, man. I'm not kidding!' There was a long pause. 'No, no, no, I am kidding,' he smiled.

At one point I broached the numerous dope busts he'd suffered as an enthusiastic user of marijuana. Did he feel victimised by the police in any way?

'A bit, yeah,' he admitted.

'It must have been like the coppers were sitting around thinking, We've got a slack day, boys, let's bust Macca,' I said.

'Well, there was a lot of that,' he laughed.

'They found plants at your farmhouse in Scotland, they had you in LA with a joint on the floor of your car,' I went on.

'That's right, yeah,' he nodded. 'That was planted. The LA thing was planted. What it was, by mistake, I ran a red light 'cause I thought, You can do that in America. Which you can. Often you can turn right on a red light. But this had a sign – No Right Turn – that I'd missed.'

'Because you were stoned?' I ventured.

He hesitated, before his face spread into a wide grin.

'I might have been.'

By the end, I realised he hadn't looked at his watch once.

Close to a week on, we met up again. McCartney invited me into his office with a beckoning head gesture, as he stood just inside the doorway, messing around on an upright bass. 'Check out my new bass, man,' he said, his fingers easily strolling up and down its neck. He looked tired, the years showing on his face. It was the end of a long day.

We parked ourselves on his office sofa again, in the same positions we'd assumed the week before. He'd obviously given our previous conversation some thought and seemed keen to play down the soft-drug angle, mainly because he figured it would be seized upon by the papers and twisted out of context.

'This is gonna get picked up by the tabloids,' he said. 'Macca Exposé. I don't wanna go on about it too much.'

I pointed out that Paul McCartney In Weed-Puffing Shock was hardly revelatory stuff.

'It's all a bit stronger these days, so I don't want to be the one who advocates it,' he argued. 'You don't want to give some kids the idea, "Well, great, man, let's go do it."'

'The Beatles got me into dope actually,' I confessed.

'See, that's it,' he said. 'But there are people these days who can't handle it, and I don't wanna be responsible for any of that.'

Firmly, and for the record, he claimed to have completely given up smoking weed himself, partly as a result of his advancing years. 'It's a bit befuddling,' he laughed. 'It's actually more important at my stage of the game to be unfuddled.'

He said his friends had noticed how his vocabulary had improved after he'd quit marijuana. 'They'd say, "Wow, your choice of words has really gone up." Before I'd go, "It's like . . . y'know . . . it's like . . . y'know . . . *good*." Whereas now, it's like, "It's kinda *exceptional*." You're actually choosing words that fit better, that I know, but I could never remember.'

If the public perception of Paul McCartney is pretty much frozen in stone, he sometimes seems to be entirely at odds with it. At one point I mentioned the 'Fab Macca' image of him as the irrepressibly chirpy Scouser, gooning for the cameras with his thumbs aloft. Surprising me, it lit his fuse and prompted a sweary explosion of only partly comedic rage.

'I have been chastened by the world opinion on that,' he said, his hackles beginning to rise. 'You will not actually see me do it.'

'Is that right?' I said, not entirely buying this.

'Well, have you seen me do it in the last ten years?' he said.

I admitted I hadn't.

'Because I'm suitably chastened by people saying, "You shouldn't do that." It's like fucking school! "One thing you must not do is put your fucking thumbs up, you twat!" So much of what happens reminds me of school. And I think my attitude's the same as it always was. "Yes, sir." Waits till sir has gone out the room and then goes, "Fuck off!" Y'know, that's what we *really* think. Anyone dares to tell us we're . . . *cunts* . . . is a *twat* . . .

Excuse me, I've just gone all sweary. You said I was Wacky Thumbs Aloft, you see.'

'Still,' I contended, 'it's quite a handy two-dimensional public image to have, isn't it? It kind of conceals the guy who gets annoyed or angry or tells people what to do.'

McCartney seemed temporarily thrown.

'Uh, y'know . . . I don't know,' he said. 'Maybe it is. Like I say, man, I really don't know. It seems natural to me, y'know. I'm not always feeling in that mood. But I am optimistic and want to remain optimistic.'

It was in moments such as this that I realised that Paul was not nearly as self-aware as you might expect. Ask him what he himself imagined was the popular image of him, Wacky Macca aside, and he was similarly, and perhaps surprisingly, stumped.

'Oh . . . I don't know, man . . . I don't know . . . no, I don't know.'

In many ways, it seems, it's this lack of self-analysis that stops him going entirely mad. Perhaps if he thought too deeply about the fact that he is 'Paul McCartney', he might not be able to function.

One of his more peculiar traits is that he constantly refers to The Beatles as 'they' ('They were the greatest little rock band going'), and even to himself in the third person ('If anyone's gonna make a decision,' he said, looking from the outside in at the warring in Wings, 'it should probably be him.'). It's as if divorcing himself from reality allows him to unburden himself of the weight of his legend.

He spoke about not quite believing he had in fact been in certain situations – such as lining up with the other Beatles for a photo-opportunity in Miami in 1964 as Cassius Clay (later Muhammad Ali) pretended to knock them all out – until he was presented with the actual pictorial evidence. He further expressed this sense of unreality in 'That Was Me', from his 2007 album *Memory Almost Full*, offering lyrical snapshots of himself playing with The Beatles on the *Royal Iris* ferry on the Mersey, at the Cavern and on TV shows, while struggling to take it in that he'd actually done all of this.

As time passed, I found myself interviewing McCartney once or twice a year, both for major features for *Mojo* and *Q* and for smaller bits and bobs. The playful approach seemed to work well with him, though he never quite let me forget that I was in his company as a journalist and, ultimately, like any big star burned by the tabloids, he had his misgivings about 'reporters'.

'But they're not bastards, they're lovable rogues,' he joshed, though a touch spikily. 'They're just not as lovable as they used to be.'

'Is it worse now than it was in the 1960s?' I asked him, perhaps stupidly.

'Well, you know it is,' he said. 'You don't have to ask me. You're *with them*.'

'I'm not with those bastards,' I protested, slightly affronted. 'I work for music magazines.'

'No, but . . . OK,' he said, softening his tack. 'You're on the side of the fence that gives you *access* to those bastards.'

All the same, one later incident in particular highlighted how he didn't really believe that I was in cahoots with the tabloid scummers. We were going over his experiences of the noughties, taking in the high points and, of course, the low points. It had only been nineteen months since his ugly divorce from Heather Mills.

What was the one thing he'd done in the past decade that he wished he hadn't?

He laughed, a touch edgily. 'Oh God, I dunno. Well, I did wish I didn't . . . not really . . . can't think of any.'

'There is one obvious one,' I said, knowing I was veering into dodgy territory.

'What're you saying?' he shot back, suddenly cool.

'Getting married again?' I said.

He laughed once again, more easily this time. 'Well, OK, yeah. I suppose that has to be the prime contender. But I don't wanna down anyone. I mean, these things happen, y'know. It's the ups and downs of life. And it was a pity that it happened that way. But I tend to look at the sort of positive side, which is that I have another beautiful daughter.'

Inevitably, perhaps, once it was published, the *Daily Mail* pounced on this quote and reprinted it under the sleight-of-hand headline 'Sir Paul McCartney Admits Marriage to Heather Mills Was His "Biggest Mistake"'. Of course, this was entirely beyond my control, and, through a writer friend, I heard that even though Paul was irked by it, he didn't blame me.

Increasingly, a more informal tone began to characterise our conversations, often conducted via phone when he had half an hour spare, shooting from somewhere to somewhere in the back of a car in Europe or America. Once I had to wait in for almost an entire dreary week, his publicist telling me that Paul – on holiday at the time and so virtually impossible to pin down – would call me between 4 p.m. and 11 p.m. on any number of given days. Another time, we spoke for ten minutes two days before Christmas and both of us had colds, and it was clear that neither of us was really in the mood.

At the end of one call in the middle of his summer holiday in the Hamptons, he seemed at a loose end and clearly wanted to carry on nattering away, talking about what we both had planned for the rest of the day.

'You know what?' he said, making the rest of *his* day sound a touch more idyllic than mine. 'I'm actually going to have a sail on my wee sailboat. It's a nice day here and it's only four o'clock in the afternoon.'

I told him that a long-lens shot had appeared in that morning's papers, strangely enough, of him posing behind a dress hanging on a clothes-line. It turned out that he and his then girlfriend, now third wife, Nancy Shevell had been wandering past a clothes stall when Paul spotted a shifty photographer.

'It's weird, 'cause I saw him and I thought, I bet that's a pap,' he said. 'And I thought, Nah, I'm being paranoid. But my instincts are too damn good on that stuff and I was right. I sort of went up to him, but he was a coward and he drove off.

'I did say to Nancy, "D'you know what? Look, it's us having fun on holiday, we're having a laugh." Y'know, standing behind a dress. I was originally trying to get her to stand behind it to see if it fitted her. So I got behind it and I must admit, as I did it, I thought, He's gonna get this, this'll be the one.'

Still, he admitted that on numerous occasions such a laissez-faire attitude to the paparazzi is hard to maintain. He comically fumed that he finds it hard to relax on a beach, lest a concealed snapper grab a few frames of him looking paunchy. He recalled enviously spying another bloke of a similar age on holiday one time. 'Just a family man and his belly was hanging out,' he said wistfully. 'He didn't give a shit, he's playing with his kids. But I'm looking to see who's in the hotel room with a long lens.'

Talking to him on the phone over three nights in spring 2013, as he rather nervously drove himself to the studio in Los Angeles in 'a low-slung sports car . . . I'm used to a big, high, strong SUV', he swung between bursts of annoyance about the intrusions caused by his celebrity and being gently tickled by the notion that he has one of the most famous faces on earth. He broke off our conversation at one point, having been spotted by a fan, to bark under his breath, 'Oi! No. Pfff-fucking hell. Everyone's got a camera these days.'

At another point he suddenly began killing himself laughing for no apparent reason. 'I've got a funny thing happening here, Tom,' he explained. 'I'm driving along, and right behind me there's one of those buses doing the Star Tours. I always want to stop and get out and go, "Hey, guys, how're you doing?" I love the irony of it. They're going around, saying, "Oh, here's so and so, here's so and so." And I'm *right* under their noses, man.'

He arrived at the studio and seemed to be having a bit of trouble parking the sports car. 'Whoops,' he cried out. 'I've just clunked me car. Shit. Hold on. It's a lesson in parking – how to not hit things in front of you.'

In Los Angeles, against his better judgement, he'll find himself jumping red lights in an effort to escape the paps. 'You think, This is dangerous,' he said. 'It's like a spy chase and you think, Spies get killed doing this. And I didn't do anything.'

In New York, more gallingly, he'll try to placate tailing photographers only to have his peace offering thrown back in his face. He'll pull the car over and three or four others will screech to a halt behind him. He'll get out and make them a deal: take your picture, then leave me alone.

'These days, of course, they've even got video cameras,' he pointed out, 'which is embarrassing 'cause I used to love gritting my teeth and going, "I hate you but I'm smiling." So I say, "OK, guys, that's it, you've got your picture." Get back in the car and they just *keep on following*.'

'Ever hit a photographer?' I asked him.

'*Nah*,' he said, softly and without any real conviction, before changing his mind. 'Well, I have, actually. But it didn't get reported. I got lucky. I think he thought he deserved it.

'But I always remember the famous story that gives you pause for thought, which was Mick Jagger was allegedly in Paris one night and he comes out of a nightclub and there was a photographer. Mick went up to the guy to clock him one. The guy turned out to be into karate. Went *foo-foo-foo-foo-foom*. Got Mick on the floor, *then* took a picture.'

Only once did I witness McCartney dealing with photographers first-hand. I was charged with chaperoning him at the *Q* Awards in 2010, where he was picking up an award for the remastered *Band On The Run*. Arrangements had been made for him to arrive at the service entrance at the back of the Grosvenor House Hotel, to save him having to negotiate the red-carpet rat-run beloved of artists with a record to plug.

He arrived, with only one security guard in tow, in a car driven by his long-time personal assistant, former Wings guitar tech John Hammel, and good-naturedly elbowed his way through a clot of snappers and fans who had made a hasty dash the few yards down from the gate where the other attendees were shuffling in.

Once I'd ushered him inside and into an ante-room reserved for him by the organisers, he was chipper, if a touch confused – as is sometimes the way up in the dizzy altitudes of the superstar – by the exact nature of the do. 'Is this the *Q* Awards or the *GQ* Awards? Are there film stars out there or just musicians?' he asked me, trying on a couple of jackets and seeking my approval and Hammel's, before settling on a navy-blue number with matching epaulettes.

Ten minutes later followed a bizarre moment when myself, Hammel, the security guy and a couple of the awards organisers marched down the corridors in convoy, like a presidential procession, to show the former Beatle where he could take a leak.

En route, a bloke who claimed to be from *Q* (though I'd never seen him before) stopped McCartney, grabbed his hand and nervously burbled, 'Oh wow hi Paul I just wanted to say it's a total honour to meet you,' as McCartney calmly and politely responded – as he has doubtless done thousands of times – 'Well, thanks, great to meet you too.'

But then the guy wouldn't let go of his hand, continuing to shake it maniacally, visibly tightening his grip. The disbelief began to spread across McCartney's face. From what I've seen and experienced, one of the worst things you can do when meeting a famous person is lose the plot in the manner of a frothing, hyperventilating fan (fan, of course, being short for *fanatic*).

'I'll let you go then,' said the bloke, sensing McCartney's discomfort and finally loosening his grasp.

As we continued on our way down the corridor, Paul, in a revealing moment, turned to me, laughing, completely at ease, and said, 'That was fucking big of him to let me go, wasn't it?'

An hour or so later, onstage, in front of an assemblage comprising, as he put it, 'All the younger bands . . . which is pretty much everybody,' McCartney accepted the award for Classic Album for *Band On The Run*, dedicating it to Linda in a characteristically jocular though properly heartfelt speech.

'The Beatles were a pretty hard act to follow and we were gonna follow them,' he said into the microphone, to whoops and cheers. 'Linda was getting slagged off for being in my band. *I* was getting slagged off for letting her in the band. This album was quite a struggle to make.'

If any word sums up Paul McCartney in the 1970s, it is *struggle*. Another is *escape*.

In essence, he spent the decade struggling to escape the shadow of The Beatles, effectively becoming an outlaw hippie millionaire, hiding out on his Scottish farmhouse, before travelling the world with makeshift bands and barefoot children. It was a time of numerous drug busts and brilliant, banned and sometimes baffling records. For McCartney, it was an edgy, liberating, sometimes frightening period of his life that has largely been forgotten.

When discussing this period in depth with him, a notion sparked in my head that led to the writing of this book. For me, a very different figure was beginning to emerge, in sharp contrast to the oft-perceived slightly cosy, head-wobbling (inter)national treasure who these days opens the Olympics or performs for the Queen.

Between 1969 and 1981, Paul McCartney was a man on the run – from his recent past as a Beatle, from his horrendous split from his bandmates, from the towering expectation that surrounded his every move. Behind his lasting image during that period as a Bambi-eyed soft-rock balladeer, he was actually a far more counter-culturally leaning individual (albeit one overshadowed by the light-sucking Lennon) than he was ever given credit for – freewheeling in his hippiefied way, taking to the road with a 'bunch of nutters' for an impromptu, disorganised university tour with the proto-Wings, viewing the world though perma-stoned eyes and defiantly continuing to flick two fingers at authorities the world over who sought to criminalise him, all the while adopting a shrugging, amused attitude to it all.

These days he marvels at a photograph taken of him carrying the naked infant Mary through Dublin Airport in the early 1970s ('I could not imagine that now'), yet he is still slightly disbelieving of the Victorian attitudes that saw him being forced to put swimsuits on his nude, pool-diving children by the staff of an exclusive country club in Lagos during the making of *Band On The Run*. 'I'm going, "You're kidding? They're aged *nothing*."'

If there was one key insight that struck me during my conversations with McCartney and the research and writing of this book, it was his eccentricity, which often gets lost behind his deceptive façade of straightness. As his devoted 1970s Wings sidekick Denny Laine told me, 'Paul *is* a bit eccentric, and whatever he wants he usually gets.'

This eccentricity is perhaps the key to everything – from the release of the bewildering 'Mary Had A Little Lamb' single to his 1972 European tour in a gaudily painted open-topped bus, to the beautifully dreamy, softly psychedelic US number one written about his uncle Albert, to his incarceration in Japan in 1980 after attempting to sneak half a pound of marijuana into the country.

In this way, *Man on the Run* sets out to tell the tale of a man living outwith normal society and, for better or for worse, acting on his own tangential whims, during a chaotic and fascinating period of his life.

Back in the late 1960s, much to Lennon's delight, his Beatle bandmate had come up with the idea of recording a wholly experimental album entitled *Paul McCartney Goes Too Far*. While that never came to pass, in many ways, in the 1970s, Paul McCartney did go too far, and not always in the right directions.

'You have to be honest about your past,' he confessed to me at one point. 'I was such a daring young thing. We were on this wacky adventure.'

Your first solo album, *McCartney*. You recorded that at home, in secret, in the midst of all of your wrangles with The Beatles.

Yeah. It was really . . . kind of . . . therapy through hell. It was one of the worst times of my life.

I

On the Run

He knew he was in trouble the morning he couldn't lift his head off the pillow. He awoke, face down, his skull feeling like a useless dead weight. A dark thought flashed through his mind: if he couldn't make the effort to pull himself up, he'd suffocate right there and then.

Somehow, as if it was the hardest thing he'd ever done, he summoned the energy to move. He flipped over on to his back and thought, Jesus . . . that was a bit near.

Day by day, week by week, his condition had been steadily worsening. His often sleepless nights were spent shaking with anxiety, while his days, which he was finding harder and harder to face, were characterised by heavy drinking and self-sedation with marijuana. He found himself chain-smoking his untipped, lung-blackening Senior Service cigarettes one after another after another.

Later, he would look back on this period and tell everyone that he'd almost had a nervous breakdown. From the outside, there appeared to be no 'almost' about it.

For the first time in his life, he felt utterly worthless. Everything he had been since the age of fifteen had been wrapped up in the band. Now, even though he couldn't tell the world, that period of his life was almost certainly over.

It was as if he'd suddenly and unexpectedly lost his job, been made entirely redundant. He was 27 and of no use to anyone any more. Even the money he'd earned up to this point was no comfort, made no real difference. This was an identity crisis *in extremis*: who exactly was he if he wasn't Beatle Paul McCartney?

On the mornings when he forced himself to rise, he'd sit on the edge of his bed for a while before defeatedly crawling back under the covers. When he did get up and out of bed he'd reach straight for the whisky, his drinking creeping earlier and earlier into the day. By three in the afternoon, he was usually out of it.

'I hit the bottle,' he admits. 'I hit the substances.'

He was eaten up with anger – at himself, at the outside world. He could only describe it as a barrelling, empty feeling rolling across his soul.

Out of work and with nothing to distract him, the ghosts from his past would rise up, whispering in his head, telling him, in spite of everything he'd achieved, that they knew he'd never really amount to anything. That he should have got a proper job in the first place, just as they'd always said.

He realised that up until this point he'd been a 'cocky sod'. And now there was this: the first serious blow to his confidence he'd ever experienced. Even when he was fourteen and the mastectomy couldn't save his mother's life, he had known that that horrific event had been outwith his control. Somehow, now, in the depths of his muddied thinking, he was starting to believe that everything that was happening was nobody's fault but his own.

His wife of less than a year felt the situation was 'frightening beyond belief'. Within a matter of months, her new partner had gone from being a sparky, driven, world-famous rock star to a broken man who didn't want to set foot out of their bedroom. But even if Linda was scared, she knew she couldn't give up on Paul. She recognised that her husband was sinking into emotional quicksand, and she knew that it was down to her alone to pull him out before he went under for good.

'Linda saved me,' he says. 'And it was all done in a sort of domestic setting.'

It had been two years since they'd first met at the Bag O' Nails nightclub in Soho, four days later being seen deep in conversation at the press launch for *Sgt. Pepper*. It was only a year since they'd managed to float unnoticed together through the streets of New York (where, in Chinatown, he had comically tried to pull her into a temple offering Buddhist weddings), before flying from coast to coast, landing in Los Angeles and disappearing for days into a bungalow at the Beverly Hills Hotel. It was still only six months since they'd giggled their way through their wedding ceremony at Marylebone registry office in London, amid a fog of seething female jealousy that seemed to spread across the world.

He had been the last single Beatle, the one seen about town, haunting the clubs and hanging with the artsy crowd. She was the American single-mother divorcee who had earned some renown as a rock photographer and who had apparently had flings with Mick Jagger and Jim Morrison. To Paul, Linda appeared deeper than the frothy, starry-eyed girls who tended to flock around him, less buttoned-up than his then paramour, actress Jane Asher.

Linda would take Paul out on long drives, saying 'Let's get lost' in her drawly, stoney way, showing him a new kind of freedom. She had surprised him by telling him, 'I could make you a nice home.'

Now it was autumn 1969, and the McCartneys were in Scotland, 'hiding away in the mists' as Paul puts it. They had escaped here, far from London and the heavy weather of intra-Beatle feuding that refused to lift.

But High Park Farm was no rock-star country pile. Paul had bought the run-down farmhouse, set on a hill overlooking Skeroblin Loch in 183 acres of rough Scottish landscape, back in June 1966, the year he became a millionaire. His accountant had suggested that McCartney invest in property to wrestle some of his earnings away from the clutches of Harold Wilson and his Labour government's painful 95 per cent super-taxing of high earners.

The ever frugal Paul, of course, leaped at such an opportunity, picking High Park Farm out of the reams of property documents his accountant sent him. The asking price was a not insubstantial £35,000, more than ten times the cost of the average family home in the mid-1960s. It was, says Paul, 'wee', consisting of only three rooms: a bedroom at either end separated by its kitchen-cum-living area. The hole in the roof of the farmhouse was included in the deal.

But it was another eighteen months after the purchase, in December 1967, before Paul, with Jane Asher in tow, made the trip north to check out his new investment. High Park was set more than a mile up a bumpy single track, and visitors unprepared for the terrain would moan that the drive would virtually wreck their offroad-unworthy vehicles.

The sorely neglected property was in a wild and windswept location, fourteen miles from the southern tip of the remote Kintyre peninsula. Three miles west from the hill lay the six-mile sweep of beach at Machrihanish Bay. A five-mile drive south-east down the A83 sat the small fishing port of Campbeltown and the closest amenities.

When Paul first came here at the tail-end of 1967 – equally the Beatles' annus mirabilis and annus horribilis (the marvel of *Sgt. Pepper*, the paralysing shock of Brian Epstein's death, the trials of *Magical Mystery Tour* and the sense that nothing would ever be the same again) – he'd tried to make High Park habitable on a characteristically thrifty level.

He'd dispatched Beatles gofer Alistair Taylor into Campbeltown, from where he'd returned with a second-hand Formica table and chairs, an electric stove and a couple of beds. The pair fashioned a sofa out of a pile of Sharpe's Express wooden potato boxes, with an old mattress found in the barn folded over the makeshift frame.

After his split from Asher, Paul first went back there with Linda in November 1968. The eldest daughter of the moneyed New York Eastman family had immediately fallen in love with the place and the idea of roughing it in this remoteness – no hot water, mice and rats in the walls and all – but had suggested to Paul that they do the place up a bit. It was a notion that hadn't even occurred to the airy McCartney.

She encouraged him to pour a cement floor in the kitchen, replacing the wooden planks laid over the bare earth. He began making a table to replace the flimsy Formica one. He scaled a ladder and climbed on to the roof to fix its hole, Linda soundtracking his handiwork by spinning the newly released *Tighten Up* reggae compilation LPs.

If you had walked through the door of the farmhouse in the latter months of 1969, according to Paul, you'd have seen 'nappies, bottles, musical instruments, me and Lin, like a couple of hippies . . . it wasn't sort of dirty, but it wasn't clean.'

High Park wasn't entirely cut off from civilisation, though it certainly had that feel. Linda in particular romanticised this notion, imagining that the McCartneys were living in another era, as if they were pioneers in this isolated place. She loved the fact that they were, as she fancifully saw it, 'at the end of nowhere'.

As the months passed, Paul and Linda grew into their rural personas. At Christmas, he bought her twelve pheasants; she bought him a tractor, which he used to plough a vegetable patch where they grew parsnips, turnips, potatoes, green beans, runner beans and spinach.

Their acreage was home to around 150 to 200 sheep, which

Paul learned to clip using hand-shears before the fleeces were sold to the Wool Marketing Board. Already leaning towards vegetarianism, they would baulk at the notion of killing their lambs, although they were forced to send some off to market if the numbers grew too high. They tried to separate the ewes from the rams, but sometimes one of the male sheep would enthusiastically spring over the fence. In time, they had six horses, including their retired racer Drake's Drum, bought for Paul's father Jim and a former winner at Aintree, alongside Honor (Paul's), Cinnamon (Linda's) and three ponies, Sugarfoot, Cookie and Coconut.

Revving up a generator, Paul put together an ad hoc four-track recording facility in High Park's rickety lean-to, which he named Rude Studio. It was in here, gently encouraged by Linda, that his songwriting slowly began to return to him, as he effectively used music as therapy to alleviate his depression. 'She eased me out of it,' he remembers, 'and just said, "Hey, y'know, you don't want to get too crazy."'

Paul would shy away from admitting that there was a strong autobiographical element to some of these new compositions, but his protestations rang hollow. The lyric of 'Man We Was Lonely' spoke of how his and Linda's self-imposed exile was not as idyllic as it outwardly seemed, that their spirits had been low, but how, under the comfort blanket of domesticity, their positivity was returning.

'Every Night', a song he'd first begun messing around with during the *Let It Be* sessions, was more confessional still – its singer painting a grim picture of a routine involving getting wasted and struggling to drag himself out of bed. The chorus, as was increasingly becoming a McCartney trait, pledged his devotion to Linda. As a song, it was a deceptively breezy affair. While elsewhere Lennon was screaming his pain, it was typical of

McCartney to mask his with melody. Only if you listened closely would you really be able to detect the songwriter's anguish.

As Paul seemed to stabilise, the McCartneys settled into a daily routine, riding their horses across the land or taking sheepdog Martha for long walks. They drove into Campbeltown in their Land Rover, which they'd nicknamed Helen Wheels, the Beatle becoming a regular sight wandering around in his wellies and sheepskin-lined brown leather jacket. In the evening, he would light the fire while Linda cooked, before stepping into Rude to work on songs. At night, they would cuddle up, get stoned and watch TV. 'We were not cut off from the world,' said Linda. 'We were never hermits.'

Aside from anything, to playfully distract Paul from his troubles, there were the children to look after: the newborn Mary, and Linda's child from her first marriage, shy Heather, only six. For the kids, High Park was a cross between a playground and a junkyard. As soon as she began to walk Mary was free to toddle outside through its abandoned gypsy-encampment-like clutter of scrap wood, sheets of corrugated iron and teetering log piles (noting incredulously as an adult that she'd effectively been brought up in a 'lumber yard').

It was a messy scene but, for McCartney, one filled with increasingly frequent spells of happiness. Nevertheless, in a corner of his mind, knowing that there was a Beatles-shaped storm brewing back down in London, Paul was still filled with unease.

It didn't help that everyone was arguing about whether or not he was dead.

The rumour had first circulated amongst the bloodshot-eyed student populace of Drake University in Iowa, around the same time as McCartney had first holed up in Scotland. The signs were all there if you cared to dig 'deep' enough, to stop just rolling joints on the covers of Beatles albums and decipher the hidden messages in the artwork and between the grooves. They listened to Lennon's daft murmur of 'cranberry sauce' in the fade-out of 'Strawberry Fields Forever' and imagined it to be 'I buried Paul'. They would spin *The White Album* backwards with an index finger and convince themselves that a voice could be heard saying, 'Turn me on, dead man'.

In many ways, The Beatles had brought this upon themselves. In their touring absence and with their increasingly cryptic music, they had laid playful clues and red herrings – with the opening lines of 'Rain' played backwards at the end of the song; with the garbled, wonked-out voices locked in the play-out groove of side two of *Sgt. Pepper*; with Lennon's head-game assertion in 'Glass Onion' that the walrus was Paul.

'We'd done them for fun, just for something to do,' says Paul, in admitting the Beatles' surprise that their penchant for japery was taken so seriously. 'Then everyone analysed them and we thought, *Ah*. We were completely oblivious to all those other "hidden" messages.'

That was until the clue-heads began to air their tangential theories. The sixteenth of September 1969 saw the first piece, in the Drake University student paper, under the tantalising head-line 'Is Paul McCartney Dead?' A week later, the *Northern Star*, the campus inky of Northern Illinois University, went one better: 'Clues Hint At Possible Beatle Death'.

A student identifying himself only as Tom called Detroit DJ Russ Gibb to inform him of the rumours. Listening in, a college writer named Fred LaBour decided to turn prankster, taking it upon himself to 'kill' McCartney, adding arm upon leg to the growing myth. Two days later, the *Michigan Daily* printed his fabricated revelations under the more contentious banner: 'McCartney Dead: New Evidence Brought To Light'. Then the rumour spread countrywide when Roby Yonge, on his networked show from WABC in New York, discussed the theories on air in the small hours, when the stoned were at their most receptive.

It all made sense to the herbally enhanced mind, of course, and somehow an elaborate back-story began to emerge. Instead of, as the real tale went, having suffered a chipped tooth and badly cut lip in a moped accident in Liverpool in December 1965 (Paul had been 'looking at the moon', hit a rock and gone flying over the handlebars), McCartney had in fact stormed off from a Beatles session at Abbey Road on 9 November 1966 in a huff, following an argument with the other Beatles, and crashed his Aston Martin, decapitating himself. The panicked band had subsequently replaced him with a doppelgänger, the winner of a secret Paul McCartney lookalike competition, a Scotsman named William Campbell, who was then given plastic surgery to render him identical.

There were other clues, apparently. The palm of a hand held above McCartney's head on the cover of *Sgt. Pepper* was a mystical sign of death (it wasn't). Paul was barefoot in the 'funeral procession' zebra-crossing cover shot of *Abbey Road* to indicate that he was a corpse (the duller truth being that it had been a hot August day, he was wearing sandals and he'd slipped them off). The licence plate of the white Volkswagen Beetle in the background of the image that ended 28IF was symbolically stating the age McCartney would have been had he survived the rumoured accident (in fact, photographer Iain Macmillan had attempted to have the car towed out of shot). The word 'walrus' was Greek for corpse (it isn't). The 'one and one and one is three' that Lennon sang about in 'Come Together' was referring to the surviving Beatles (rather than being just a throwaway line in a surreal, pinballing lyric). Paul is facing away from the camera on the back cover of *Sgt. Pepper* because it is in fact William Campbell, hiding his surgical scars (although that didn't explain why he is shown facing forwards on the front cover). And on and on and on it fantastically went.

By November, the story had made it to the pages of *Rolling Stone*, albeit in a piece with an eyebrow-raised, slightly mocking tone. Nevertheless, Beatles publicist Derek Taylor soon found himself having to fend off calls from reporters the world over. And still the rumour persisted, not least when Dr Henry Truby of the University of Miami studied three pre- and post-1966 recordings of McCartney singing and rather vaguely stated he couldn't conclude that they were in fact the work of the same person.

But even for its chief propagator, the whole affair was getting out of hand. Fred LaBour was invited to appear on TV in California in a mock trial where he presented evidence to back up his claims. Before the recording, however, he confessed to the show's host, lawyer F. Lee Bailey, that he had made the whole thing up. It was too late, pointed out Bailey. They would have to go with it, to air the legend.

Finally, Paul issued a statement through the Beatles' press office. 'I'm alive and well,' he said. 'But if I were dead I would be the last to know.'

Of course, maddeningly, it was such a ridiculous myth that it was almost impossible to disprove. It hinged on McCartney somehow managing to prove that he was who he said he was. But even if he underwent and passed a fingerprint test, the naysayers could crow that it was all down to forgery and conspiracy.

Given McCartney's distinctive voice, features and physical demeanour, the Paul Is Dead fiction was of course absurd. In London, even his long-time barber was forced to respond to a New York radio reporter's probing by saying that the last time he'd cut Paul's hair, a flaw in his parting had still been there.

In the end, it came down to one simple, rumour-puncturing

poser – if this imposter William Campbell had managed not only to win the McCartney lookalike competition, had gone under the plastic surgeon's knife, had learned to sing like Paul and written songs of the calibre of 'She's Leaving Home' and 'Hey Jude', why would he or any of the other Beatles leave a trail of clues to blow his cover?

More tickled than annoyed, and mindful of Mark Twain's famous quote, after the publication of an erroneous obituary, about the rumours of his death being greatly exaggerated, McCartney was aware that there might be a positive, publicity-friendly angle to all of this. It couldn't do the just-released *Abbey Road* any harm, and in the end the rumpus sent its sales rocketing skywards, making it the biggest-selling Beatles album in the US since *Sgt. Pepper*.

Nevertheless, dying, as McCartney now jokes, 'wasn't easy . . . it took a lot out of me.'

It also drew the unwanted attentions of the press directly to the door of High Park. The first journalist to make the long and difficult journey from London to Scotland and out to the Argyll peninsula was dogged *Daily Express* pop scribe Judith Simons, who in the past had interviewed The Beatles on many occasions.

The trek was clearly more arduous and involved than the writer had expected, since she showed up at night, in the dark, timorously knocking on the door of the farmhouse. Paul, considering Simons 'a little sweetheart', wasn't particularly irritated by her intrusion, instead being quietly impressed by her tenacity and bravery.

'She was totally scared shitless of being in the middle of this place,' he says. 'I mean, there were no lights on the road.' Still, he remained vague and nonplussed when Simons started firing what he viewed as wholly trivial questions at him. 'She was just asking me about some story. I'm saying, "What can I tell you?"'

In truth, Paul had stopped doing interviews because he still felt far too exposed and emotionally raw. There was one question he dreaded above all others: 'Are you happy?' In his precariously balanced state, it would almost make him burst into tears.

Nevertheless, as time went on, his patience was beginning to fray, resulting in eruptions of other emotions entirely. When a pair from the London offices of the US magazine *Life* – writer Dorothy Bacon and photographer Terence Spencer – flew to Scotland, schlepping all the way to High Park to get a reaction about the death rumours, McCartney's anger boiled over.

It was a Sunday morning in late October and Paul, unsurprisingly, was still in bed. The *Life* duo had cannily assumed that it was a good time to catch the McCartneys at home and that their journey was less likely to be hindered by interfering local farmers. Intrepidly, they hoofed up to High Park from the main road, trudging across the fields for close to an hour.

Arriving at the door of the farmhouse, Bacon knocked. Paul, having got up as soon as he realised what was going on outside, jerked the door open, a bucket of slop from the McCartneys' rudimentary kitchen in one hand. He was unshaven, his hair an early Beatle-ish mop-top grown out and gone pineappleishly unkempt. His face was beetroot with fury. Spencer raised his camera to take a shot.

'I threw the bucket at him,' Paul says. 'It was nearly the cover of *Life*.'

The bucket flew past the photographer's head, but Spencer had got the shot and Paul knew it. Enraged, he stepped forward and punched the snapper on the shoulder. Having covered six wars and experienced nothing in the way of physical violence until faced with a raging Beatle, the startled Spencer turned to Bacon, saying, 'I think we've run out of our hospitality.' The pair turned tail and quickly marched away.

Alone, calming down, Paul reflected on what had just happened. He'd utterly lost his cool, and now the photographer definitely had the shot of him looking furious and demented. Ever the PR man, Paul realised he had to try to mend the situation if the shot wasn't to appear on the cover of *Life* and in the world's papers thereafter, making him look like a lunatic.

Bacon and Spencer, meanwhile, were shaken but happy enough: they had pictorial proof that McCartney was still alive.

As they made their way back down the farm track, the McCartneys' Land Rover, with Paul, Linda and the kids inside, pulled up behind them. Spencer was initially afraid, saying to Bacon, 'For God's sake, be careful, because that man is mad.'

But it was an altogether more amiable and contrite Paul who emerged from the Land Rover, apologising, proffering a handshake and offering, in return for the roll of film containing the offending snap, to give a short interview and, albeit still reluctantly, to have his photograph taken with the family.

'We agreed to pose on the Land Rover,' he remembers. 'But I was definitely not in posing mode.'

A slightly haunted-looking image of the McCartneys made the cover of *Life* dated 7 November 1969, along with the accompanying splash 'The Case Of The "Missing" Beatle: Paul Is Still With Us'. In the shot, one of two that would illustrate the piece, Paul appears bed-headed and morning rough, his left arm curled protectively around a wind-blown Linda, his right cradling baby Mary, as in front of him, Heather, perhaps sensing her parents' hostility towards these unannounced visitors, wields a walking-stick like a club. In the second, the family are arranged on the front bumper of the Land Rover, Paul trying to appear upbeat, raising his hand in a friendly, open gesture as Linda nuzzles his neck.

In the interview, he addressed the Paul Is Dead rumours. 'It is all bloody stupid,' he said. 'Perhaps the rumour started because I haven't been much in the press lately. I don't have anything to say these days. I am happy to be with my family and I will work when I work. I was switched on for ten years and I never switched off. Now I am switching off whenever I can. I would rather be a little less famous these days.

'The people who are making up these rumours should look to themselves a little more,' he went on. 'They should worry about themselves instead of worrying whether I am dead or not.

'I would rather do what I began doing, which is making music. But the Beatle thing is over. It has been exploded, partly by what we have done, and partly by other people.

'What I have to say is all in the music,' he concluded. 'If I want to say anything, I write a song. Can you spread it around that I am just an ordinary person and want to live in peace? We have to go now. We have two children at home.'

Upon publication, the piece appeared to lay to rest the ghosts of the Paul Is Dead furore, although in some heads the doubts and conspiracies rumble on to this day.

One crucial point was completely missed, however: the fact that Paul had let slip that 'the Beatle thing is over'. *Life* had in fact got the world exclusive that the former Fabs had secretly imploded. But, amid all the fuss, no one even noticed.

In private, The Beatles had fallen out and fallen apart, prompting McCartney's state of panic and depression. As if to spotlight the emotional distance and physical remove of the four former friends, each was filmed separately with their respective partners for the promotional clip for 'Something', Apple MD Neil Aspinall having travelled to High Park to shoot the jokey, smoochy segments featuring Paul and Linda.

The critical episode in what Lennon called the 'slow death' of

The Beatles had come at a meeting at Apple on 20 September 1969. Three of the band members, minus George Harrison (whose mother had just been diagnosed with cancer), had convened at the office to ink their names on a new deal with Capitol Records, their label in the US and most other international territories. The deal had been hammered out by Allen Klein, a hate figure to Paul, who represented the others, while McCartney had divisively chosen to be looked after by his new in-laws, father-and-son lawyer team Lee and John Eastman. A touch gallingly for Paul, the contract Klein had brokered carved out an impressive 25 per cent royalty cut for The Beatles, the highest of any recording artists in the world.

On the day, in the preamble to signing the deal, a self-consciously babbling Paul had attempted to rah-rah-rah his downbeat colleagues into trying to recapture their fire. He suggested they could perhaps do this by way of a tour of small clubs where the band – who had last performed for a paying audience more than three years before – could turn up unannounced or billed under a pseudonym (he proposed Rikki and The Redstreaks). He argued that this might prop up their sagging confidence in their live abilities and help them get back in touch with who they were.

'I think you're daft,' a scowling Lennon abruptly informed McCartney, before announcing, 'I'm leaving the group. I want a divorce.'

Following this jaw-dropping declaration, the three signed the contract (which would in any case ensure that they earned far more from their future record sales, whether or not they stuck together) 'in a bit of a daze', according to Paul. All involved would look back on this as being the moment when the illness that had been affecting The Beatles finally became terminal.

As he would later attest when the press and fans cast him as the pantomime baddie in the drama of the Beatles' separation,

Paul was actually the only member who up until that point hadn't previously walked out on the band. Ringo, feeling like an outsider and, worse, a musician of dwindling talent, had announced during the sessions for *The White Album* in summer 1968, that he was quitting. On his return from a cooling-off-period holiday in Sardinia, he walked into Abbey Road to find the studio festooned with flowers to celebrate his return.

George, meanwhile, had stormed out of the rehearsals for *Let It Be* in the cold environs of Twickenham Film Studios during the Beatles' winter of discontent in January 1969. Harrison, who would later gripe that McCartney had treated him with a 'superior attitude' for some years, had bitterly argued with Paul over the guitar part for 'I've Got A Feeling', as seen in the final cut of the painfully candid documentary. On the day he walked, however, he had been battling with Lennon over a matter long since forgotten, though serious enough to enrage both sufficiently that they ended up trading blows.

After Harrison's departure, The Beatles spent the rest of the day rehearsing without him. That afternoon, with a significance that can't have escaped anyone, Yoko Ono took over George's position and began wailing into his microphone. The others reacted – Lennon with enthusiasm, McCartney and Starr in frustration – by erupting into an accompanying barrage of feedback and thunderous drumming.

George, of course, returned to the band a week later, though the schism between him and Paul was now even wider, if papered over for the purposes of band morale.

In the aftermath of the ultimate Beatles split, of course, the wives would take the blame. But it was Allen Klein, rather than Yoko Ono or Linda McCartney, who broke up The Beatles.

Klein walked into the Beatles' world like something from a bad cartoon, a squat, cigar-sucking caricature of a Jewish showbiz manager. The New Yorker divided and conquered John, Paul, George and Ringo when they were lost and insecure and lacking in impetus and direction. He was also a master of casual intimidation; in one meeting in the Apple boardroom, he smirked at Lennon while nonchalantly brandishing a hammer.

He had served his apprenticeship as an accountant at an entertainments firm before moving into management, initially handling 1950s crooner Bobby Darin. But Klein's special skills soon became apparent: meticulously auditing accounts and sniffing out discrepancies, and, later, prising enormous advances from record companies. He had pulled off something of a coup by securing $1 million for American soul singer Sam Cooke. More significantly, however, in 1965, The Rolling Stones had appointed Klein as their business manager and he'd renegotiated their contract with Decca, resulting in a record-breaking $1.25 million advance that wouldn't have escaped the attention of The Beatles.

It was Lennon who first became captivated by Klein, before convincing Starr and Harrison that this mouthy character could plug the holes in their business affairs. McCartney was not so sure. He'd already put forward Lee Eastman as a possible candidate for, if not exactly Beatles manager, then at least some form of financial controller for Apple. 'But they said, "Nah, nah, he'd be just too biased for you and against us,"' Paul says. 'Which I could see.'

Significantly, Eastman had informed McCartney about the shady flipside of Klein's reputation in America. At the point when Klein first approached The Beatles, he had just been investigated for both insider trading (he was in fact cleared, though he immediately changed his company name from Cameo-Parkway to ABKCO) and tax evasion.

Then Paul received a letter from Mick Jagger, pointedly warning him, through his own bitter experience – the New Yorker having managed to con the Stones into signing over their hits up to that point to his company – about getting involved with Klein. Paul, feeling that at last he had someone to add weight to his serious misgivings about the manager, invited Jagger to Apple to meet the others and explain his feelings about Klein. McCartney remembers the Stones' singer backing down when faced with all four Beatles: 'He said, "Well, he's alright if you like that kind of thing." He didn't say, "He's a robber."'

The bad feelings festering among The Beatles came to a head one night when George, John and Ringo turned up at Olympic Studios during the *Abbey Road* sessions with Klein in tow. The three informed Paul that he would have to sign the ABKCO management agreement right there and then, as Klein had to report to his board. McCartney refused to put pen to paper, pointing out that it was Friday night anyway and, since Klein was 'a law unto himself', the board theory didn't wash. The others then told McCartney that Klein was asking for twenty per cent of their future earnings. Paul, enraged, insisted that Klein would take fifteen, since The Beatles were, with no little understatement, 'a big act'. The three accused him of stalling and walked out of the studio.

On 8 May 1969, John, Ringo and George signed the ABKCO agreement. Only three days before, The Beatles had begun recording Paul's melancholic and resigned 'You Never Give Me Your Money', a barely disguised attack on Klein. McCartney remembers that Lennon, perhaps typically, appreciated the twisted humour of the lyrical gesture.

But now, no one could even laugh about where The Beatles had ended up. 'It was,' Paul says, 'just fucking awful.'

McCartney greeted the dawning of the 1970s back in London in his St John's Wood townhouse at 7 Cavendish Avenue, within walking distance of Abbey Road. Here, Linda and Heather, still relative newcomers to England, attempted to fit back into London life.

For Linda it was a frequently claustrophobic experience, thanks to the often bitter and vicious attentions of the feral girl fans who stalked her every time she stepped outside the house, tried to trip her up, or, if she was in a car without Paul, hammered on its roof and lobbed abuse at her. They scrawled messages on the walls outside: 'Fuck Linda'. They broke into the house and stole her photographs. They posted her cruel letters and parcels containing human turds.

For Heather, naturally reticent and in possession of an incongruous American accent, life at Robinsfield, the local private primary school in which the McCartneys had enrolled her, was equally as tough. She found it hard to make friends and often appeared sad and isolated, a situation only made worse by her elongated breaks from school as she travelled with her mum and soon-to-be adoptive dad, in an arrangement that was only to become looser as the decade progressed.

At the time, the McCartneys professed a wholly laidback attitude towards their child's education. 'I leave Heather to herself pretty much,' said Linda. 'I'm not interested in breathing over her shoulder.'

'I'm not fussy about education,' said Paul. 'Linda's not very well educated. I know a lot of people who aren't and they're still really great people. So I don't place very heavy emphasis on it.'

For Paul, returning to the capital from Scotland made him quickly realise that the destructive animosity that had set in to The Beatles was, if anything, beginning to intensify.

Business woes aside, there was still the matter of the unreleased tapes of the troubled Twickenham sessions (which had been transplanted to Apple Studios in Savile Row upon Harrison's return to the group). Throughout 1969 and into early 1970, two intensive attempts were made by producer Glyn Johns to boil down the hours of unvarnished, often sloppy takes – inspired by the bare-bones live jams of The Band – into an album that deserved to be released under the Beatles' name.

Test acetates had been found lacking in one way or another, although a mocked-up sleeve had been designed for the planned album, to be named *Get Back*. It featured The Beatles assuming the same positions and poses they'd adopted on the balcony of EMI's Manchester Square offices for their *Please Please Me* debut album six years earlier, the four now decidedly hirsute, with Lennon the most dramatically changed of all.

Back in Beatles headspace, Paul sat in a room at Cavendish Avenue and, with fresh ears, reviewed the results of the second version of the *Get Back* LP. To his mind, the music was stark, unadorned, frighteningly bare, but ultimately thrilling.

Klein, meanwhile, bluntly deemed it 'a crock of shit' and conspired with Lennon to bring in Phil Spector, who had just overseen the rousing production of 'Instant Karma!', to rework the tapes. Unknown to McCartney, Spector booked studio time in March and began slathering strings and brass, fairytale harp and *aaahing* choir onto 'The Long And Winding Road', making it sound hopelessly corny, like a BBC orchestra backing Engelbert Humperdinck.

At this stage, however, Paul remained unaware of this development, his thoughts somewhere else entirely. Secluded in his music room at Cavendish Avenue, McCartney began recording his first solo album, without the knowledge of the others. He wheeled a cooker-sized four-track machine from Abbey Road into his home and, free of the emotional and artistic complications of the Beatles' most recent sessions, began to play, in the childlike sense of the word.

'It was very liberating,' he says. 'But very necessary at that time, 'cause otherwise, I wouldn't have anywhere to go to get away from the turmoil.' In these solo sessions, it became clear to Paul that treating his music as therapy was yielding positive results: 'It's a bit like after an operation, where you want to rest but you've got to push it.'

He was able to record entirely alone, and even without a recording engineer, thanks to a device built by an Abbey Road technician which allowed him to plug directly into the back of the tape machine. He muffled boomy tom-toms with towels or simply moved the cymbals further away from the microphone if they sounded too loud and splashy on the recording. 'It was brilliant, actually,' he says of this unfussy approach. 'You're talking pure sound.'

When it became clear to him that he would have to step outside his house to finish the recordings, Linda booked time for him at Morgan Studios in Willesden, north-west London, under the name Billy Martin, making explicit the necessity for secrecy.

Inside Morgan, the troubles of the outside world seemed to evaporate, as noted by the facility's house engineer, Robin Black. 'You would never have guessed that he had any problems at all, quite frankly,' he says. It was 'like a holiday', according to Paul. He and Linda would even turn up with a packed lunch: 'We'd take some sandwiches and a bottle of grape juice and put the baby on the floor.'

The sense of fun and games spilled over from Cavendish Avenue and into the Morgan sessions. One day, inspired by a TV documentary he'd watched the previous evening about the Kreen-Akrore tribe of the Brazilian Amazon region, Paul fashioned a slightly daft ethno-rock instrumental of the same name. Feeling that something was lacking from the track, he disappeared for an hour and returned from Harrods with a longbow and arrow set, which he fired at a target to add percussive effects to the recording. 'I had microphones the whole way across the studio,' says Black, 'to try and capture the sound of the release of an arrow and the swish and the thud as it hit the target.'

Home-made and hand-made, the resulting album, *McCartney*, was less the grand launch of his solo career, more an insight into Paul's creative practices, being a precursor to the lo-fi recordings that would be in vogue decades later. But without the critical input of the other Beatles or George Martin, McCartney's creativity ran rampant, and to many the record seemed too random and sketchy, especially coming off the back of the polished *Abbey Road*. In many ways, the freedom and playfulness resulted in Paul's quality control slipping. For every track with the sophistication of the dreamlike and nostalgic 'Junk' or the gold-standard McCartney ballad 'Maybe I'm Amazed', there was the cloyingly simple snippet 'The Lovely Linda' or the throwaway one-man jam of 'Oo You'.

But before the listening public even had the opportunity to make up their minds about Paul's first solo effort, it was to provoke an almighty ruckus.

Ringo Starr stood on the doorstep of McCartney's house at Cavendish Avenue, unaware that he was about to precipitate the end of The Beatles. His tricky diplomatic mission, which he had chosen to accept in his role as the chirpy drummer, was to convince his increasingly estranged bandmate that there was an unacceptable clash of release dates between the long-delayed *Get Back* – now renamed *Let It Be* – and Paul's freshly minted eponymous solo album, which was due to be issued only a week before.

With him, he had a letter, dated 31 March 1970, handwritten by John Lennon and co-signed by George Harrison. It read: 'Dear Paul, We thought a lot about The Beatles and yours [*sic*]

LPs – and decided it's stupid for Apple to put out two big albums within 7 days of each other. So we sent a letter to EMI telling them to hold your release date 'til June 4th (there's a big Apple-Capitol convention in Hawaii then). We thought you'd come round when you realised that The Beatles album was coming out on April 24th. We're sorry it turned out like this – it's nothing personal. Love, John and George.'

Paul – his patience already strained, his temper on a hair-trigger – invited his friend inside and very quickly absorbed this information. Then he erupted.

'I told him to eff off,' Paul says. 'Everyone, to my mind, was completely treating me like dirt. It was kind of like, "We're the big guys, we're the grown-ups." And I said, "No way, man. Get out."'

Ringo swiftly departed with the sound of Paul's fury ringing in his ears. McCartney refused to budge and his solo album was released on 17 April 1970, forcing *Let It Be* back another two weeks to 8 May.

It was the moment when Paul McCartney finally gave up on The Beatles, the point where he mentally quit the group. Interview-phobic as he was at the time, when it came to promoting *McCartney*, Paul sidestepped face-to-face encounters by inserting a press release-cum-self-interview with the review copies of the album.

In the mock questionnaire, however, he sounded sulky, revealing more of his unhappy state of mind than perhaps even the most probing interviewer might have been able to. Was it true that Allen Klein and ABKCO weren't to be involved in the manufacturing or distribution of the new album? Not if Paul could help it. Was he planning any new records with The Beatles? No. Due to 'personal differences, business differences, musical differences'. Did he see himself writing songs together with John in the future? No. What were his plans now? 'My only plan is to grow up,' he wrote.

Not that anyone could tell from the tone of the pseudo-interview, which was stroppy and childish. Later, McCartney said it made him shudder to look back at it.

The news exploded across the front pages of the world's newspapers. The *Daily Mirror* in Britain, on the morning of 10 April 1970, was the first to break the news of the band's split, with the unfussy words: 'Paul Quits The Beatles'. In the days that followed, a wave of outrage began to build, with fans and reporters alike stunned that McCartney would dare to walk out on their beloved Fabs. Lost in the roar was the fact that at no point in the 'interview' had McCartney actually stated that he was walking out on the band.

Overwhelmed by the reaction, Paul thought, 'Christ, what have I done?', as he vainly attempted to back-pedal. Forced to break his year-long British press silence, he asked Derek Taylor to arrange an interview with a trusted journalist, Ray Connolly of London's *Evening Standard*. The pair met for lunch, along with Linda, at a packed seafood restaurant in Soho. It was apparent that Paul was desperate to set the record straight.

'It was all a misunderstanding,' he protested. 'I never intended the statement to mean "Paul McCartney quits Beatles". I didn't leave The Beatles. The Beatles have left The Beatles, but no one wants to be the one to say the party's over.' He went on to spend much of the remainder of the interview venting and moaning: about Klein, about the previous flounce-offs by Ringo and George, about how John had demanded a divorce from The Beatles, about how this 'trial separation' wasn't working.

If Paul was trying to redirect the finger of blame towards John, then it suited Lennon fine, since he was fuming that Paul had broken the news. John had in fact told Ray Connolly the previous

December that he had left the band, but asked the writer not to print the story, since Klein didn't want the news to leak until after the release of *Let It Be*.

Now, of course, Lennon was furious that McCartney had beaten him to it. Ray Connolly would later wonder whether Lennon had attempted to set him up with the Beatles Split exclusive, figuring the journalist wouldn't be able to resist printing it and that John could shruggingly walk away from the band, blaming the writer for letting the cat out of the bag.

McCartney, meanwhile, now viewed Klein with out-and-out contempt. On 14 April 1970 he wrote him a flinty letter, addressing what he saw as the vandalising of 'The Long And Winding Road', informing him that 'in future no one will be allowed to add to or subtract from a recording of one of my songs without my permission', though only going as far as to insist that the orchestration be toned down. Menacingly, though, he ended it with a threat: 'Don't ever do it again.'

But Klein was no pushover. For the US release of *McCartney*, he further incensed Paul by taking out ads in *Rolling Stone* provocatively proclaiming that the album was being released by Apple, 'an ABKCO-managed company'. The battle, it seemed, was on.

In the fall-out, the McCartneys once again ran away to Scotland. But Klein continued to haunt Paul. He would appear in his dreams as a demented dentist, chasing after him with a hypodermic needle, determined to, as he imagined, 'put me out'. McCartney confessed his fears to those close to him and they laughed. 'No,' Paul insisted, 'it's really fucking scary.'

For the first time in his life, he noticed grey in his hair. He gritted his teeth and read the music-press reports of how he had apparently stitched up the other Beatles and about how, vain and reclusive, he was 'sitting up in Scotland, looking into his mirror, admiring his own image'.

It drove him back to the bottle. One evening, in front of his wife, Lee Eastman and another unnamed guest, Paul began swigging whisky and jabbering, mumbling repeated phrases to himself: 'Fuckers . . . fucked me up . . . fucking carve-up.'

Eventually Linda led him to bed. Again, it was down to her to straighten out her husband's head. 'If I'd been doing that on my own,' Paul says, 'I'm not sure I'd have got out of it.'

Come summer, Lennon and McCartney entered into an odd correspondence, in an attempt to untangle the legal binding of The Beatles. First, Paul sent a twelve-page document to his bandmate, listing his many dissatisfactions. The gist was: 'I want to leave.' John artily responded with a photograph of himself, upon which he'd drawn a speech bubble containing the words 'How and why?' Paul wrote back saying he wanted the band's partnership to be officially dissolved because there was no partnership left. John sent him a curt postcard: 'Get well soon. Get the other signatures and I will think about it.'

The words 'I will think about it' unsettled Paul. For the first time, he considered the sickening notion that he might have to resort to legal action. It was something that had already occurred to Lee Eastman, the 60-year-old legal veteran, music publisher and expert in copyright law. Eastman senior had a reputation as a strong-headed negotiator himself and had already lost his composure in meetings with Klein. In June, he wrote an official letter to his adversary seeking the dissolution of the Beatles' partnership. Klein didn't reply. Eastman could read the signs that this had all the makings of a dirty fight.

For their part, the other Beatles had their reasons for being distrustful of McCartney and the Eastmans, particularly given the superior, almost Kennedy-like air of the latter. During the carving-up of the Beatles' business affairs between the two New Yorker factions, Lee Eastman had furtively advised Paul to buy up extra shares in the band's publishing company, Northern Songs, in an effort to strengthen his bargaining power. Upon his discovery of this, Lennon flew at Eastman, attempting to thump him.

Amid all of this viciousness and spite, a touch ludicrously, US promoter Sid Bernstein chose this moment to publicly offer The Beatles $1 million to perform at a music festival in Holland in August 1970. If at that time it seemed to McCartney that a reunion had never been less likely, in fact it wasn't quite as ridiculous a concept as it appeared.

Suddenly concerned that he had inadvertently slit the throat of his golden goose, in October Klein was behind a sneaky attempt to bring the band back together, when he tried to trick McCartney into returning to the fold. He instructed John to call Paul and say, 'We're recording next Friday, are you coming?' Dutifully, John did just that, having been advised by Klein that any signs of détente might limit Paul's powers in being able to legally extricate himself from the group.

Paul simply didn't show up. The three others then proceeded to work on a song called 'Early 1970', sung by Ringo and set to become the B-side to his subsequent single, 'It Don't Come Easy'. The loping, light-hearted number addressed each of the other Beatles in the first three verses, before mocking Ringo's own musical limitations in the final stanza. In the opening lines, concerning Paul, Starr noted that his estranged friend not only lived on a farm but, in addition, apparently had 'plenty of charm'.

If it was any kind of serious attempt at reconciliation, it was too little, too late. That same month, the McCartneys travelled to New York to 'get away from everything', not knowing that both Harrison and Lennon were coincidentally to be in the city at the same time.

While there, John arranged a meeting with Paul. McCartney cancelled, and Lennon later claimed that he hadn't planned to turn up anyway. Paul and George did meet, however, though their conversation quickly turned argumentative. McCartney stressed that he wanted off Apple. 'You'll stay on the fucking label,' Harrison hissed, before reflexively adding, 'Hare Krishna'.

And so McCartney's mind was set, even if, torn and procrastinating, he let the situation drift on for another couple of months before making his final move.

That December, back in Argyll, on a bright, cold day, McCartney stood high on a hill overlooking Skeroblin Loch, at the end of a long walk and deep conversation with Lee Eastman, in which, Paul says, 'we'd been searching our souls'. There was no other way, he concluded.

Surveying this peaceful scene, he decided that it was time to sue his bandmates, to legally kill The Beatles.

Taking the other Beatles to court must have been a huge, difficult decision for you to make.

It was just something I knew I had to do. I could not let Allen Klein get away with it. I just knew that very clearly. And unfortunately, nobody else did. You've got to imagine yourself in my position then. Being, in my mind, the only person without the blindfold on.

2

Across the Water

Three days into the new year of 1971, the SS *France* pulled out of Southampton harbour, en route to New York, with the McCartneys aboard. Unusually for Paul, visibly reflecting his desire to be distanced from the 'straights' he was forced to share the luxury ocean liner with for six days, he spent much of the voyage sporting dark glasses.

This starry behaviour disgruntled one female passenger in particular, who was affronted by the singer walking one evening into the dining-room without first removing his shades. She duly accosted him, saying, 'Take your sunglasses off. Elizabeth Taylor is on this boat and she doesn't wear them.'

In response, Paul accurately pointed out, 'Well, I'm not Elizabeth Taylor.'

McCartney was intent on putting some miles between himself and the legal ructions beginning to rumble back in London. Effectively, this trip to the States would find him, for a limited period, in self-imposed exile.

On the final day of 1970, he had filed to dissolve The Beatles & Company, listing his three estranged friends as defendants. There were still almost seven years left to run in the ten-year partnership agreement that the four had signed together in April 1967. In the light of the recent aggravations, however, McCartney couldn't bear the prospect of every financial or creative move he made having to be filtered through the clogged Beatles bureaucracy.

At the same time, he also sought a receiver for Apple to be appointed until the dispute was settled and asked that Klein be charged with the mismanagement of Apple funds, since he claimed not to have had accurate accounts from the New Yorker for either Apple or the band's partnership. Access to the band's recent income, totalling nearly four million pounds, was accordingly frozen.

From here on in, no one could get their hands on any of the money earned in the name of The Beatles.

To Paul's way of thinking, Klein had ripped off The Rolling Stones, and The Beatles were next. 'I was the lone voice,' he says. 'It was really painful, but I knew I had to take a stand.'

Compounding the agony, John and Paul's feud was intensifying and, worse, going public. Lennon fired the first shot in the press war, lambasting McCartney in his lengthy, Beatles-demolishing *Rolling Stone* interview, published in two parts early in 1971.

It caught John in a coarse, purgative mood. Far from being adorable mop-tops, The Beatles, he said, were 'the biggest bastards on earth'. He even took a dig at the mild, inoffensive George Martin, dismissing the producer's crucial role in the band's development. But, of course, he spewed most of his bitter rage in the direction of McCartney.

Paul had elected himself bandleader after Brian Epstein's death, he said, but in the end McCartney had only led The Beatles round and round in circles. Eventually, Lennon began to think of his role in the band merely as a day job. Paul would only toss him a guitar solo on Beatles records when he was feeling 'kindly' or guilty that he'd commandeered the A-side. The other Beatles had grown sick of being merely sidesmen for McCartney. Given Paul's casually domineering nature, there was a ring of truth to all of this.

But then Lennon twisted the knife: the *McCartney* LP was

'rubbish'. The *Let It Be* film had been 'set up by Paul, for Paul'. McCartney had fallen for the Eastmans' 'bullshit' because he was hopelessly entranced by this 'east coast suit . . . with Picassos on the wall'. They were cut from the same cloth, anyway, Paul being 'all form and no substance'. Now, Lennon seethed, McCartney would only talk to the others through lawyers because his attitude was 'I'm going to drag my feet and try and fuck you'.

Lennon's rant blindsided McCartney and, privately, it began to further deplete his already pitifully low self-esteem. Paul sat down and pored over every sentence, thinking, maybe Lennon was right, maybe he was this horrendous, vain, pig-headed, self-serving bastard. He voiced these thoughts aloud: 'He's captured me so well,' he said. 'I'm a turd.'

Again, Linda tried to talk her husband out of his black fug, saying, 'Now you know that's not true.' But Paul was wary of being drawn into a public battle with the merciless, acidic Lennon. Deeper than the worry of merely losing face, he feared being humiliated: 'He'd do me in.'

In New York, Paul kept his head down, scruffy-bearded and dressed-down in combat jacket and jeans to look 'like any junkie on the street'. One night, he and Linda rolled up to the Harlem Apollo to check out the talent night. Typically late, Linda had to sweet-talk the doorman to let them in. At the tail-end of an era violently stirred by the Black Panthers, they were the only two white faces in the theatre, blithely assuming that they would be safe in the crowd.

Still, elsewhere, paranoia was in the air. As a father, Paul worried about the kids being photographed by fans or, unthinkably, kidnapped, and tried to maintain as low a profile for his family as for himself. At the same time, there remained an oddness to his behaviour. One New Yorker Beatles fan, Libby Fields, claimed to have discovered a rumpled-looking McCartney very early one morning, spaced and jaded, in his army fatigues jacket, sitting on a bench in Harlem's Marcus Garvey Park. Shocked by his demeanour but thrilled to have this surprise one-to-one with even an apparently down-and-out Beatle, she asked him if he could wait five minutes until she ran home to grab her camera.

'Why not?' said Paul. 'I'm not going anywhere.'

A week into January, drummer Denny Seiwell, booked for a nameless demo session, turned up at an address in an unsettlingly heavy area in Manhattan, on 43rd Street between 9th and 10th. Immediately, he felt something was not right: the building looked burned out and appeared to have no electricity.

Through the opened door of the lobby he saw a guy sitting at a desk. Seiwell tentatively asked, 'Is there something going on?' The doorman nodded and gestured: 'Yep, down there.' Seiwell felt uneasy but made his way downstairs. There, in the damp, seedy basement, to his relief and surprise, he found Paul and Linda, sitting beside a battered old hired drum kit.

'They said, "Do you mind playing for us?"' says Seiwell. 'And I just went into Ringo on the tom-toms.' His playing aside, the drummer scored extra points for not being thrown by the idea of performing for a Beatle. 'I was young, and I don't mean to sound egotistical, but I knew I had something good. I felt like I deserved to be in there.'

Two days beforehand, New York session guitarist David Spinozza had found himself auditioning for Paul in a filthy loft on 45th Street. Linda, now acting as day-to-day organiser for Paul, had called the guitarist, introducing herself as Mrs McCartney, before vaguely asking him if he would like to meet her husband. The much-in-demand Spinozza copped something of an attitude straight away, playing hard to get and forcing the cagey Linda finally to name Paul. 'Like I'm supposed to know Paul McCartney was calling my house,' he huffed.

Post-audition, the guitarist got the gig and was asked if he was available to work five days a week for the next six weeks. He said he wasn't, but that he could manage two days a week. And so began the loose, three-handed recording sessions, featuring McCartney, Seiwell and Spinozza, for what would become *Ram*.

While the album was to be credited to Paul and Linda McCartney, Spinozza claimed – their increasingly accomplished and characteristic harmonies aside – that the latter's input was minimal. The sessions at Phil Ramone's A&R Studios on West 48th Street were markedly clean and efficient: McCartney and the two session men working regular hours, with no imbibing of alcohol or dope, usually knocking off late in the afternoon. Emphasising the McCartneys' growing attitude that they were a travelling musical family, Linda and the kids were always present, even on the rare occasions that the session dragged on and on until four in the morning.

During the making of *Ram*, Seiwell and McCartney grew closer. 'I'd never seen that kind of talent before,' says the drummer. In this setting, far from London and the battling Beatles, working with musicians paid to follow his every musical instruction closely, Paul was at last free to let his creativity flourish in a band setting without argument or interference. For the time being, this arrangement was highly productive, McCartney directing the musicians through song after song, great take after great take. To Seiwell's ears, one stand-out number, 'Another Day', the mundane daily routine of a female office worker set against a dreamy, hooky acoustic-guitar-strummed backing, sounded like 'Eleanor Rigby' transported to inner-city New York.

But while the sessions were creatively successful, Seiwell

remembers that the money deals with the musicians were done, in a pre-echo of the troubles to come, purely 'on a hippie handshake'.

Sorely disrupting the creative flow, on the other side of the Atlantic there was the tangled mess of the Beatles' legal affairs still to unravel. On 19 February 1971, a Friday, Paul stepped back into the eye of the storm, gently shoving through the crush of reporters outside the High Court in London for the first day of the case to settle the dispute in the partnership. Even if it was weighed down with negativity, there was still the thrill of a Beatle-styled happening in the air.

John Eastman had insisted that Paul appear in court every day wearing a suit and tie. McCartney initially protested, until he was reminded exactly what was at risk. If Allen Klein and the other Beatles retained control of the band's interests, then McCartney would effectively wind up bound to Apple or, cripplingly, ABKCO.

Paul turned up for the first day in court in the dark grey Tommy Nutter-designed suit he'd worn on the cover of *Abbey Road*, matched with an open-necked shirt, in a minor show of defiance. Conforming to the point of wearing a tie, he told his brother-in-law, would feel like 'humiliation'. Though his hair was trimmed, his bushy beard remained, signifying his recent rough times and desire to shield himself psychically.

In tow was Linda and Paul's counsel, David Hirst QC. The McCartneys entered the court and settled into the second row facing the judge's bench, with Hirst directly behind and, two rows further back, Klein, in trademark brown turtleneck sweater, along with his legal team. Paul shot a blank stare at the New Yorker and then turned away.

In a prelude to the proceedings, there was a moment of

lightness to lift the tension. The court attendant whispered to Paul that he expected the imminent arrival of John and Yoko, since it was unlikely they would be able to resist turning up. Paul bet him two shillings that they wouldn't show, and won. None of the other Beatles would make an appearance during the twelve-day period in which the case lumbered on.

Facing Mr Justice Stamp, Hirst set about dismantling Klein's professional character – a task made far easier by his opening announcement that the manager had been convicted of ten tax offences by a New York jury only three weeks before. 'It has obviously not enhanced Mr McCartney's confidence in Mr Klein,' Hirst pointed out dryly. He further argued that Klein couldn't be trusted to look after the partnership and its assets, and accused him of already overpaying himself in commission.

McCartney sat before the judge, using body language as a weapon, shaking his head sadly every time an erroneous statement was read out by Klein's defence. Then, having made this first-day appearance, he disappeared to New York once again.

On day two, Klein's counsel, Morris Finer QC, declared that Klein had effectively saved The Beatles from bankruptcy and that the current partnership could be advantageous to McCartney since, under the arrangement, all four Beatles shared in the profits of one another's solo records. Harrison's 'My Sweet Lord', he pointed out, had earned nearly £1 million, close to twice what Paul's solo releases in 1970 had brought into Apple. 'No one is getting at Mr McCartney on this,' he stressed.

On the third day, the affidavits from the other Beatles were read out. Lennon's was long and, in places, persuasive. He didn't agree with Paul that The Beatles had begun to drift apart after their touring days ended in 1966. In fact, he claimed, they had argued more on the road, and since then had got on better and were regular visitors to each other's homes. The Beatles were, however, he admitted, largely clueless about business, which is why Apple had become a hopeless mess.

Klein, Lennon reckoned, was 'certainly forceful to an extreme, but he does get results'. John said he had brought in Klein to clear out the 'hustlers' and 'spongers' responsible for the haemorrhaging of Apple funds. Further, he claimed that he had initially only wanted Klein to be his personal manager and that he hadn't tried to force him on the other Beatles. He concluded by declaring that Paul was acting 'selfishly and unreasonably'.

Harrison was clearly keen to air his grievances too. The major rift within the band had between himself and Paul. Since George had walked out of the Twickenham *Let It Be* sessions, however, Paul had treated him more as a 'musical equal'. This, he reasoned, showed that an intra-Beatles argument could be beneficially resolved. He had been stunned by Paul's legal letter seeking to dissolve the partnership: 'I still cannot understand why Paul acted as he did.'

Ringo's statement at first flattered Paul, calling him 'the greatest bass guitar player in the world', but went on to say that McCartney was also 'determined . . . he goes on and on to see if he can get his own way.' This, the drummer argued, had led to musical disagreements, even if these often proved to be the grit that produced the pearls. In December, he said, Paul had apparently agreed to sit down for an air-clearing meeting with the other Beatles in January, and so the writ had shocked the drummer too.

'Something serious, about which I have no knowledge, must have happened after Paul's meeting with George at the end of December,' he reasoned, apparently entirely unaware of the damage the guitarist had done by angrily telling McCartney he would make him stay on the label. Starr ended on a positive note, however, in hoping that 'all four of us together could even yet work out everything satisfactorily'.

On day four, Klein launched his defence in an affidavit read out to the court, pointing out that he had vastly improved the Beatles' financial affairs. In 1969 their earnings had doubled; in 1970 they had increased fivefold. He then griped that: 'Mr McCartney has made attacks on my commercial integrity'.

One of Paul's chief grievances was that Klein had sold the rights to the *Let It Be* film to United Artists without his approval. Klein argued that the sale had 'made an absolute fortune for all four Beatles'. In this way, he was virtually holding up his hands and admitting he was a music-business hustler, while pointing out that all four Beatles were better off as a result. This was, of course, undeniable: Paul had profited from the deals Klein had made. 'McCartney has accepted the benefits,' the manager stated, 'which I have negotiated in that capacity.'

A week into the proceedings, 26 February, Paul returned to the court, entering the witness-box. He rejected Lennon's earlier claim in his statement that the band 'always thought of ourselves as Beatles, whether we recorded singly or in twos or threes'. He quoted, almost as evidence, the fact that in the mantra-like 'God', from the *John Lennon/Plastic Ono Band* album, released two months earlier, his former bandmate had listed all the things he no longer believed in, the final one being, simply, 'Beatles'.

He then tried to undermine Lennon and Klein's relationship. In a phone conversation Klein had apparently told Paul that John was only angry with him because 'you came off better than he did in *Let It Be*'. In the witness-box, McCartney stirred the situation further, saying Klein had also warned him that Yoko was 'trouble . . . she's the one with ambition'. Openly and brazenly playing an intra-Beatles mind game, in a court of law, he disingenuously said that he'd wondered what John might make of this.

The main problem, as he saw it, was that when The Beatles signed the 1967 agreement, none of them had really considered the wording. Spotlighting his apparently guileless attitude to business, Paul said he always thought that he could just walk away from the deal at any point. In response to his colleagues' bewilderment when it came to his current legal action, he stated that his reasoning behind it was simple: The Beatles had broken up. In his mind, there could be no partnership if there was no band.

When summing up, David Hirst for McCartney said there were four major factors to their argument that the 1967 contract was unworkable: its assets were in jeopardy, one partner was being excluded, there existed a 'lack of good faith towards a partner by other partners', and the likelihood was that a dissolution was inevitable.

Morris Finer, for Klein and the other Beatles, rather poetically accused Paul of living 'in a world where everyone is either a seraphim or angel, ape or viper'. Moreover, he asked the judge not to grant a receivership order, since this would trigger the band's business organisation descending further into 'chaos'.

McCartney's defence team, having sifted through a three-foot-high pile of Beatles- and Klein-related documents, finally showed their hand. Hirst produced a cheque from Capitol to Klein for £852,000. The manager had of course increased the Beatles' US royalty rate from 17.5 per cent to 25 per cent, contractually entitling him to a fifth of the 7.5 per cent rise. But this was commission for a fifth of the band's entire cut. Paul argued that Klein had invoiced for at least £500,000 more than he should have done. 'We couldn't send him to jail for that,' he later said, 'but at least we could get a judgment.'

On the ropes, Klein's team cited a letter from the other three Beatles, dated January 1970, that seemed to rubber-stamp this new commission agreement. McCartney's team rightly argued that his former bandmates weren't allowed to alter management terms without his permission. Mr Justice Stamp instantly backed them, denouncing Klein's protestations as 'the prattling of a second-class salesman'.

After all the debate and deliberation, on 12 March 1971 Justice Stamp granted McCartney's request for a receiver to oversee the band's interests 'pending a permanent fix'.

James Spooner, a City-based chartered accountant, was appointed to oversee the Beatles' business affairs. Later, as he dug deeper into the paperwork, he discovered a different partnership agreement that appeared to have Paul's signature on it. He concluded that it was a forgery, which was a distinct possibility, given that through years of signing countless records, The Beatles had successfully learned to copy each other's signatures. 'It was a very crooked piece of paper,' Spooner noted.

Whatever the truth behind this strange postscript to the whole chaotic affair, McCartney had unequivocally won the first crucial round in the Beatles' legal battle, even if he now found himself hated by the press, the fans and the other band members.

'There was a lot of hostility going around,' he says now. 'But I had to do that to not let Allen Klein own The Beatles. If I hadn't done it, everything we'd ever done would've just gone down the drain. A few years later, they all recognised that.'

That was to be some way into the future, however. On the day, after the verdict was announced, according to the eyewitness accounts of the constant scrum of fans outside Paul's house, John, Ringo and George turned up at Cavendish Avenue in Lennon's white Rolls-Royce.

Lennon emerged from the car with two bricks, scaled the wall and, reverting to the furious teenage Teddy boy who used to wreck phone boxes in Liverpool, smashed McCartney's windows.

Meanwhile, Paul was three thousand miles away, back in New

York. Three days after the end of the court case, with the recording of *Ram* completed, he flew to the west coast with Linda and the girls to oversee its mixing in Los Angeles. For the duration of their stay the family rented a Santa Monica beachside house, owned by the Getty family. Their routine quickly began to resemble a working holiday: leisurely laps in the pool while listening to Linda's reggae records, lengthy dinners in hip restaurants on Ocean Park Boulevard.

In his final act of Beatle duty, Paul attended the Grammys with Linda, padding up to the podium to pick up the award for Best Original Score for *Let It Be* from, a touch surreally, famously swaggering Western screen legend John Wayne. As the McCartneys left, a reporter asked him if he was planning to do any recording while in LA. Paul, in a line that sounded prefabricated, said, 'I have a knife and fork and I'm here to cut a record.'

The New York leg of the album having been cleanly and successfully marshalled, the LA sessions were fuelled by dope. Paul would usually arrive mid-afternoon, spark up a joint and then tinker around endlessly. This mood of stoned whimsy extended to the album's artwork, featuring a black-and-white shot of McCartney manfully handling the horns of a Blackface sheep on the Scottish farm, framed by crude felt-tip scribbling in yellow, purple, green and red. The inner art was similarly childlike, incorporating photos of Paul and Linda and random horses into a purposely rough-cut collage with slightly bizarre found elements: grass from the garden, a few strands of human hair.

Upon the release of *Ram* in May 1971, keen artwork-scanners soon found in it what they assumed to be an oblique jibe: a nature photography library shot of two beetles copulating. This was interpreted in various ways: fucking Beatles, fuck The Beatles, fucked by The Beatles. Paul insists that its inclusion was purely accidental. 'It was just a funny shot,' he protests. 'A photograph of two beetles shagging. I mean, that *had to* get on the cover. Then afterwards, you go, "Oh, but they were beetles." To me they were just a couple of little ladybirds or something. I swear to God I didn't think about that. The thing is, whatever you do gets interpreted. And I don't see half of it coming.'

Less considered still was a strange promo disc put out to press and radio to publicise the album, entitled *Brung To Ewe* and featuring a sound collage of sheep noises, nonsensical snatches of Paul-and-Linda dialogue and in-jokes over snippets of the album's songs. Recurring throughout was a gospel number, 'Now Hear This Song Of Mine', that hadn't even made it onto the record. Those in the music industry who heard it were slightly baffled: rather than summoning the spirit of Beatleish playfulness, it sounded like a lot of stoned rambling.

Nevertheless, although not viewed as such at the time in many quarters, given the Olympian expectations of the solo Beatles, *Ram* was something of a marvel. Really the true successor to *Abbey Road*, in its baroque detail and flights of imagination, it was variously funny, daft, touching and knowing. It was also deliberately eventful in its structure, featuring songs within songs and unexpected dips and turns.

'I tried to avoid any Beatles clichés and just went to different places,' says Paul. 'So the songs became a little more episodic or something. I took on that kind of idea a bit more than I would've with The Beatles. I suppose I was just letting myself be free. So if I wanted to do "Monkberry Moon Delight" with "a piano up my nose", then I figured, that'll be OK.'

Unlikely US number 1 'Uncle Albert/Admiral Halsey' spotlighted the new McCartney method: its trippy sentimentality giving way to rain and vocally impersonated ringing telephone effects before restlessly tempo-shifting upwards through its lengthy coda. Elsewhere, Beach Boys references abounded, not least in the ornate arrangement of 'Ram On' and the multi-voiced teenage swoon of 'The Back Seat Of My Car'.

Artwork aside, *Ram* also seemed to be carefully mined with lyrical digs at Lennon and the other Beatles. McCartney insists that the apparent pot-shots in '3 Legs', particularly the parts where he laments being betrayed by a former friend, were misinterpreted: 'That was just kind of a joke blues song in my mind.'

'Too Many People', though, was directed squarely at the 'preaching practices' of John and Yoko. 'I felt that was true of what was going on,' says McCartney. '"Do this, do that, do this, do that."' If there was dark anger at the heart of *Ram*, however, it was deeply hidden. Even the song's opening words, 'piss off', were veiled by a weak pun.

'It's actually "piece of cake",' Paul says, 'which was thinly disguised as "piss off, cake". And, hey, come on, how mild is that? It's not exactly a tirade.' The withering put-downs of 'Dear Boy', meanwhile, were penned not with any of The Beatles in mind, but for Linda's first husband, Mel See. In it, the singer derided See for not recognising the wonders of the now Mrs McCartney, who Paul further admitted in the lyric, had emotionally revived him when he was low.

If relatively slick compared to its scrappier predecessor, *Ram* only made number 2 in the US, where *McCartney* had reached number 1, though it topped the album chart in the UK. Critics on both sides of the Atlantic, however, were unkind, verging on brutal. *Rolling Stone*'s review was particularly vitriolic, loftily claiming, '*Ram* represents the nadir in the decomposition of 1960s rock thus far . . . so incredibly inconsequential and monumentally irrelevant.' *Melody Maker*, meanwhile, struck a nerve: 'It must be hell living up to a name . . . you expect too much from a man like McCartney.'

Asked about *Ram*, Lennon admitted that he liked the

beginning and end of 'Uncle Albert/Admiral Halsey', but griped that the rest of it 'just tripped off all the time'. Ringo, quizzed about the record elsewhere, came across as bitter and hurt when it came to Paul. 'I don't think there's one tune on *Ram*,' he said. 'I just feel he's wasted his time. He seems to be going strange. It's like he's not admitting he can write great tunes.' The fact that, in May, Paul and Ringo had hung out together at Mick Jagger's wedding to Bianca in St Tropez – the first time they'd socialised since the Beatles split – seemed to have no bearing on the drummer's negative feelings.

For McCartney himself, *Ram* was an entirely successful endeavour, both creatively and commercially, if not critically. In the end it served its purpose, in driving on his post-Beatles career, as – he pointed out – suggested by its determined, dual-meaning title: 'It meant . . . ram forward, press on, be positive.'

If McCartney's ongoing process of creative therapy now found him with his head happily back up in the musical clouds, where it had been in the best times with The Beatles, it wasn't long before various realities began to drag him back earthwards once again.

In April 1971 came the word that Klein and the other Beatles weren't going to appeal against the court's judgment and had decided to grant McCartney his freedom from the partnership. But, with most of his money still tied up in Apple, Paul was suddenly faced with financial embarrassment. On the last day of March, the newly formed McCartney Productions Ltd submitted its first annual accounts for the period 1970 to 1971: £3,017 incoming, £5,417 outgoing, resulting in a deficit of £2,400.

Day to day, the McCartneys were actually living on the money that Linda had earned as a photographer in New York before meeting Paul. As a kept husband, McCartney used to joke to his wife that at least one of them was keeping them afloat.

But in December 1970, before announcing that he was to sue the other Beatles, Paul had tried to make a business manoeuvre that, depending on your perspective, was either prescient or crafty. He had asked for there to be a further definition of the terms of his contract with Northern Songs – the company formed by Brian Epstein, The Beatles and music publisher Dick James in 1963, which owned the rights to all of the group's songs and which James had sold in 1969 to media magnate Lew Grade's ATV, without first consulting The Beatles. McCartney was arguing that the deal shouldn't cover any material that he wrote with anyone other than John Lennon.

Now, with *Ram*, he was claiming that seven of its fourteen tracks were straight 50–50 co-writes with Linda, despite the fact that she wasn't a recognised songwriter. Grade, perhaps understandably, thought he was being stitched up and that Paul was underhandedly trying to claw back some of his songwriting royalties to McCartney Productions.

This, of course, was reasonable, but tough to prove. Only those in the room when the songs were being written, Paul and Linda, knew exactly who was responsible for what. 'If my wife is actually saying, "Change that", or "I like that better than that", then I'm using her as a collaborator,' Paul reasoned. In the event, an entirely unconvinced Grade slapped the McCartneys with a lawsuit for an arbitrarily round one million dollars, in a dispute to be settled, in a wholly unorthodox fashion, a little further down the line.

As the spring of 1971 turned to summer, the strangeness that came with Paul's extraordinary fame began to creep back into the McCartneys' lives. In June, an odd-looking parcel addressed simply to 'Paul McCartney' was delivered to the BBC's Bush House in London's Aldwych. Suspecting it to be a letter bomb, the staff there immediately called in the police. Once carefully opened, the package was revealed to be a gift of wineglasses and crockery from a fan, ahead of Paul's upcoming twenty-ninth birthday, along with a letter that said 'I love you' in Spanish.

Other, more determined devotees would sometimes make the long pilgrimage to Argyll, since it was no secret now that the McCartneys spent much of their time near Campbeltown. Their neighbours would sometimes be shocked to find a frazzled-looking hippie peering through their windows, thinking they had found where Paul lived. Once the McLean family, who lived nearby, found five longhairs hiding in their shed, claiming they had merely wanted to practise yoga in the vicinity of the supposed McCartney aura.

More worryingly, a young girl, a Mormon from Utah, had taken to camping on the edge of some woods just beyond the boundary of High Park, meaning she could get close to Paul without trespassing on his land. The McCartneys often saw her, partially hidden by the trees, watching them through binoculars. One day in summer 1971, Paul apparently snapped and, according to the girl, came out of the house, drove towards her in his Land Rover and angrily emerged, shouting and swearing.

The girl claimed that she couldn't remember much of what happened next, except that, in the aftermath, her nose was bleeding. The inference, obviously, was that McCartney had assaulted her, which Paul denied. 'I have been asking her politely – pleading with her – to leave me and my family alone,' he stated. 'She refuses to recognise that I am married with a family.'

The greater solution to all of this was simple, if expensive, and required much in the way of patience. Now, whenever any of the McCartneys' neighbours put their properties on the market, Paul snapped them up. In time he became the owner of two other neighbouring farms, Low Park and Low Ranachan, using the barn of the latter as a makeshift rehearsal space. Acre by acre, Paul bought back his privacy.

That summer, in the light of the pressures of the first half of the year, the McCartneys decided to escape further into Scottish solitude by taking a trip to Shetland. 'We just took off in the Land Rover,' Paul says. 'We piled everything in the back, kids and us in the front, dogs in the back too. The potty on top of everything and off we went.'

The McCartneys drove to the small port of Scrabster on the north-eastern coast of Scotland, with the notion of taking a ferry to Orkney, from where they could fly on to Shetland. But the plan was thwarted when, two cars ahead of them, the announcement came that the ship was full. Still determined, Paul began enquiring around the harbour about the possibility of hiring a fishing boat, romantically fancying that it might involve giving the skipper a salmon or a bottle of whisky.

Rousing from his slumber the Shetland-jumper-wearing captain of a modest vessel named *The Enterprise*, Paul successfully offered him £30 to take the McCartneys aboard. The kerfuffle involved in getting all of the family's stuff on the boat at low tide, including gently easing sheepdog Martha down in a net, drew a crowd to the quayside. As Paul and Linda and the girls and the dogs pulled out of the harbour on their rented craft, the locals cheered and waved them off.

Once into their voyage, passing around beers, the choppy waters ensured that the McCartneys began feeling green around the gills. The baby Mary was first to be sick, quickly followed by Linda. Paul manfully gripped the mast and tried to keep his nausea at bay. Soon, it became obvious that this wasn't going to be possible. The skipper, George, gestured towards the fishing baskets, saying, 'Do it in there!'

And so, far from the luxuries of the SS *France* six months earlier, there at the edge of the world, Paul leaned over and threw his guts up.

McCartney and *Ram* weren't the first records of yours that Linda appeared on, were they?

No. She sang back-ups on 'Let It Be'. She'd done a real good job. I'd just taken her in the studio quietly one time and said, 'We need a high note on the top of the chorus.' She just went bang, hit it. Great, y'know.

3

Knee Deep in the River

Picture the scene, he asked her. Imagine us standing behind a curtain and it parts to reveal a waiting, expectant audience.

'Would it completely freak you?' he said.

She suspected it might, but she was at least up for finding out whether or not it did.

The McCartneys were in bed one night when Paul first floated the idea by Linda: 'Do you think you could handle being in a band?'

'He made it sound so glamorous,' she said, 'that I agreed to have a go.'

Aside from anything, as he pointed out, if she decided not to come on the road with him, it would curb the family's self-fash-ioned lifestyle as 'roving hippies'. This, it seems, sealed the deal.

In the days and weeks that followed, Paul began to map out the basic piano chords for Linda, in her new role as keyboard player. Fourteen years earlier he'd done something similar with John: shown him how to retune his guitar from the banjo stand-ard taught to Lennon by his mother Julia, demonstrated how to reposition his fingers to play rock'n'roll shapes.

With Linda, though, Paul didn't display as much in the way of tolerance or enthusiasm. 'He has no patience,' she moaned. 'I had to learn it myself. The few things he'd show me, if I didn't get it right, he'd get really angry. So I said, "Like, forget it."'

His frustration with Linda's lack of natural musical ability aside, there was a part of McCartney that was tempted to indulge in the current vogue for the supergroup. In his mind, he saw himself surrounded by Eric Clapton, John Bonham, Billy Preston; even, in a parallel, ideal world, John Lennon.

But then he cast his mind back to how The Beatles had begun and the camaraderie that couldn't be faked with a bunch of 'name' musicians. 'All I thought was, How do you start a band?' he says. 'Well, you start with nothing and you just learn and you improve. The idea was to get a bunch of mates together. I wasn't interested in putting it together professionally.'

Elsewhere, skint and sleeping on an old mattress in the back room of his manager Tony Secunda's office in Mayfair, Denny Laine was about to get the call that would reroute the next ten years of his life. The Birmingham-born former singer with The Moody Blues, frontman of their yearning 1964 hit 'Go Now', was on his uppers, his life after quitting the band being the slightly desperate one of the nearly-but-not-quite-successful musician.

Laine had gone on to form the proto-classical/rock cross-pol-lination act the Electric String Band, whose performance at the Saville Theatre in June 1967, supporting Jimi Hendrix, had been witnessed by McCartney three days after the release of *Sgt. Pepper*. In time it proved too expensive for him to keep such an ambitious project on the road, particularly after, comically, the tapes of the band's third single were lost after being posted to their own record label, Decca.

The apparently luckless Laine drifted to Spain where, in Andalucía, he lived with gypsies, rented an artist's hut neighbour-ing a pigsty and learned flamenco guitar. Returning to England in 1969, he formed the unfortunately named Midlands supergroup Balls, which quickly disintegrated. Feeling sidelined by Secunda after the manager turned his attentions to his new charge, soon-to-be-superstar Marc Bolan, Laine was half-considering a solo career when McCartney phoned him, mooting the idea of a band.

'I was needing the money, really,' Laine admits. 'But I wouldn't have just gone out and done anything either. So when I got the call from him, it was like, Oh, this is gonna be fun. I know Paul, I know I can make some dough eventually in doing this and I'll be back to doing what I like doing.'

McCartney and Laine already knew one another, from the days when both The Beatles and The Moody Blues were managed by Brian Epstein's NEMS outfit and shared tour buses together. Reconnecting now, Laine sensed a surprising nervousness in the newly ex-Beatle. 'I think his confidence was a little bit in question because, trying to follow The Beatles, what are you gonna do?'

Paul was certainly looking for a vocal foil to replace Lennon, if not exactly a songwriting partner. 'Just a fellow vocalist so we could harmonise together,' he says. 'As far as composing was concerned, probably I was spoilt with John as a collaborator.' The New York sessions for *Ram* had made McCartney hanker for the musical closeness of The Beatles. For various reasons, he missed being in a band. 'Camaraderie was one thing,' he says. 'Musical turn-on was another.'

To this end, in June 1971, he invited Denny Seiwell and New York guitarist Hugh McCracken (who had filled the boots of the increasingly errant David Spinozza as the making of *Ram* progressed) to Scotland for a part-holiday, part-potential-band sound-out. Perhaps harbouring over-romantic ideas about Scotland, the Americans – Seiwell and McCracken and their respective wives, Monique and Holly – found themselves living in basic, unglamorous rooms at the Argyll Arms in Campbeltown. Neither did they take to the nation's famously stodgy, greasy food.

On the day they arrived, the party drove over to the McCartneys' farm for drinks. As they were leaving, though, the men were pulled aside by Linda and asked not to bring their wives the following day, since the plan was for the band, including Mrs McCartney, of course, to work. This did not go down well with the women, for whom this wasn't turning out to be much of a holiday.

Within days the McCrackens returned to New York. Clearly not at one with the farm-centred or hippiefied existence, Paul reckoned that Hugh 'didn't want to go that far out with his life'. Seiwell, however, apparently did. Although he and Monique initially followed the McCrackens back to the States, two months later, in August 1971, the drummer returned.

Denny Laine first hooked up with Denny Seiwell at Glasgow Airport, where the two met to take the 40-minute flight across the Firth of Clyde and over the Isle of Arran, down to Campbeltown. Having made their way to High Park, the evening was spent drinking and, for Paul and Denny Laine, reminiscing, while sketching the plans for the new band.

Laine was impressed that Paul was apparently now 'just a farmer who plays guitar . . . out on his tractor, growing vegetables . . . he's not a Beatle any more'. Paul would joke that, in green-fingered terms, whether digging the vegetable patch or tinkering around in their recently assembled greenhouse, he remained second to Linda. 'She's the lead gardener,' he quipped. 'I'm the rhythm gardener.'

But, as the band started to rehearse, Linda struggled to keep up. Initially there hadn't even been any mention of her being part of the band, says Laine. 'She was taking pictures and Paul would just say, "Linda, can you just try and play that note or sing that line there?" They were seeing whether it would work.'

Privately, Laine thought that the outfit would get tighter far quicker with a professional keyboard player, while slightly resenting having to coach an amateur. However, both the drummer and the guitarist understood that Linda's influence on the group, through her love of design and photography, would be great, and that, crucially, she provided unconditional support and stability for Paul.

'She was his security blanket, his inspiration, his wife and mother of his kids,' Seiwell says. 'She was the one who got Paul off his ass when he was having to sue the other Beatles. His heart was broken. He would've sat up there in Scotland and just become a drunk. If she hadn't got on his case, none of it would have ever happened.' At the same time, the drummer acknowledges that Linda wasn't an important addition to the line-up on a musical level. 'Not musically. But she was more than an important element, she was a necessity.'

'The thing is,' says Paul, 'we wanted to be together and we said, "What right has anyone got to say we shouldn't be together in a band? Whose affair is it but ours?"'

For the musicians, life at High Park was rough and ready. With no room in the small family house for them, Seiwell and his wife rented nearby Brechie Farm, at Kilkenzie, while Laine, ever the gypsy, pitched up in a caravan on the McCartneys' land. All visitors to the farm were expected to live the basic rural life, although some extra efforts would be made for special guests. When his father Jim and Jim's second wife Angela came to stay, Paul scrubbed the floor of the garage before laying a mattress down for them.

Seiwell and Laine were both put on a £70 weekly retainer – not exactly a fortune, but a decent working wage for the early 1970s. Paul's money remained tied up in Apple, and there was a casual understanding that there was more to come for the musicians in the future.

Inside the small, low-ceilinged, wood-panelled musical den that was Rude Studio, the band quickly moved on from jamming rock'n'roll standards to picking their way through Paul's latest, half-finished songs. On days when the weather was fine, the musicians would move their amps and instruments outside and play al fresco.

A snapshot from the time captures the four of them rehearsing on the grass in front of the studio lean-to – all in muddy wellies, toasting the birth of the group with glasses and cups of whisky and Coke. Seiwell, tellingly, wears a white T-shirt printed with a green marijuana leaf, revealing the other key ingredient in their bonding. 'We weren't Bob Marley and the Wailers by any means,' he laughs. 'We enjoyed a bit of the herb for the creative conscious, you know what I'm saying?'

The sound of the nameless band would echo freely out over the hills, but trying to confine this unbridled noise to the environment of the recording studio was to prove far harder.

Enthralled by his new group, McCartney was suddenly gripped by the notion of spontaneity. Bob Dylan had the year before recorded most of the light country breeze of *New Morning* in an impressively tight five-day period. 'Coming off the back of taking a long time over records,' says Paul, 'it just seemed like an interesting idea to do a record quickly.'

Thus inspired, McCartney blocked out a week in August at Abbey Road and the band nailed eight songs, five of them in the first take. This sense of urgency is captured right at the top of the album that was to become *Wild Life* when, in the opening seconds, McCartney can be heard to excitedly shout 'Take it, Tony' to engineer Tony Clark, asking him to roll the tape at the height of the jam that became 'Mumbo'.

'Paul wanted to give the world a real true look at a new band,' says Seiwell. 'We did not mess around with that record. It was done quickly and honestly.' Still, there remained a feeling that these tracks were just being carelessly thrown down. The other engineer on the sessions, Alan Parsons, thought as much: 'I was so excited to be working with Paul, but I did feel a certain lack of precision.'

For all that the band appeared to be a democratic arrangement, Parsons says that when the other members pitched in their ideas, 'they would occasionally be shouted down' by Paul. Meanwhile, Linda's keyboard contributions to the album were competent, and made all the more impressive by the fact that she was eight months pregnant.

Out in the wider world, it was impossible to tell whether McCartney's commercial stock was rising or falling. Within weeks of one another, 'Uncle Albert/Admiral Halsey' made US number 1, while the far hookier 'The Back Seat Of My Car' struggled to number 39 in the British singles chart – notably Paul's most miserable performance to date, whether solo or as a Beatle.

It was a sign, among others, that the last of the shine was coming off the previously untarnishable Fabs, whose post-split interpersonal relationships were further deteriorating. McCartney was invited by George Harrison to appear on 1 August 1971 at Madison Square Garden in New York alongside Bob Dylan, Ringo Starr and Eric Clapton at his Concert for Bangladesh, hastily arranged as a benefit for the flood-stricken nation. Paul flatly declined. Visa problems were cited as the reason for his non-appearance when, in truth, it was due to Allen Klein's involvement and the ongoing Beatles friction.

Klein, never one to miss a media opportunity, immediately jumped on the no-show to inform the press that Paul was refusing to perform for the suffering refugees. But if he and Harrison were pushing for a Beatles reunion to crown the event, both Lennon and McCartney were less than keen. John said he couldn't be bothered rehearsing and getting into the whole 'showbiz trip' that the occasion entailed. 'I thought, What's the point?' Paul said. 'We've just broken up and we're joining up again? It just seemed a bit crazy.'

In the meantime, over the summer, Lennon had sharpened his blade for what would be regarded as his deepest and most vicious stab at McCartney. The deceptively laidback rocker 'How Do You Sleep?', from his *Imagine* album, released in October 1971, was a swift and hateful response to what John perceived as Paul's cryptic digs at him and Yoko in 'Too Many People' and '3 Legs' from *Ram*, released only four months earlier.

'How Do You Sleep?' attempted to demolish McCartney's character. The vengeful lyric accused Paul of living with 'straights' buffing the ego of the king who, with an irony surely not lost on Lennon, was utterly controlled by his wife-cum-mother-figure. His music was 'Muzak'; the 'freaks' had been right in saying Paul was dead; his best work was far behind him and even his doe-eyed good looks would only distract the public from his shallow talent for 'a year or two'. Using a sibilant echo effect on his voice, Lennon ended the choruses mimicking the hissing sound of a snake.

It was a precision attack that hit hard at the still fragile McCartney. Cruelly, if amusingly, Lennon even poked fun at McCartney's new country life, with a postcard tucked into *Imagine*'s sleeve featuring a piss-take of the cover of *Ram*: a photograph of John holding the ears of a snuffling pig. Harrison, playing slide guitar on 'How Do You Sleep?', was silently complicit in the hazing. Starr didn't contribute to the track, but was there when it was being written, growing visibly upset as the lyrical taunts became more and more barbed, before finally saying, 'That's enough, John.'

Lennon was unrepentant, however. At one point, during a run-through of the song, he turned and stared into a camera documenting the proceedings for the *Imagine* film, remotely eyeballing McCartney and asking him, 'How do you sleep, ya cunt?'

'The joke was,' says Paul, 'my answer – although I never rang him up and told him – was, "very well". That was the one thing, I was sleeping very well, 'cause I was in the countryside. Fresh air.' He admits, nonetheless, that the track did needle him. 'Oh yeah. It was a massive, massive bug. I was just really *sad*, y'know, 'cause we'd been really tight mates since about sixteen or something. So it was a very, very strange turnaround.'

Upon its release, Lennon back-pedalled when questioned about the savagery of 'How Do You Sleep?', explaining that it was written as a bitter studio in-joke, with chipped-in contributions from Yoko and Allen Klein. He admitted, however, that he'd been blinded by fury and determined to wound McCartney. Even if Paul only had himself to blame, he argued, since he had started it.

'Listen to *Ram*, folks,' Lennon instructed the public. 'It's an answer to *Ram* . . . a moment's anger.'

Though hurt, McCartney, as ever, ploughed on. Toying with band names ranging from the half-decent (Turpentine) to the dreadful (The Dazzlers), the trading name of the new group was to come to Paul in a moment of acute panic provoked by life-or-death crisis.

In mid-September, Linda went into labour and was taken to King's College Hospital in Southwark. Upon examination, it was revealed that there was a likely complication to the birth: she was suffering from placenta previa, a condition where tissue covers or part-covers the uterus, restricting delivery and causing heavy bleeding.

The decision was made by the doctors to perform an emergency Caesarean section. Hurried into a waiting-room, Paul, in his green surgical gown, suddenly found himself alone, 'praying like mad', for his wife and unborn child. Into his racing thoughts came an image of an angel's wings, striking him with its simple, calming beauty.

The drama over, the McCartneys found themselves with a second natural daughter, Stella Nina, and a name for their new band: Wings.

For the next two months, the newly extended family disappeared to Scotland. As soon as October, however, the music press was announcing the name of the new band and reporting that they were rehearsing on the farm for upcoming live dates.

On 7 November, the McCartneys came out of hiding, reportedly wasting no unnecessary costs by travelling second-class on the train from Scotland to London in preparation for the following night's launch of Wings and their album, *Wild Life*. Re-engaging with the music industry, Paul and Linda had decided to throw a party at the Empire Ballroom in Leicester Square.

Indicating just how big a deal the bash was for the McCartneys, Paul had handwritten every one of the 800 invitations. In some ways, though, the party served to highlight how far removed the couple now were from hip London. Along with an incongruous raffle, the assembled guests – including Elton John and members of Led Zeppelin, The Who and The Faces – were entertained by former Cavern owner Ray McFall's jazz band and a kitsch turn by Frank and Peggy Spencer's ballroom dancing team. Then the guests were plied with food and drink as *Wild Life* pumped out of the club's speakers.

The four members of the newly minted Wings grouped together for photographs: the moustachioed Seiwell looking 1970s-suave in grey suit and black turtleneck; Laine skinny in a retina-scorching red jacket; Linda hiding her post-pregnancy curves in a roomy dress adorned with white doves; and Paul, a touch bizarrely, in a wide-lapelled checked suit with rough white stitching. It turned out that when he had gone to pick the suit up from his tailor that morning, he'd been told that, sorry, it wasn't ready.

'Maybe not, but it's a look,' Paul replied, before deciding to wear the two-piece exactly as it was. All evening, puzzled members of London's in-crowd came up to him to point out that his suit wasn't finished. To this he would beamingly respond, 'Yeah, I know. Great, huh?'

A reporter from *Melody Maker* asked the McCartneys why they'd chosen to launch the band on a Monday night in Leicester Square.

'Why not?' Paul responded, with typical elusive cheerfulness.

'We thought it would be a nice idea,' said Linda, making it sound like an office do, 'to invite a whole lot of our friends to a big party where they could bring their wives.'

'EMI are paying for it,' Paul pointed out, unwittingly revealing that under no circumstances would he have shelled out from his own pocket for this kind of shindig.

The party did the trick, though, in heralding the arrival of the new band. Five days later, the first shot of the quartet appeared on the cover of *Melody Maker*, along with the words 'Wings Fly!' Inside, under the provocative headline 'Why Lennon Is Uncool', McCartney attempted to dispassionately respond to the public abuse hurled at him by his former friend, which, as suspected, had stung him far more than anything he could throw back at John. Touching on 'How Do You Sleep?', he said, 'I think it's silly. So what if I live with straights? I like straights.'

It was perhaps with this comment alone that, in the eyes of the excruciatingly cool rock elite, McCartney indelibly cast himself as 'straight', sounding more like a bowler-hatted banker, commuting into the city every morning on the 8:12 from Cheam, than an eccentric millionaire rocker living in remote Scotland in a rundown two-bedroomed farmhouse, subsisting on joint after joint.

'He says the only thing I did was "Yesterday",' Paul added, sounding a touch more bruised. 'He knows that's wrong.'

Further riled, having read the interview, Lennon fired off a blistering letter that appeared in the next edition of the music paper, ending: 'If we're not cool, what does that make you?'

Wild Life was met with a colossal wave of disappointment. As a Dylan-inspired attempt to bottle the lightning of live recording, it was lacking in thrills. Paul's second album in seven months, it sank faster than even the poorly received but creatively buoyant *Ram*. The record-buying public seemed baffled by how this formerly perfectionist creator of so many peerless Beatles classics could turn out such half-finished scraps. For those weaned on the mini-symphonies of *Sgt. Pepper* and *Abbey Road*, this really wasn't good enough.

The truth seemed to be that McCartney, high and happy, was simply indulging himself, without anyone to tell him no, or to edit or jettison his weaker ideas. Worse, with the gibberish words of side-one leading tracks 'Mumbo' and 'Bip Bop', he apparently couldn't even be bothered writing lyrics any more. Later, when listening to the latter, Paul would cringe. 'When you allow yourself to be playful,' he says, 'the morning after or the month after or the year after, you can just think, Oh, maybe that was a bit *too* playful.'

The best moments in *Wild Life* were to be found further down the track list: the early stirrings of the McCartneys' animal-rights sympathies in the mournful rocker 'Wild Life', the lovely Paul-and-Linda-do-the-Everly-Brothers cooing of 'Some People Never Know'. Amid the gentle waves of harmony in 'Tomorrow', a follow-up song of sorts, an insecure McCartney pleaded with his lover not to let him down, as if recalling the female figure in 'Yesterday' who had once broken his heart by leaving.

At the end of the record, in the orchestrated piano ballad 'Dear Friend', Paul addressed John directly, declaring his love for him and, in a highly sentimental tone, sadly asking if this really was the 'borderline', the end of their friendship. 'That's much more loving,' Paul says of the conciliatory song. 'It's like, "Oh come on, mate."'

Sales-wise, in Beatle terms, the album stiffed, prompting EMI to cancel the release of the proposed double A-side single 'Love Is Strange/I Am Your Singer'. 'I like the record,' Paul now says of *Wild Life*, before accepting, 'It wasn't perhaps as good as some of the others.' At the same time, McCartney points out that validation for his records can sometimes come from the most unlikely or fleeting of encounters. Shortly after the release of *Wild Life*, he was motoring down Sunset Strip in Los Angeles when a camper van, driven by 'a typical Woodstock type', pulled up beside him. Spotting McCartney, the grinning hippie waved a copy of the record out of the van's window before shouting over to tell him that he was heading up into the hills with the LP, doubtless to get high and listen to the album in much the same state as it was created. 'He said, "Great record, man",' remembers Paul. 'To me, that was it.'

Others weren't so enthusiastic. *Rolling Stone* head-scratchingly wondered whether the LP was 'deliberately second rate', theorising that it was perhaps an exercise in creating banal music that would infuriate Lennon by outselling his apparently more meaningful records. This ridiculous notion was instantly disproved by the fact that, in a perhaps commercially hobbling move, on its initial release in the US it didn't have any words at all on its cover. In an effort to prop up the record, Capitol hastily affixed a sticker to the remaining stock bearing the legend 'Paul McCartney & Friends'.

Still, the photograph that appeared on the front of *Wild Life* seemed to say it all: Paul was now just a member of a band, and one that, to his mind, needed no introduction. In the pastoral scene, foregrounded by hazy sunlit foliage, the barefooted members of Wings – positioned at the bottom of the picture, almost as an afterthought in the framing – balance on a horizontal branch a few feet above a stream.

Second from left in the line-up, McCartney stands knee-deep in the river, strumming an acoustic guitar, too distant from the camera for anyone other than the sharp-eyed – and maybe this was the entire point – to recognise him as Beatle Paul.

As Wings were splashing around in the country, the glitter-and-glue stomp of glam rock was fast becoming the soundtrack of the times, making The Beatles, and their solo efforts, seem hopelessly passé, only a year and a half after their demise.

In an effort to toughen up his new band's sound, as hard-rock-tinged pop began creeping into the charts, Paul decided to expand Wings to a five-piece by drafting in a lead guitarist. Over twelve intensive days of rehearsals in January 1972 at the Scotch of St James club, an old hangout for The Beatles and The Stones just off Piccadilly, McCartney worked up new songs with the band, inviting down, through a tip-off from a roadie, Henry McCullough.

Painted by *Melody Maker* as 'an eternal drifter wandering from gig to gig', McCullough, from Portstewart in Northern Ireland, was a proper road-worn rocker with many touring miles to his name. Three years earlier, during Joe Cocker's star-making set at Woodstock, McCullough had been part of the backing Grease Band who had successfully heavied-up Lennon and McCartney's 'With A Little Help From My Friends'.

As such, he was only slightly daunted by the prospect of

working with a Beatle. 'But I was a little bit,' McCullough admits. 'I mean, this is Paul McCartney. I grew up with The Beatles. But we had a long talk and he told me what the score was going to be and it was all very exciting. I wasn't scared. He was easy to be about if you were in the gang, y'know. After a month or two, you got used to his face.'

McCullough further proved himself to be a perfect fit when he quickly settled into life on the McCartneys' farm: 'It was all good fun. You could get dirty. There was nobody afraid of getting shite on their boots.'

The band now complete, Paul began itching to get out on the road. But, recognising how difficult a high-profile re-entry into touring might be, nearly six years after The Beatles had taken their last bows at San Francisco's Candlestick Park in 1966, he began formulating a plan.

This time, he would do things differently. He hinted as much in the press. 'I just want to get into a van,' he said, 'and do an unadvertised Saturday-night hop at Slough town hall or somewhere.'

Or, as it turned out, anywhere.

You banned yourself from playing any Beatles songs live with Wings in the early days . . . that must have been tough?

Yeah, but I wanted to grow Wings from a seed. And that was what we ended up doing. However, this meant that, y'know, if you had a bad spring and you didn't get enough rain or enough sunshine . . . you were fucked.

You'd find that you'd had a pretty poor song harvest?

Yeah! And we had some pretty bad weather in the early days.

4

Road to Anywhere

They gathered on the pavement for one last photograph before leaving. Out in the road at the front of the Cavendish Avenue house they stood, a scruffy assemblage of longhairs. At its centre were the McCartneys and their daughters, along with the Seiwells – Denny's wife Monique holding baby Stella, underlining the sense that they had now become one big family. To their right, looking like tufty escapees from The Faces or The Stones, were brother-in-law roadies Ian Horne and Trevor Jones. To their left, Henry McCullough and Denny Laine, the latter pulling a comically vacant Stan Laurel face. All wore big winter coats to keep out the February chill. All waved to the camera, except for the too-cool-for-school McCullough, who kept his hands deep in his pockets.

Behind them stood a green Transit van and an Avis rental three-ton lorry stuffed with their equipment. Given his head entirely, Paul was at last getting his wish – as expressed to the uninterested Beatles during their dying days – of embarking on a low-key, last-minute tour of small venues or civic halls. The plan for this upcoming jaunt was a similar one, if far looser, and in keeping with the laidback mood of the times. Everyone – musicians, roadies, kids, even dogs – was to pile into the vehicles and take off up the motorway, heading for university towns, in search of somewhere to play.

This tapped into McCartney's romantic notion of the

vaudeville or circus troupe heading off over the horizon, en route to anywhere. Moreover, the scheme allowed him to ward off his fears about returning to live performance. He was, he confessed, 'very nervous'. The nightmare scenario, in his mind, was facing row after row of reporters at the front of the stage, sitting in judgement with their pads, scribbling snippy notes about how he wasn't as good as he used to be.

Instead, by not pre-announcing shows, he could keep one step ahead of the press. In effect, he thought, he could outrun his critics.

And so, on the morning of 8 February 1972, this strange coterie of hippies, kids and animals set off, pointing the noses of their vehicles in the direction of the M1 motorway, destination unknown. 'We were,' says Paul, with barely disguised pride, 'a bunch of nutters on the road.'

It was an emboldened Paul who faced the beginning of 1972. With Lennon's cutting accusation that McCartney created anodyne 'Muzak' still ringing in his ears, he determined to push into new and, for him, uncharted territory, by toughening up his sentiments and stepping into the unlikely arena of the protest song.

After the low-blow trading of the previous year, John and Paul had reached some kind of détente. Surprisingly, given his growing reputation as a peacenik in all areas except for his more bitter personal relations, it was Lennon who first extended the hand of friendship. Trying to repair the damage, John used journalist Ray Connolly – the same writer who had faced McCartney's swift denials that he'd quit The Beatles in the infamous Q&A press release – as a go-between to hand-deliver a letter to Cavendish Avenue. A visiting Jim McCartney took the envelope from Connolly at the front door, before unhappily warning the writer, 'If I were you, son, I wouldn't get involved in all this.'

On the last weekend of January, Lennon and McCartney hooked up for the first time since the ruckus began. Saturday saw Paul and Linda fly to New York and accept an invitation to come over to the apartment the Lennons were renting at 105 Bank Street in Greenwich Village, where the couple had now taken up permanent residence. Over dinner, John and Paul chatted amicably, if still a touch guardedly, and agreed to stop slagging one another off in public, whether in the press or in song. At the same time, it seems, the fact that Lennon was living in such a febrile counter-cultural environment, hanging with hirsute radicals and becoming increasingly politicised, rubbed off on McCartney.

The following day, as events quickly unfolded on the other side of the Atlantic, Paul found his cause to support, his enemy to kick against, however lightly. On Sunday 30 January, in the Bogside area of Derry, Northern Ireland, a march by a civil rights organisation representing the Catholic minority suddenly descended into rioting. Under attack, albeit from a group of rowdy teenagers, British soldiers fired live rounds at the protesters, resulting in 26 unarmed civilians being shot. Thirteen died on the day, escalating the Troubles that were to violently stain the UK for decades.

McCartney, along with much of the civilised world, was outraged. Giving an interview to US radio station KHJ in the hours after the event, Paul talked little about Wings, instead railing against the British government, reportedly using 'strong language' that needed much in the way of editing by the station before it could be broadcast. The next day, the McCartneys flew home, but not before booking a session at Island Studios in west London for an impromptu recording session on Tuesday 1 February for Wings' first single, the hastily penned response 'Give Ireland Back To The Irish'.

Paul had always thought that Lennon was 'crackers' to write

overtly political material. This, however, doubtless because of McCartney's Irish heritage, felt different. 'It took us aback,' says Paul. It wouldn't harm his image, either, of course, to be seen to be making such a potent statement. 'I knew what I was doing,' he admits.

At the studio, a TV crew from ABC in the States filmed the band rehearsing a harder-edged version of the song than would appear on the slightly vanilla-sounding 45, with Paul seen in the footage lustily belting out his lyrical protest. In truth, it was fairly tame stuff: Great Britain was 'tremendous', but its creation of a police state in Ireland and its imprisoning of those with a passion for 'God and country' was totally unacceptable.

In the two-minute TV news segment, Paul sat with Linda, being interviewed, while laughing at the continual interruptions of one of their dogs howling in the background. No, said Paul, he wasn't worried about being an entertainer making a political statement. In fact, from his impassioned demeanour, it was clear that he was enjoying having an agenda.

'I don't now plan to do everything as a political thing,' he told the unseen reporter, before repeatedly stabbing the air with his finger to emphasise his point. 'But just on this one occasion I think the British government overstepped the mark and showed themselves to be more of a sort of repressive regime than I ever believed them to be.'

EMI chairman Sir Joseph Lockwood, more used to having to deal with the controversies stirred by Lennon than McCartney, tried to talk Paul out of releasing the single: 'He rang me up and said, "Woo, y'know, don't do this." I said, "Hey, man, y'know, although I'm not a protest songwriter normally, this time there's no stopping it. I've gotta do this. It's gotta happen."'

For his part, as a young Northern Irishman recruited into a band who were overnight making such a pointed comment about the divisions in his homeland, Henry McCullough was strangely ambivalent about the whole affair. 'I never thought about it once, and that's the God's truth,' he says. A travelling musician, the guitarist had been out of the country and on the road when the Troubles began to intensify in Ireland in the late 1960s. 'I don't think it was a bad thing to miss that tragic period,' he points out.

Not that his involvement in the record was to go unnoticed, however. Amid the fuss to come with the subsequent release of the single, the guitarist's brother was thumped in a pub in the Irish expatriate stronghold of Kilburn, north London: 'It was, like, "Are you Samuel McCullough?" "Yeah." "Is your brother Henry that played on 'Give Ireland Back To The Irish'?" "Yeah." *Bang.*'

For a line-up of individuals who might as well have bumped into one another while queuing for a bus, the five-piece Wings quickly bonded in rehearsals. As manufactured in some ways as any toothsome teen-scream pop band, the group, all except Linda, of course, were nothing if not professionals who could adapt to any musical scenario.

Mirroring the segment in *Let It Be* where the four Beatles are each shown separately arriving at Apple Studios in Savile Row, the members of Wings were filmed coolly rolling up one by one to the Institute of Contemporary Arts on The Mall, the location for their first intensive batch of rehearsals. Inside, on the stage, the quintet were filmed rattling through old rock'n'roll standards such as 'Lucille' before working their way through a raw live take of 'Wild Life', along with the stomping 'The Mess I'm In', which owed much to The Band's 'The Shape I'm In', released two years earlier.

More and more, Linda appeared comfortable and to be grow-ing in confidence behind her keyboard set-up. But in truth there were already murmurs of dissent within the ranks over her role in the band. The forthright Henry McCullough even brazenly suggested to Paul that the band get a 'proper' piano player. 'I'm quite ashamed of it,' he says. McCartney instantly rebuffed the guitarist, firmly informing him that it was his decision alone who was in or out the band. 'I was, like, "Alright",' says McCullough. 'It was never brought up again, on my part anyway.' But, at certain points, it seemed Paul wasn't entirely convinced either that having his wife in the band had been such a great idea. Once, in a moment of irritation, he threatened to replace her with Billy Preston, the American keyboard player who had done such a fine job augmenting The Beatles during *Let It Be*. Later, a little uncharitably, he'd admit that Linda had been 'absolute rubbish' when she'd started playing. Then, in a spot of double-damning, he tried to qualify this harsh assessment by saying that George Martin had dumped Ringo from The Beatles' 'Love Me Do' session for exactly the same reason. His circuitous, slightly cack-handed point seemed to be: she's getting better.

'It was the weirdest thing,' he says today. 'There was me, having been one of the world's most famous people, a member of The Beatles, suddenly playing in this semi-professional band kind of thing.'

There was no little amount of defiance in Paul's decision to stick by Linda, not least when his contemporaries began to mock him: 'We had people like Jagger saying, "Oh, he's got his old lady in the band." We had to take all that. I would think, Oh, fucking thanks a lot . . . tosser.' Linda herself was ambivalent about the prospect of being a touring musician, telling a friend that she'd 'just as soon have stayed on the farm with the horses and kids'. But Paul wanted her there, and so there she was.

Ultimately, McCartney saw Wings as an experiment. Acknowledging that he couldn't replicate The Beatles, he was striking out in another direction entirely and now road-testing the band with this freewheeling, haphazard tour. 'We didn't even have hotels,' he points out, almost incredulously. 'Anyone else at least would've booked a hotel.'

Once they'd hit the road, the Wings touring party motored northwards and began scanning signs for a likely place to stop. Taken with the exotically named Ashby-de-la-Zouch in Leicestershire, they exited the M1 and headed for the small market town. Passing through its centre, Paul and Linda spotted a pony tied to a lamppost and, prone to making impulsive equine purchases, tried to find the owner and make him an offer for it, to no avail. Getting back to the matter in hand, the group discovered that, of course, there was no university in the tiny Ashby-de-la-Zouch. Undeterred, they headed back on to the motorway.

A safer bet, they decided, was to aim for Nottingham, a city where they reckoned they'd be guaranteed a gig. Arriving on the university campus around five o'clock, they sent roadie Trevor Jones ahead into the building to scout the location. Jones asked around for the social secretary and was directed to the bar, where he found student Elaine Woodhams. He told her that he was with Paul McCartney's new band and they were looking for somewhere to play a spontaneous gig. In fact, he said, Paul was already waiting outside.

Initially sceptical and suspecting a practical joke, Woodhams was led by the roadie out to the van. The door slid open to reveal McCartney, turning the social secretary's expression into a goldfish gape. A gig was duly arranged for the following afternoon and announced in a scrawl on the blackboard in the bar: *Entrance – 50p*. The word that the ex-Beatle was to break his concert silence here, of all places, quickly filtered through the campus. 'It was a big deal for them,' says McCullough. 'But it was a bigger deal for us. It was, like, "This is it, the first fucking gig . . . let's see what happens."'

The following lunchtime, in the dinner-hall-cum-ballroom, Wings publicly took to the stage for the first time – Paul wearing a red-and-white pinstripe shirt under a pair of denim dungarees – before a crowd of 800, their number constrained by the fire safety limit. The band sounded lively, if a touch scrappy. Proudly displaying his rock'n'roll roots, Paul launched into 'Lucille' as an opener, before leading into the first airing of 'Give Ireland Back To The Irish'. The rest of the set was largely comprised of songs from *Wild Life* ('Bip Bop', 'Some People Never Know'), one from *Ram* ('Smile Away'), and a filler blues jam fronted by McCullough ('Henry's Blues'). Running out of material, since McCartney had self-imposed a rule not to perform Beatles songs, they played 'Give Ireland Back To The Irish' and 'Lucille' again. In a moment of dopey dizziness, they slipped into 'The Grand Old Duke Of York'. Paul admits that not allowing himself to play any of his most famous tunes was 'a killer . . . we had to do an hour of other material and we didn't have it'.

Strangely, perhaps, one of the most satisfying elements for Paul in all of this was being handed the band's agreed half-share of the door profits at the end of the gig, a bag of 50p coins, which were then evenly distributed by the singer among the musicians. Given the fact that, after signing with Brian Epstein's NEMS management company in January 1962, The Beatles never handled actual money earned from their performances, this was something of an unanticipated thrill. It was the first time in ten years that Paul had seen any cash after a show, and he enjoyed the working musician's dignity-of-labour aspect of it, feeling like 'Duke Ellington divvying out the money' to his band. 'Two for you and two for you,' says Henry McCullough. 'We were like children. But it was all 50ps. You walked out of the university and your trousers were tripping you.'

By day two, the press were already gaining on them, and Wings felt they were losing the chase. Exiting the van at Leeds University, the band were accosted by a gaggle of reporters and TV crews. As their hunted leader, Paul immediately made the call: the gig's off, everyone back in the van. Instead they headed for York, where a show was arranged at York University's Goodricke College, only six hours before stage time. Too late to book the union's theatre, the refectory was again the scene of the performance, with 550 students crammed into the space and another 400 stuck outside.

But Paul hadn't quite managed to shake the reporters tailing him. A stringer from the *Guardian* was in the audience at York, noting that Wings seemed slightly old-fashioned when faced with a crowd that, in the hippie fashion, sat on the floor for most of the duration. McCartney was 'seemingly oblivious of the passage of time', since the highlights of the set were 'old dancing numbers'. By the end, though, the crowd were apparently on their feet. 'Give Ireland Back To The Irish' was played twice, with Paul quipping that they needed 'to get some practice'.

The still-unreleased single was already drawing some heat. On the day of the York gig, the BBC banned it on the grounds that it was politically biased and didn't account for the suffering caused to many on the other side of the divide. Asked by the *Guardian* whether the gigs were actually secret fundraisers for the IRA, Paul 'refused to be drawn'. The fact that his reply was noncommittal shows the strength of feeling in the wake of Bloody Sunday: the idea of passing around the collection hat for the IRA – who only months later intensified their terrorist bombing campaign – was not yet considered taboo. 'We're simply playing for the people,' Paul said.

Literally escaping the controversy, one night Wings were forced to drive through a mob of protesters. While trying to leave the campus in their van, passing through the gates, students menacingly crowded around the vehicle, frightening everyone inside.

Denny Laine, driving that night, says, 'I put my toe down and they all jumped out the way. They were pretty threatening.'

For the most part, though, McCartney successfully managed to give both the media and his detractors the slip. Back in London, his assistant Shelley Turner playfully fielded calls from journalists fishing for information about the next destination of the tour. 'They have taken a lot of sandwiches with them,' she offered cagily. 'They could turn up anywhere.' Countering growing rumours that EMI, in the wake of the BBC ban, was refusing to issue 'Give Ireland Back To The Irish', Turner said that the record company was '100 per cent behind it . . . it will probably be in the shops next week.'

As the tour progressed, Wings and crew developed something of a routine around these guerrilla gigs. Each morning they'd pick up the map and decide where to go that day. Sticking mainly to larger towns and cities, they would arrive at a university in the early afternoon; Trevor Jones would be dispatched to make the gig arrangements, then a local B&B would be found before the roadies returned to the venue to set up the equipment.

Post-gig, the bounty of 50p coins was dished out and the party returned to the B&B for fish and chips or cheese sandwiches and a game of darts. Baby Stella would be placed in a makeshift cot fashioned from an opened drawer lined with blankets and pillows. Bottles of wine would be uncorked, smokes sparked up and the guitars whipped out for a jam through old rock'n'roll numbers. One night everyone sat around and listened to the tapes of the gigs recorded from the sound desk by Trevor Jones on a couple of reel-to-reels borrowed from Abbey Road. Disappointingly, they sounded rough. There was still much work to do.

If the universities jaunt was distinctly lacking in glamour day to day, and far removed from the luxury afforded to The Beatles during their touring years, it was overall an enjoyable experience for everyone, peculiarly British and very 1970s. Henry McCullough likens it to 'a black-and-white *Sgt. Pepper* . . . you were staying with Mrs McGonagall on the promenade.' The buzz for all involved was getting up in the morning and not knowing what the day was going to bring, or, even where you were going to end up. 'It was just as exciting travelling in a green Transit as it was in a fucking Rolls,' says the guitarist. 'You probably had more room in the van.'

Before long, the touring party began to suspect that the student organisers were preparing in advance on the off-chance that Wings would drop in. On their arrival at Hull University, the PA was already set up in the concert hall. Driving around looking for accommodation, the band were forced a mile out of the centre of town to Pearson Park, where they booked into what McCartney remembers being a 'third-rate' hotel, run by, in Denny Laine's opinion, an 'asshole' landlord. 'Some little weird old guy,' says Paul. 'Got very annoyed with us because apparently one of the roadies was smoking something.'

Here there was an altercation between McCartney and the landlord, though not, as Laine remembers, because of dope-smoking. After the gig, the band returned to the bar, helping themselves to drinks (but leaving money) and eating their fish and chips, though neglecting to tidy up after themselves. 'When the guy came down in the morning and saw all the mess,' says Laine, 'he got upset.'

McCartney happened to walk into the room at breakfast-time as the landlord was loudly telling off the roadies. An argument broke out and Paul – 'accidentally on purpose', according to Laine – elbowed the proprietor in the nose. Enraged, the landlord threatened to call the police. Nine-year-old Heather ran around the band members' rooms, knocking on the doors to rouse them. The group and entourage quickly fled before they found themselves deeper in trouble.

A week into the tour, Linda talked to *Melody Maker* about how the tour was going and, specifically, how her eldest daughter was coping with rock'n'roll road life. The McCartneys, she said, had given Heather 'the choice of school or coming with us, and she chose the latter'. Revealing her blasé, university-of-life attitude, Linda added, 'I mean, this is an education in itself, isn't it? We're just a gang of musicians touring around.'

On one key date, however, Linda's credentials as a musician were once again called into question. Having aborted the Leeds University gig due to the press attention, the band arranged a date for 16 February in the city's town hall, a larger and more imposing venue. Taking to the stage a touch intimidated, Paul sang the opening bars of 'Wild Life' solo before turning to his wife and counting in her staccato piano introduction. There was silence. Linda had frozen. She mouthed to Paul, 'I've forgotten the chords.'

'The audience thought, This is good . . . this is a little joke they've got going,' McCartney remembers.

Paul stepped over to his wife's side of the stage and placed his hands on the keyboard before realising that he too couldn't remember how the song began. Nervous laughter began to rise up from the stalls. 'It looked even more like a joke, like a great big set-up thing,' Paul says. 'For a moment, there was panic.' Then Linda suddenly remembered the sequence, began playing the simple, descending three-chord riff and the band fell in behind her. 'We went into the song, our hearts beating fast,' says Paul.

Very quickly, the novelty of the tour began to wear off. In Manchester, Wings played in a theatre in Salford where the owners worried that the band's low-end rumble might somehow damage the scenery of the venue's current production. In Birmingham, Wings visited Laine's parents and then played a very average show at the university. In Swansea, with only 75 minutes' notice, 800 fans – by now wise to Wings' modus operandi – suddenly appeared. The element of surprise was gone. The game, it seemed, was up.

On 23 February, after eleven dates, the tour was over, with the plan to continue for another week abandoned. Denny Seiwell says it was proving a bore to have to find a B&B every day that had six free rooms and allowed animals. In addition, there were only so many fish and chip suppers an American drummer could stomach.

Two days later, 'Give Ireland Back To The Irish' was released, a mere three weeks after it had been written and recorded. Following the BBC's lead, the Independent Television Authority and Radio Luxembourg immediately banned it. Paul's response was one of faintly comic defiance. 'Up them!' he said. 'I think the BBC should be highly praised, preventing the youth from hearing my opinions.' Radio 1 DJ John Peel was the sole voice to speak out in defence of McCartney, saying that the ban disturbed him. 'The act of banning it,' he argued, 'is a much stronger political act than the contents of the record itself. It's just one man's opinion.'

For better or for worse, 'Give Ireland Back To The Irish' marked the beginning and the end of Paul McCartney's career as a protest singer. As relatively weak a song as it was, at least it was better than Lennon's awful folk dirge 'The Luck Of The Irish', released later that year on his worst album, *Some Time In New York City*. In the end, the first Wings single reached number 1 in two countries – Ireland and Spain. 'Basque separatists loved it,' says Paul now.

As Abbey Road was to The Beatles, Olympic Studios in the southwest London suburb of Barnes was the preferred recording hive of The Rolling Stones. McCartney had used the facility in the past, not least during the sessions for *Abbey Road* (only partly recorded at the famed St John's Wood studio), which, although producing a fine Beatles album, had been troubled. As was quickly to be proved, it was not a lucky environment for Paul.

It was here that, irritating the other Beatles, Yoko Ono had laid up in a double bed installed in the studio, recovering after the car crash that she and John had suffered in Scotland in the summer of 1969, Lennon giving her a microphone so that she could, as she now remembers, 'just experiment or do something'. It was here that Paul had fought against being press-ganged into signing the Allen Klein management agreement by his bandmates, a decisive moment in the disintegration of their long friendship. And now it was here, in March 1972, that he returned for the beginning of the difficult sessions for the second Wings album, *Red Rose Speedway*.

Employing a producer for the first time in his post-Beatles career, Paul brought in Glyn Johns, the studio name of the day thanks to his recent wave of successes with The Rolling Stones, The Who and Led Zeppelin after his dedicated if ultimately failed attempts to create the *Get Back* album. A self-assured, headstrong character, Johns was in no way intimidated by McCartney on any level.

Wings set up in the grand, ballroom-like live room in Studio One at Olympic and began jamming their way through Paul's new songs. Roundly unimpressed by the sounds emanating from the studio, Johns sat with his feet up in the control room, reading the paper and refusing to roll the tape. On day one, McCartney had asked the producer to consider him just the bass player in the group, in an attempt to underline his apparent desire for Wings to be a democratic and 'normal' band. Of course, when the blunt Johns began to treat McCartney just as he would any old musician, the shirking bandleader, he says, grew disgruntled.

Very quickly the pair began to rub one another up the wrong way.

Laine says that Johns wasn't willing to accommodate McCartney's more experimental ideas, like 'going into funny little rooms to get weird guitar noises'. The producer declared the music that Wings were making to be 'shite'. Inevitably, this provoked a shouting match between Johns and McCartney. 'Anything like that, I always stood five feet behind Paul,' says McCullough. 'That's his territory, that's his business. He was speaking on his own behalf, but he was letting us in on it and holding us together, like, "OK, boys, I'll take care of this. You don't want to get involved."'

Four weeks in, Glyn Johns walked out of the sessions for *Red Rose Speedway*. 'I think he felt we were too lackadaisical,' says the guitarist. 'He got quite angry about the whole thing.'

Whether right or wrong in his motives and manoeuvres, Paul's next step would have almost everyone wondering if he'd entirely lost the plot. Back in January, on the farm in Scotland, mainly to entertain his middle daughter, Mary, he'd started tinkering around with a new composition that set the nursery rhyme 'Mary Had A Little Lamb' to a new melody.

This lilting and inoffensive, if bizarre track was to become, in May, the second Wings single, bamboozling a large portion of the rock-buying public, who were then enjoying glammier or harder, hairier sounds. Still, as bewildering a record as it was, touted as 'a song for spring to make people happy', 'Mary Had A Little Lamb' reached number 9 in the UK charts, purely on novelty value. Over in America, discerning US DJs simply ignored the track, flipping the single over and playing its New Orleans-flavoured B-side rocker 'Little Woman Love'.

For Paul, this kind of children's song was part of the strain of his writing that had produced 'Yellow Submarine', 'When I'm Sixty-Four' and 'Maxwell's Silver Hammer', a bit of singalong fun that harked back to the old days and the music-halls. Public tastes had moved on, though, and such featherweight fare was considered utterly uncool. When the record was slated by critics, Paul quickly realised just how out of step he'd become, admitting, 'I do things that aren't necessarily very carefully thought out.' He even blamed his star sign for giving him this trait: 'Geminis are supposed to be changeable. I'm crazy. I've always been crazy from the minute I was born.'

At the same time as holding his hands up in defeat, McCartney tried to claw back some of his cool, claiming the daughter of The Who's guitarist, Pete Townshend, had pestered her dad to buy the single for her. 'I like to keep in with the five-year-olds,' Paul remarked. Then, even more wrong-headedly, he tried to justify the song in 'deeper' terms, using the hippie-hangover parlance of the times – pointing out that the lamb follows Mary to school, but then, after having been thrown out by the teacher, hangs around like a devoted child.

'To me, that's a heavy trip, those lyrics,' he mused, like the stoner who has just discovered an entire universe on his fingernail. 'It's very spiritual when someone hangs around because it's loved. I'm sure no one ever thinks about those kind of things.'

To spotlight the incongruity, on 25 May Wings performed the fluff-light nursery rhyme on a *Top of the Pops* bill that included Elton John, offering the stirring, other-worldly ennui of 'Rocket Man (I Think It's Gonna Be A Long, Long Time)', and the utterly of-the-moment T. Rex thundering their way through 'Metal Guru', one of the 45s that would define the era.

Capping it all, Wings' next appearance was a slot on *The Basil Brush Show*, miming their way through a performance of 'Mary Had A Little Lamb', spliced with cheap cartoon sequences illustrating the words, in a break from the antics of the starring fox puppet. On TV, the otherwise wine-slugging, weed-puffing band members sang along through sprayed-on grins. They all now admit they were slightly bemused by their new-found roles as children's entertainers.

'Listen, how do you think I felt?' says Henry McCullough. 'I was coming off the road after three years in America with Joe Cocker and I end up playing "Mary Had A Little Fucking Lamb".'

'We're supposed to be a rock band,' says Denny Seiwell. 'I said, "What's with all this shit?"'

Even the ever loyal Denny Laine, it seems, suffered a moment of doubt, admitting he was privately thinking, I didn't sign up for this, Paul.

Looking back on 'Mary Had A Little Lamb', Paul confesses that he's slightly stumped himself as to why he made this unarguably odd record. 'I can't believe that now,' he says. 'It seemed like a good idea at the time.' Perhaps it highlights the fact that McCartney always acted impulsively and instinctively, and then did the heavy thinking later.

This whimsical, semi-detached part of McCartney's character was quickly understood, however, by McCullough, who says that even if Paul is generally seen as being down-to-earth, then in some respects he's quite the opposite – spacey and often somewhere else. 'He does what he does,' says the guitarist. 'We were put into his bubble, basically.'

And so, by the summer of 1972, the members of Wings had every right to be confused: they didn't know whether they were supposed to be angrily shaking their fists at the British government over their actions in Ireland or singing story-book lullabies for the under-tens. They were en route to somewhere, but sometimes the musicians must have wondered where exactly Paul was taking them.

It was always hard for you to lock in a line-up with Wings. As a band, you always seemed to be in a state of flux.

Yeah, exactly.

What would you put that down to?

Um. Musical differences.

5

Life in the Slow Lane

The bus was an open-topped Bristol Commercial Vehicles double-decker whose top speed was an unimpressively chugging 38mph. Yet, for Paul, this was the ideal vehicle to ferry Wings around for the duration of their first European tour.

There was method in this apparent madness: if his band and family were to spend the summer months motoring around the continent, he figured they might as well make it a pleasant experience. Rather than be stuck inside a van or coach, gasping for air in the breathless heat of July and August, they could all be lazily sunning themselves on the upper deck.

The notion recalled *Magical Mystery Tour* and, more directly, Cliff Richard in *Summer Holiday*. McCartney had the bus painted in a screaming, multi-hued psychedelic design that might have been hip five years previously but already looked out of date. Where the bus's advertising strip had once been was now written the legend *Wings Over Europe*, atop a cartoon mural depicting verdant, sunlit mountain peaks against a duck-egg-blue sky.

On the back of the bus, the band members' names were stencilled in a telling pecking order: Paul & Linda McCartney, Denny Laine, Henry McCullough, Denny Seiwell. On the front, backdropped against a deeper shade of blue, a pair of white wings fanned out, framing the spinning destination indicator for which a new set of names had been printed: Châteauvallon, Juans-les-Pins, Arles and so on, to be rolled out as the tour trundled onwards.

Inside, the lower level had been carpeted and fitted with a galley kitchen at the rear. There were bunks for the kids, and four of the original seats remained behind the driver's cockpit. The upper level, meanwhile, was basically a hippie crash space – albeit one with a play-pen – its floor strewn with fraying sofa cushions and enormous, puffy bean bags. 'Bit of dope in the fridge,' says Henry McCullough. 'Magical. Like being part of a movie.'

The McCartneys really had become a touring family. Wherever the band were, so were the kids. During rehearsals in London at Manticore Studios, a converted cinema in Fulham owned by the notoriously unrestrained progressive rock trio Emerson, Lake and Palmer, Wings had pounded away on the stage while the kids, clearly quite used to this kind of thing, mucked around and enjoyed a picnic on carpets and mats in the empty auditorium. Paul and Linda would sometimes have to break from rehearsals to go and change Stella's nappy.

There was never ever any question of the kids being left with nannies or sent away to boarding school or summer camp while the band were on the road.

'That's right, and we even got slagged for that,' Paul says now. 'I remember somebody saying "Oh, they're dragging their kids around the world". And our answer for that would be to say "Yeah, look, the thing is, number one, we love 'em. Number two, what are we gonna do? We're gonna be in Australia, and a nanny's gonna ring up and say 'Ooh, your kid's got a fever of 105'." Shit. We would wanna be there, so that was it.'

From here on in, tutors were to be employed wherever possible. 'We'd get them to talk to the school first and find out what subjects they were gonna cover,' he remembers. 'We kind of kept up. The kids tell me now they didn't really keep up. They did inevitably sort of fall behind a bit. But we had the freedom to do what we liked with our family and we were just careful to not have it sort of damage them.' Attracting criticism for forcing their offspring to join the circus, Paul would shrug and laugh, saying, 'It's a geography lesson.'

'Mary's friends used to call her a hippie commune kid,' he recalls. 'But it was just kind of a question of mucking in. It was more like gypsies than anything else. This family was gonna move around.' But this easy-going attitude wasn't always prevalent. If one of the kids got ill, it would cause Paul and Linda to bicker. 'It would be a strain on our relationship,' Paul admits. 'But at least we were doing what we wanted to do. Life causes arguments and there were plenty of reasons for that. I don't think having the kids on tour was particularly stressful. I think just people living together can be stressful. Y'know, it was a great love affair, but nobody's perfect.'

The first show of the European tour was booked for a deliberately out-of-the-way location – a 2,000-seat Roman amphitheatre at Châteauvallon, high in the pine-forested hills above Toulon on the south-eastern coast of France. Here, before the gig, on Sunday, 9 July 1972, Paul gave an informal press conference.

'I'm starting all over again and working my way upwards,' he accepted. 'You don't fight Cassius Clay on your first time out.' He hinted at his recent crisis of confidence and the worry of being smothered by the weight of his reputation: 'A year ago, I used to wake up in the morning and think, I'm a myth. I'm Paul McCartney. And it scared the hell out of me.'

Pre-echoing Lennon's later declaration that Yoko had 'showed me what it was to be Elvis Beatle and to be surrounded by sycophants', Paul admitted that his time with Linda, particularly his 'hermit' period in Scotland, had similarly opened his eyes. 'It wasn't until she came along that I realised what was happening to me,' he said. 'She made me see I was surrounded by con men and leeches.'

This statement underlined just how much Paul now relied on

Linda and explained why she was a constant presence by his side. Not that her role as her husband's musical co-conspirator was getting any easier – a fact that she sometimes chose to hide from her partner. Before their show at Châteauvallon, Wings were apparently 'scared shitless', though none more so than Linda, who was so terrified that she cried on Denny Seiwell's shoulder. 'She was unhappy and frightened,' says the drummer. 'But she had a lot of chutzpah. She wasn't much of a piano player or a singer, but, boy, she had the heart for it.'

'I didn't want to let Paul down,' Linda reflected. 'I didn't want to let the band down. It was too much to hope that I'd be ignored, like I deserved.'

In the end, she coped, and the Châteauvallon show was a success. In the wake of the chaotic university tour, Wings were becoming a more polished operation. Where before the band would just rock up and play, there were now some production values. Paul sported a glittery black stage suit; there were backdrop films of scenes from Argyll – crashing waves, galloping horses – and climactic explosions of confetti as the band charged around the stage and Henry McCullough fell to his knees soloing.

If Wings were now beginning to resemble a credible rock band in step with the early 1970s, there was still daftness afoot. Throughout the tour, McCartney roped the band into making sideline appearances for a planned but unreleased film called *The Bruce McMouse Show*. Intended to be a mixture of animation and live action, interspersed with Wings performances, it was to feature the titular cartoon mouse and his family, who lived under the stage on which the band were performing. The group were even taught a choreographed music-hall dance routine, though it was clear that their hearts weren't in it. McCullough admits he 'never quite made the grade' in this particular respect. Seiwell recalls the moment he had to stand in a crowded backstage room, speaking prepared lines to an imaginary mouse, as agonisingly embarrassing and 'one of the hardest things I ever had to do in Wings'.

In other ways, in spite of their outward family image, Wings attracted much the same kind of attention as other rock bands. The European tour was the first time that predatory females began turning up backstage. Post-show in Zurich, the intimidating, omnivorous Anita Pallenberg made an appearance. Her considerable reputation preceding her, having already counted three members of The Rolling Stones – Brian Jones, Keith Richards and Mick Jagger – among her conquests, she apparently made a beeline for Denny Laine.

The guitarist, however, in a recent development, was already spoken for. In Juans-les-Pins, three dates into the tour, a strikingly pretty, almond-eyed brunette by the name of Joanne Patrie, a Boston-born model working the European catwalks, managed to manoeuvre her way into Wings' dressing room. Jo Jo, as she preferred to be known, already had a rock-star-devouring past, having lost her virginity to Jimi Hendrix backstage at Woodstock, spent a 'wild night' with the booze-soaked, in-decline Jim Morrison and enjoyed a two-year on-off relationship with Rod Stewart.

Linda was instantly suspicious of Jo Jo, and, as it transpired, with good reason. As a seventeen-year-old Beatle fan, Patrie had written devotional fan letters to Paul, before turning up in Britain three years later with the express intention of meeting and marrying him. Following the Juans-les-Pins show, she had ended up seducing one of Wings' roadies, securing herself a place on the crew's tour bus, which drove in convoy with the band's more colourful transporter. In the days that followed she made a play for Denny Laine, making flirty eye contact with the guitarist whenever the group's open-topped bus pulled level with the roadies' vehicle. Later, Laine walked in on Jo Jo taking a bath in her roadie beau's room. Within days the two were an item and inseparable. It was at this point that Jo Jo stepped into the inner circle.

The McCartneys were less than happy about this development. A week into their relationship, Denny sat Jo Jo down and told her that Paul and Linda were 'very uptight about you being around'. Linda, especially, was convinced that Jo Jo was simply using the guitarist to get close to Paul. Patrie began crying, having effectively suffered the rejection of her former pin-up. While the guitarist and the groupie's affair was to prove far more enduring than these flaky beginnings promised, the future Jo Jo Laine's relationship with the McCartneys was to remain painfully strained.

Meanwhile, the tour rumbled on. Sometimes, if the struggling double-decker clearly wasn't making the distance, and it looked as if Wings were going to miss their stage time, an emergency convoy of vehicles would be dispatched from the venue to collect them. This, if anything, added to the general air of hilarity and joie de vivre within the band. Paul, meanwhile, was becoming increasingly playful with reporters. At a press conference in Paris, he introduced the band members one by one before turning to his wife with the words, '. . . and Yoko.' Embarrassingly, though, and unthinkably for a returning Beatle making his first live appearances in France since 1965, the show in Lyon had to be cancelled due to poor ticket sales.

Unperturbed, the group booked studio time at EMI's Pathé Marconi Studios in Paris, where they knocked out the Linda-fronted reggae-lite song 'Seaside Woman', written as the result of a playful challenge from her husband when ATV first accused her of not being a capable songwriter. It would be another five years before this sweet if slight offering was released under the band name Suzy and the Red Stripes.

As the tour reached Sweden in the first week of August, the carefree mood began to darken. First of all, the press there began trashing the McCartneys, claiming that they'd been horrible to staff at various hotels when they'd complained about being forced to accept, as one report put it, 'conventional Scandinavian single beds . . . their attitude seems to be, I want it, therefore it must happen'.

Out drinking one evening in a nightclub, things turned disturbingly nasty. A young man in a green jacket sidled up to Paul, calmly informing him that he had a revolver in his pocket and that he planned to kill him. Having coolly revealed this threat to McCartney, the youth swaggered over to the bar and stood there staring and grinning at the singer.

McCullough and Laine arrived not long afterwards. McCartney, clearly shaken, whispered to his bandmates, telling them what had just happened and gesturing towards the stranger. The guitarists, particularly the streetwise McCullough, who had begun his musical career as a showband player in the rough Northern Irish dancehalls of the early 1960s, quickly took control of the situation. Pulling a knife out of his boot, and with Laine in tow, he wandered over to the bar. The pair flanked the now flustered wannabe thug, who began to protest his innocence, claiming it had all been a misunderstood joke. Laine and McCullough quickly wrestled him to the floor and searched him, producing no weapon. As soon as they let him go, the youth scrambled to his feet and took off into the night.

In McCullough's opinion, it was 'one of those incidents that happens a thousand times on a Saturday night in any given city. I felt very protective of Paul because of his vulnerability . . . he needed a strong helping hand from whoever was around him.'

It was four dates into the Swedish leg, in the west coastal city of Gothenburg, when trouble really hit. On Thursday 10 August, at the Scandinavium Hall, as Wings finished the last number in their set, a fiery 'Long Tall Sally', the power to the PA was unceremoniously cut. A line of armed policemen then appeared in the seated upper levels of the arena. 'They all came shuffling round with rifles,' says Henry McCullough. 'We're thinking, What's going on?'

When the band tried to make their way to the dressing-room, their path was aggressively blocked. Paul, Linda and Denny Seiwell were forcefully peeled away from the others and told they were being arrested for possession of marijuana. The McCartneys, as it transpired, had collected a postal package containing weed, addressed to Denny Seiwell, from their hotel earlier that day – unaware that they were being watched.

The scenes in the concert hall quickly descended into chaos. As the police gripped the suspects more firmly than was strictly necessary, Linda shouted to tour photographer Joe Stevens to keep on taking shots: 'Just get the pictures,' she yelled. One dramatic frame caught the McCartneys amid the tumult – Paul burying his head in the bosom of a distressed Linda, who was bawling furiously at the policemen. In the event, the three suspects, along with tour secretary Rebecca Hines, were dragged off for questioning.

Throughout an intense grilling, all sorts of threats were thrown at them, not least that the police would refuse to let the McCartneys and Seiwell leave until they offered their confessions. Any denials were in any case worthless: the Swedish police had been snooping on McCartney, a known marijuana smoker since his Beatle days, since he had arrived in the country. They'd even recorded a call that Linda had placed three days earlier, from Stockholm to MPL in London, arranging for two cassette boxes of weed to be posted to the band.

'Where shall they send it?' Linda could be heard asking Paul on the recording. 'Do you have a copy of the itinerary?'

'Send it to Gothenburg,' Paul said, 'to the hotel.'

It was a system that had worked until now. Henry McCullough remembers that at the beginning of the tour they'd 'set off with a small bit each, and then there was weed sent from the office'. In each new country, there would be an agreed destination for the band's postal drop. As a result, Jo Jo Patrie remembered, when leaving one country for another, Paul would force everyone to jettison their remaining supplies before the party reached the border. Together, they would dejectedly perform a ritual where they chucked 'big handfuls' of weed over the side of the open-topped bus, as if scattering the ashes of a dear departed one.

At the police station, in the early hours of the morning, after three hours of questioning, Seiwell and the McCartneys finally admitted that the weed was theirs. It was a hefty amount – seven ounces – and revealed how heavy their intake was, considering this was only intended to last them for the remaining two days they were to be in Sweden. The police later claimed that the three confessed that they smoked marijuana every day and they were effectively addicted to it.

Ultimately they were forced to convince the authorities that the dope was for their own personal use and not for sale – the charge of intent to supply being a far more serious one than personal possession. Of course, in the end it was not difficult to persuade the police that the ex-Beatle had not become a pot dealer to help make ends meet.

Nevertheless, tour manager John Morris, likely anticipating the unwanted knock-on effects the bust would have in terms of acquiring international visas in the future, attempted to play down the situation. 'Lots of people send drugs to the band,' he told reporters. 'They think they are doing them some kind of a favour. Instead it causes all kinds of trouble. It was simply a case of pleading guilty, paying the fine and getting out of the city. As far as we're concerned, the whole business is finished.' The three were fined a total of $1,800 and sent on their way.

The bust made the front page of the *Daily Express* in Britain the next day, with the ambiguous if unwittingly accurate headline 'McCartney Fine After Police Raid Concert'. Rather than being ashamed, all involved were defiant, and quietly tickled by the thought that this kind of notoriety would lend Wings an air of outlaw cool.

The day after the bust, an unrepentant Paul and Linda gave an interview to the *Daily Mail*, published under the provocative splash 'Why I Smoke Pot – By Paul'.

'You can tell everyone that we're not changing our lives for anyone,' he stressed. 'We smoke grass and we like it, and that's why someone sent it to us in an envelope. At the end of the day, most people go home and have a whisky. Well, we play a gig and we're exhausted, and Linda and I prefer to put our kids to bed, sit down together and smoke a joint. That doesn't mean we're heavily into drugs or anything. You can't expect us to pretend we don't smoke for the sake of our fans. But now that I've been caught, I'll say, "Yeah, it's true."

'We're not the kind of people who can't go on without it,' he added, perhaps disingenuously. 'We wouldn't be on tour if we were.'

In the wake of the arrest, Linda clearly now saw herself and Paul as pro-pot campaigners, publicly arguing the case for marijuana use. 'Every time we appear in public and people see that we are smoking hash or pot, it'll make things just a bit easier for an ordinary person,' she stated. 'I'd love to be one of the reasons for people changing their minds about soft drugs. But people must lead their own lives. They must make up their own minds. And I know that Paul and I like weed. To us, it's just like nothing, and when other people share that point of view, I'll be happy.'

Paul, however, ended the interview on a slightly resigned and unhappy note. 'We're just easy people who like to smoke if we can,' he offered. 'But now that's out of the question, and I'm sorry.'

In reality, far from being contrite, as Denny Seiwell recalls, the band's dope supplies were quietly replenished by a local source in Lund. This, more than anything, spotlights Paul and Linda's outlook at the time on marijuana and the laws that prevented them from smoking it. By scoring more weed the very day after they'd been so publicly busted, the couple were clearly unrepentant.

If there was a trace of arrogance to be detected in all of this, it was surely rooted in the fact that The Beatles had enjoyed almost diplomatic immunity when crossing international borders. Now that the untouchable Fabs were over, though, gone too were those privileges. And so this carefree (and careless) way of dealing with their fondness for dope was, as the decade progressed, to cause the McCartneys problems time and time again.

Five weeks later, in Argyll, Norman McPhee, a police constable from Campbeltown, fresh from a drug identification course among the bright lights of Glasgow, decided to have a nose around the vacant High Park Farm. Following the publicity that surrounded the Swedish bust, he was looking for anything suspicious, on the premise that he was checking the security of the property. Peering through the glass of the McCartneys' greenhouse, among the tomato plants, he spied cultivations of an altogether more exotic nature, bearing the distinctive serrated leaves he had recently been taught to recognise.

He left, taking with him a couple of the plants to have them checked out back at the police station in the town. When they were positively identified as marijuana, McPhee returned to the farm with seven colleagues, finding more plants at the Low Ranachan property. Once the search was completed, the police had collected five tiny plants, the product of which would have amounted to very little weed.

It was beginning to look like open season on the apparently

lawless McCartneys, who were back in London at Cavendish Avenue when they were given the news. Worse, Paul's lawyer in Scotland, Len Murray, had heard that the raid had been prompted by a local tip-off. Three days after this second bust, on 20 September, McCartney was charged in absentia on three counts – two of possessing marijuana and a third of growing it.

Paul was now viewed as a notoriously open dope smoker. From 1965 on, The Beatles had used the drug to spark their imaginations, but McCartney admits that, in creative terms, by the early 1970s, it had begun to have the opposite effect at times, leaving him lost in clouds of indecision. 'In songwriting,' he says, 'the amount of times I have got stuck on a word that really didn't matter . . . It was absolutely inconsequential what the word was – it could've been "boot" or "chump". It did not matter, y'know. And you just totally come to a grinding halt, so the song never gets finished. I had a lot of that through substance misuse.'

There remained flashes of real inspiration in McCartney's songwriting, however. One day, talking to former Apple Records head Ron Kass, Paul mentioned his previously unspoken ambition to write the theme for a James Bond film. Kass said that he knew the Bond producers, Harry Saltzman and Albert 'Cubby' Broccoli, and that he was sure they would love the idea of the former Beatle penning the title song for the next movie. The connection duly made, and with the producers more than agreeable to the idea, McCartney was given a copy of the book *Live and Let Die*, which he read one Saturday in October 1972 before starting and finishing the song the following day.

Paul says he relished the idea of being commissioned to write to order. 'As a writer who thinks of himself as part-craftsman,' he says, 'the idea is akin to being asked to make a bit of furniture for the national collection or something. Y'know, there's a prestige thing. There was for me, anyway.' Working the title into the lyrics was the trickiest part of the process for him. 'I thought, live and let die . . . OK, really what they mean is live and let live, and there's the switch. So I came at it from the very obvious angle. I just thought, When you were younger you used to say that, but now you say this. So it just found its way easily into a song, really.'

The gorgeously atmospheric ballad, mined with explosive up-tempo instrumental passages, was to prove one of McCartney's most enduring creations, revealing that he worked best perhaps when given a directive or challenge or, as in his partnership with Lennon, a spot of friendly rivalry. The song was quickly recorded with Wings at Morgan Studios in Willesden the next week, with its dynamic orchestration added later by George Martin at his studio AIR London in Oxford Circus.

Once completed, Martin flew to Jamaica with an acetate of 'Live And Let Die' to play to Saltzman. The film producer was impressed but, mistaking the recording for a demo, casually wondered aloud who Martin and McCartney were planning on asking to sing on the master. It was down to the diplomatic Martin to point out that this was indeed the final version. 'I think they were looking for Shirley Bassey,' laughs Paul. 'Burly Chassis.'

In the same week as recording 'Live And Let Die' at Morgan, Wings laid down their next single, 'Hi Hi Hi', a shuffling rocker and seemingly blatant paean to the wonders of smoking dope. Paul felt the lyric invited interpretation, in much the same mischievously playful way as the 'everybody must get stoned' double entendre of Bob Dylan's 'Rainy Day Women Nos 12 & 35'. 'It was like, "Ooh, what does Dylan mean?"' says McCartney. '"Does he mean you get high? Or does he mean getting stoned, like, getting drunk?" So there was the ambiguity, and I assumed the same would apply to me.'

He was soon to learn that it didn't. Upon its release in the first week of December 1972, 'Hi Hi Hi' was instantly banned by both Radio 1 and Radio 2. Ironically, however, it wasn't the apparent drug reference that found it blacklisted, but an innocent line sexually misconstrued. The song's publisher, Northern Songs, sent a wrongly typed lyric sheet to the radio stations, someone having misheard the abstract innuendo of the line 'Get ready for my polygon' as 'Get ready for my body gun'.

The same month, Paul's trial for the High Park Farm bust was set for March of the following year. And so, for McCartney, 1972 was characterised by two drug busts and two banned singles. Interviewed at the close of the year, Denny Laine looked ahead to the upcoming twelve months with a quote that, in retrospect, would seem loaded with unintended portent.

'The next year is really going to be exciting for Wings,' he frothed. 'A lot of amazing stuff is bound to happen.'

La Mamounia – its name meaning 'safe haven' in Arabic – is one of the most exclusive hotels in Marrakesh. Once described by Winston Churchill, who regularly spent his winters there, as 'the most lovely spot in the world', it was a destination of choice for Charlie Chaplin, Charlton Heston and Alfred Hitchcock, who used it as a central location for his James Stewart and Doris Day-starring *The Man Who Knew Too Much* in 1956.

Bucking his reputation for extreme thriftiness, it was to La Mamounia in February 1973 that Paul McCartney took his Wings bandmates, treating them to a two-week Moroccan holiday. Here the musicians swam or loafed around the pool, strumming acoustic guitars, or meandered through the hotel's twenty acres of citrus trees and olive groves, or went on long camel treks in the deserts outside the city.

Ever productive, Paul spent the time writing songs for the next Wings album. 'Then it would be, "Wait till you hear this, lads,"' Henry recalls. 'It was a lovely place to be. It was also another bonding period. It was as much a holiday as Wings Over Europe was.'

Paul returned to face his trial at Campbeltown Sheriff Court. Clearly keen to waste no more time than was necessary on this jaunt north, the McCartneys hired a private plane to fly them to RAF Machrihanish. When they emerged from the plane, their QC, John McCluskey, immediately noticed that Linda appeared 'stoned out of her mind'. Arriving at the court, Paul seemed keen to treat the proceedings with something approaching respect, while his wife clearly saw it all as a bit of a laugh.

Once the trial got under way, McCluskey presented McCartney's flimsy defence: he had received the seeds in the post from a fan and, curious, had naïvely planted them. The QC told the court that McCartney's innocence could be proven by the fact that no attempt whatsoever had been made to conceal the plants. This argument seemed to sway the judge, Sheriff Donald McDiarmid, who gave McCartney a £100 fine and allowed him fourteen days to pay, prompting an outburst of open laughter in the courtroom. Speaking to a reporter in an anteroom immediately afterwards, Paul said that, if jailed, he had planned to pass his prison time writing songs. Typically ebullient, and a touch relieved, he described the judge as 'a great guy'.

Stepping out of the court building, the McCartneys were interviewed by a Scottish television reporter. Paul, in grey suit with a white scarf swept rakishly over his left shoulder, haircut now a proto-mullet, was faux-sincere, peppering his statements with knowing smiles. Linda, wearing a bowler hat pinched from McCluskey, and looking like a toddler emerging triumphant from the dressing-up box, giggled by his side.

'It was said that those seeds had been sent to you,' noted the reporter. 'How did you come to grow them?'

'Yeah, well, we got a load of seeds, y'know,' Paul replied, fixing the reporter with his doe eyes, playing the innocent wee laddie. 'Kind of in the post. And we didn't know what they were, y'know. And we kind of planted them all and five of them came up, like . . .' He paused, trying not to laugh, smiling impishly. 'Five of them came up illegal.'

'Now, of course, this conviction,' the reporter went on, 'it might affect your entry to the States, where you have considerable business interests. How do you feel about that?'

'Well, y'know, I understand that I might not get stopped from going into the States,' Paul went on, looking entirely unruffled. 'I hope not, anyway.'

Around the same time, a different legal pothole was finally smoothed over. In February, Lew Grade of ATV had tracked Paul down to Morocco and sent over an emissary with an unusual offer to settle their legal tussle over his post-Beatles songwriting partnership with Linda. If McCartney agreed to make an hour-long television special for the company, the $1 million lawsuit would be dropped. Paul immediately agreed to the deal. The resulting programme, titled *James Paul McCartney*, was an ambitious affair, being the first time since the misunderstood and derided *Magical Mystery Tour* that a major pop act had attempted a prime-time TV special.

Still, when filming began, it seemed as if the grand concepts dreamed up for the show might be upended by hubris. Shooting on location on Hampstead Heath in north London, Wings gathered on 10 March 1973 to mime to the perhaps better buried 'Mary Had A Little Lamb'. It was a bizarre performance, with the band dressed all in white – save for Denny Seiwell in unsportingly beige trousers – and looking like piously virginal New England pioneers. Wings arranged themselves under a weeping willow as Paul sat pawing away at an electric piano among a flock of actual sheep. Linda, looking like a crinoline-skirted Royal Doulton milkmaid figurine come to life, swung back and forth on a tree swing over a pond, singing and bashing a tambourine. Later, the group marched the sheep over a bridge, then juggled themselves into a rowing boat for a leisurely bob on the water.

All the members of Wings appeared entirely at ease with this scenario, except for Henry McCullough, who looked mortified. 'I had to stand playing a mandolin, dressed in white trousers and a white shirt,' he says, cringing. 'The shepherd had the sheep running round our feet. It was just a bit strange.'

There was worse to come. In the tradition of 'Your Mother Should Know' from *Magical Mystery Tour*, Paul further indulged his song-and-dance-man fantasies in a Busby Berkeley-flavoured routine, 'Gotta Sing Gotta Dance', in which dozens of dancers appeared in vertically divided half-male, half-female costumes: part slick-haired 1930s gent, part blonde-locked showgirl. An oily-mulleted and fake-moustachioed Paul fronted the routine, tap-dancing in glittery golden shoes, pink suit and tails. As daft and camp as it was intended to be, the result looked hopelessly out of step with the shaggy, bell-bottomed fashions of 1973.

But it turned out that McCartney had shied away from an even grander transformation: 'At one point I was gonna be in drag and do a full-blown impersonation of Diana Ross. But as the moment grew nearer and wardrobe started to measure me for the frock and get all serious with the wig and stuff, I started to bottle out.' When the show's US sponsors got wind of the fact that the singer was planning to go tranny for TV, they warned him to back down. 'Luckily this telegram came from the conservative Chevrolet people, who said, "Under no account must McCartney do drag impression of Diana Ross. We'll pull funding if he does."'

The special wasn't all bad. It opened with Wings performing 'Big Barn Bed' – the throwaway if grooving opening track from *Red Rose Speedway*, released under the more commercially viable name Paul McCartney and Wings in May – in front of a futuristic bank of televisions. Later in the running order, there was an impressively atmospheric, surreal clip for 'Uncle Albert', starting with a long shot of Paul scribbling solutions into a newspaper crossword and Linda making tea, as distortedly filmed through a fisheye lens. The picture melted into forks of lightning and dark thunderous clouds before fading into rows of Stepford Wives-like female typists working in a bureau. The camera passed through a throng of old men, all talking into curly-corded brown telephone receivers, before a 'straight' bespectacled and besuited McCartney appeared, sitting behind a typewriter, sadly replacing a phone on its cradle as the song ended. It was evocative stuff and richly redolent of The Beatles.

Elsewhere, there was a live recording of 'Live And Let Die', filmed at Elstree Studios in Hertfordshire, along with the other full-band 'concert' segments shot before an audience. This performance of the Bond theme was to prove more explosive than intended, however, when pyrotechnics stuffed inside a dummy balsa-wood piano turned out to be far more powerful than anticipated. When the detonation occurred at the end of the song, it threw McCartney back on his piano stool, lifted Henry McCullough clean off his feet and sent chunks of burning wood flying into the air and raining down on the shocked orchestra members.

The most misguided section of the programme, however, came with the footage filmed in a dockside pub, the Chelsea Reach, in Wallasey, Merseyside, featuring Paul's extended family and friends, who had been invited for a boozy knees-up for the benefit of the cameras. The idea was clearly for Paul to show off his working-class roots. But Linda, for one, wasn't keen on her husband presenting himself as a booze-chugging man of the people. 'She had such a go at Paul over that,' says Robert Ellis, who had become Wings' official photographer. He remembers Paul arguing long and hard about wanting to shoot this sequence. 'In the end, they filmed it and everybody in that thing is just cringing.'

It did make for uncomfortable viewing in its painful staged encounters with his relatives, including his father Jim and aunt Gin. 'I'm the only one paying for drinks here this evening,' Paul stiffly jokes, sipping a whisky and Coke and puffing on a Senior Service before being seen tapping his dad for a fiver. 'Isn't it terrible?' he said later. 'I'd come without me money.' As the drink flows, the packed gathering, and even Paul, visibly unwind and break into spirited singalongs of 'April Showers' and 'Pack Up Your Troubles In Your Old Kit-Bag'.

The members of Wings mingle with the crowd, supping nutty brown ales from dimpled pint-glasses – though, in Henry McCullough's case, worryingly overdoing it. The guitarist vaguely remembers that Paul, possibly now seeing his bandmate as something of a liability due to his increased drinking, had McCullough staying with one of the McCartney relatives.

'Get Henry out of the fucking way,' says McCullough. 'Maybe it was the right place for me at the time.' The evening ended with the guitarist having a shouting match with his wife, somehow losing his shoes and wandering, wearing a fancy rhinestone-studded coat, lost and confused through the streets of Liverpool. 'I plodded in my bare feet with this jacket that was flashing all over the place,' he dimly recalls. 'I was crawling to get home.'

When *James Paul McCartney* aired in the US on Monday, 16 April 1973 – premiering on ITV in the UK nearly a month later – John Lennon was watching at home in New York. He later commented, with notable warmth and tact: 'I liked parts of Paul's TV special, especially the intro. The bit filmed in Liverpool made me squirm a bit. But Paul's a pro. He always has been.'

The critics were brutal, however. *Melody Maker* denounced it as 'overblown and silly'. Linda's former friend, Lillian Roxon, reviewing it in the *New York Daily News*, comprehensively savaged it and its participants, slagging Mrs McCartney's various hairdos, calling Paul 'sweaty, pudgy, slack-mouthed' and loftily, if perhaps revealingly, announcing: 'I can tell you right now, she didn't marry a millionaire Beatle to end up in a Liverpool saloon singing with middle-aged women called Mildred.'

In interviews from the time, Paul stuck up for himself and the TV special, saying he'd received a wave of fan letters posted from remote locations in America after it was shown, the subtext being that it had touched the kind of ordinary people that snooty critics would never understand. 'The funny thing was, only the hip people didn't like it,' he pointed out. 'But we got millions of letters from mid-America saying they loved the show.'

More illuminatingly, he confessed to occasionally feeling burdened. 'Sometimes I feel as if I have a ten-ton weight on my shoulders,' he admitted, before shrugging off this statement with characteristic good cheer. 'There's many a person has committed suicide over the fact that his special wasn't so good,' he added. 'But I wouldn't give a crap.'

Still, even Linda felt it was 'a terribly unsure period'. Paul himself admitted that sometimes he'd come home from Wings rehearsals with the nagging feeling 'it's not right, we could do much more'. He was, he allowed, 'a born worrier'. Linda described *Red Rose Speedway*, which had been recorded in protracted sessions throughout the previous year, as 'such a non-confident record'.

'I don't remember a lot about it actually,' Paul now says of *Red Rose Speedway*. 'I think the fact that I don't remember it too well bears that out.'

The album certainly had its moments – the strident rocker 'Get On The Right Thing'; the rolling Pink Floyd-echoing instrumental 'Loup (1st Indian On The Moon)'; the dreamily strummed ballad 'Little Lamb Dragonfly', inspired by a neighbouring farmer at High Park bringing a near-frozen lamb to the McCartneys for them to nurse. 'He knew we were soft-hearted,' says Paul. 'He wasn't sure it was gonna survive, so we took it in and warmed it up and fed it and it did survive.'

To close the record, McCartney attempted to repeat the trick The Beatles had so successfully pulled off in the second half of *Abbey Road*, knitting fragments of incomplete songs into a seamless medley. Only, this time, it didn't work. The song cycle – 'Hold Me Tight', 'Lazy Dynamite', 'Hands Of Love', 'Power Cut' – was entirely forgettable, even to its creator. 'I don't remember it,' he confesses.

The fact that *Red Rose Speedway* was slimmed down to a single album from a planned double spoke volumes. 'Double albums are notoriously hard to pull off,' McCartney admits. 'If you've just got loads and loads of top, top material, then that's the way to go. And I think you can see that by pulling the songs into a medley at the end, maybe I didn't think I had loads and loads of top material.'

There was, however, one unarguable standout on *Red Rose Speedway*. 'My Love' was a magnificent McCartney ballad in the vein of 'The Long And Winding Road' and 'Let It Be', confidently recorded live with an orchestra at Abbey Road. It was also notable for a last-minute musical mutiny from Henry McCullough that produced the song's beautifully liquid, entirely improvised guitar solo.

'I was ready to put on a guitar solo along with the orchestra,' says McCullough, 'and whatever it was that was suggested to me to play, I wouldn't play it. I just said to Paul, "Look, y'know, I'm changing the solo." And he says, "Well, what are you going to play?" I said, "I have no idea."'

'I had to make a decision,' says McCartney. 'Either it was like, "No, stick to the script." Or, it was, "Do I believe in this guy?" Yeah. And he played the solo, which had come right out of the blue. I'd never heard it before. And I just thought, Fucking great.'

'The orchestra started and I hit a lick and that was it,' says Henry. 'I put my guitar down and I went into the control room and I knew that I'd either hit the jackpot or else it was shite. But if that had've been the case, then I would've withdrawn my horns. Anyway, I got lucky. To capture a solo like that in one take in a studio . . . it was just a stroke of luck, a gift from God really, and you get that in music.'

The increased respect that Henry had earned from Paul with this spontaneous move was soon to be destroyed, however. Filming a performance of 'My Love' for *Top of the Pops*, the guitarist, suffering the ill-effects of his imbibing, threw up onstage, sickening and embarrassing Paul.

Nevertheless, in May, Wings headed off around the country on their debut theatre tour of the UK, the first scheduled jaunt in Britain by any of The Beatles since 1966. Further underlining the idea that Paul felt like a variety-show turn, the bill included a hoop-throwing juggler. Interviewed backstage in Newcastle, McCartney enthused about the wonders of modern touring – better planning, improved sound systems – indicating that he wanted to do a lot more of it. 'It hasn't ground me into the ground, anyway,' he said.

The McCartneys were now almost becoming part of the show-biz establishment – throwing a party (after a sold-out three-night run at the Hammersmith Odeon) in the reception hall of the Café Royal, where Paul starrily duetted with Elton John, and attending the premiere of *Live And Let Die*, Paul wearing a tuxedo and bow-tie but, wackily, no shirt.

Wings, finally, appeared to be stabilising. One of the comments around this time, from the increasingly dissatisfied Henry McCullough, told an entirely different story, though.

'I don't suppose we'll be together forever,' he mused dolefully. 'I'm sure Paul's got more of a tie to The Beatles. Wings has all the makings of a great group, but our battle is to not let it fall apart, as it could so easily do.'

You put together a really strong set of songs for the *Band On The Run* album. Did you feel that yourself?

Yeah, I thought they were a pretty strong set of songs. I think at this point I was getting it a bit more together. I'd been through the sort of raw stages of Wings. I was now settling with the idea of it.

6

Panic in Lagos

As the nose of the jet dipped on its approach into Lagos, Paul began to get the jitters. Invited into the cockpit to witness the landing, he heard an unsettling exchange between the pilots. Flying low over a thick, misty carpet of jungle, the captain began searching in vain for the airport, turning to his co-pilot and wondering aloud, 'Is that it down there?' McCartney was thinking, Oh my God, *they* must know.

There was already much on Paul's mind. The night before, in London, he had received a phone call giving him the news he really didn't want to hear: Denny Seiwell was quitting the band and wouldn't be coming on the planned recording expedition to Nigeria the following day. Compounding the agony, two weeks earlier, Wings had suffered the first split in its ranks, when Henry McCullough had angrily walked out on the band. Virtually overnight, Wings had gone from being a sturdy quintet to an apparently shaky trio compromising Paul, Linda and Denny Laine.

Behind their happy hippie family façade, the discontent within Wings had been stewing for some time. For all McCartney's protestations and gestures to the contrary, the supposedly democratic band was in reality little more than an autocracy. Even the compliant Denny Laine would get irked any time one of his friends asked after the guitarist's 'boss'. 'He wasn't really my boss,' he now insists. 'He was just a mate I knew for many years before

I even joined Wings. But I allowed him to be the boss. That was fine by me.'

Henry McCullough, meanwhile, had become increasingly disgruntled. After appearing unannounced with jazz singer Carol Grimes at the Roundhouse in London, a newspaper review the next day mentioned that the guitarist had played on a few songs at the gig. Finding out about this, McCartney took him to one side and pointed out that he was on a retainer with Wings: 'Paul said, "Look, Henry, I'm paying the wages. And when I pay the wages, you don't play for anybody else."'

Then, one week he received his pay slip and noticed that his £70 retainer had been docked £40 for the hire of an amp. 'That's not just tight,' he laughs. 'That's *welded*, that is. I had to pay for the hire of an amp to fucking play alongside Paul McCartney.'

The guitarist had grown tired of McCartney forcing him to play the same parts over and over, and felt creatively shackled. 'It's like being in a show band,' McCullough moaned. Denny Laine had long seen the rift coming, noting that Henry essentially wanted to get stoned and rip through lengthy blues solos, which given Paul's inherent pop sensibilities, was always going to make for an awkward fit. 'He had some musical differences with Henry,' says Denny Seiwell. 'Henry was at a tough point in his life. It probably was the beginning of the demise.'

On the upside, the songs that Paul had written for the third Wings album were clearly shaping up to be the best of his post-Beatles career. Keen to hole up far from the London music business, he, Linda and the band once again escaped to High Park. Running a generator in the unheated barn at Low Ranachan over the hill, the band set up a makeshift practice space, with Paul and Linda, in rural-hippie style, arriving at rehearsals every day on horseback.

McCullough, though, was beginning to air his frustrations through his playing. The guitarist would dutifully ape the riffs written by McCartney, then continually change them from one run-through to another, frustrating the bandleader. While Paul, missing the camaraderie of The Beatles, was keen on some levels to mould Wings in their image – with the intra-band banter and jokey jams and all hands on the mixing desk in the studio – he clearly still reserved the power of veto over the ultimate musical decisions.

'Let's be honest, he wanted to be in a band in a *sense*,' Laine says. 'But he would still have the final call.'

'The thing is, if you come out of The Beatles and you go into another group, you're not just anyone,' Paul argues. 'You're the guy out of The Beatles. It was just natural for me to try and run the band in the way that I saw fit. I'm not trying to avoid the fact that I was the boss.'

Tensions between Paul and Henry escalated. 'He didn't really like the music that much,' says Laine of the latter. 'He was rebelling a lot and also drinking a lot too.' In one afternoon's rehearsal, McCartney, as he remembers, asked McCullough 'to play something he didn't really fancy playing'. Henry argued that the part 'couldn't be played'. Paul became rattled. 'I knew that it *could* be played,' he says. 'Rather than let it pass, I decided to confront him with it.'

Once the session was over, Laine and the defiant guitarist disappeared to a pub in Campbeltown and downed a few pints, the effects of which further emboldened McCullough to stand up to his boss. He returned, lightly refreshed, to the rehearsal barn. 'I'd had a couple of drinks,' says Henry. 'I wasn't falling down. But I was angry because I had drink in me.'

An argument broke out between the two which ended with each shouting 'Fuck you!' at the other. Face to face with the incensed Irishman, Paul became a 'bit choked', stormed out of the rehearsal room and huffed his way back to High Park. Henry sat alone in the barn, raging. 'Something had been cut,' he says. 'Or was just about to be cut. I think he left it to me to make up my mind and that's what I did.' McCullough dumped his guitar and amp in the back of his car and angrily revved away, never to return. 'If I hadn't got out then, I think I would have been sacked,' he says. 'It was the most unprofessional thing I've ever done in my life. I was driving off the edge of a cliff.'

Now, two weeks later, Denny Seiwell had followed. In his tense phone call to McCartney, the drummer told Paul he felt that the band wasn't ready to record following McCullough's departure. What's more, even though he accepted that McCartney's finances were tied up in the ongoing dispute with the other Beatles over the fate of Apple Records, he couldn't exist any longer on the retainer he was receiving from Wings. 'We worked for £70 a week,' Seiwell says. 'But I was making £2,000 a week in New York as a session guy.'

For the drummer, money had been a constant bugbear. While on tour, the band were forced to pay their own expenses, meaning they'd often return home skint. During Wings' downtime, Seiwell was sometimes forced to return to New York to play a few top-up studio sessions just so he could settle his American Express credit card bill. The drummer reckons that, having been fiscally cosseted during his Beatle years, McCartney wasn't in touch with the realities of financing a band.

'It wasn't just being stingy,' he says. 'Y'know, The Beatles made £50 a week in their pay packet. But if they wanted a house or a car, they went and they signed for it and Apple picked it up. But cash money in your pocket? You got £50 a week.

'And this was only a couple of years later, so we got a raise,' he laughs. 'But we couldn't sign for a house or a car. I had to go to Barclays bank and borrow £3,000 to buy an old, beat-up Mercedes to run around London.'

Gallingly, perhaps, in May Paul bought himself a Lamborghini and went on holiday to Jamaica. The loyal Denny Laine was happier with his lot: he was playing guitar with a Beatle, and he had a one-bedroom flat in London now, when only two years earlier he'd been dossing in his manager's office. During the rehearsals in Scotland, Paul, rewarding his loyalty, pulled him tighter into the firm. The pair had climbed a hillside to smoke a joint at sunset when McCartney offered to share the royalties with him on the next album, telling him, according to Jo Jo Patrie, 'Just think, man, you'll get, like, quarter of a million.' It was no coincidence, either, that it was the same month as the band were due to leave for Lagos and that Jo Jo had given birth to the couple's first son, Laine Hines, at Campbeltown hospital.

Seiwell, for his part, was getting sick of being broke and at the beck and call of the McCartneys. 'I should've sat down with him and said, "Look, I need some sort of a document, a written agreement on paper as to what my share of this band is." You're playing with a Beatle, for fuck's sake. And you're one of the top bands in the world. You're on call 24 hours a day. Whatever needs doing, whether it's photo-shoots or press interviews or rehearsals or recording or special appearances at TV shows. It just wasn't right.'

When Seiwell told Paul he'd had enough and that he wasn't coming to Africa the following day, McCartney was initially stunned. Then he boiled over into rage.

'I got off the phone,' he fumes, 'and I just thought, Well, thanks, nice. Thanks for letting me know in plenty of time. Then I just thought, *Right*, we'll show you.'

Having been ensconced within Abbey Road Studios during his time in The Beatles, Paul was increasingly drawn to the idea of location recording. Knowing that EMI, whose slogan boasted of being The Greatest Recording Organisation In The World, had various studio facilities dotted around the globe, he had staff at the label draw him up a list of their locations. For a time he mulled over whether the band should decamp to Bombay, Beijing or Rio de Janeiro. But, given his burgeoning interest in African rhythms – and a vague notion that the trip could in essence become an intensely creative working holiday – he settled on Lagos.

'We thought, Great . . . lie on the beach all day, doing nothing,' he says. 'Breeze in to the studios and record. It didn't turn out like that.'

Once their plane had safely touched down in Lagos, on 30 August 1973, the Wings party – Paul and Linda and the kids, Denny Laine and engineer Geoff Emerick – suffered severe culture shock. It was the monsoon season in Nigeria, characterised by heavy storms and oppressive heat. Given the McCartneys' freewheeling ways, no one had thought to check the weather forecast.

The scene that greeted them at Ikeja Airport was one of forbidding military presence. Machine gun-toting soldiers, under the rule of General Yakubu Gowon, who had violently seized power seven years earlier in 1966, stone-facedly stalked the terminal. Nigeria in the summer of 1973 remained a hazardous, volatile location. Only three years before, the country had been riven by civil war, which had led to almost three million casualties, whether through the direct effects of the conflict or its grim, lasting hangover of disease and starvation.

It quickly became apparent to the group that Lagos was in chaos. Hurtling to the studio through the alarming traffic, Laine was shocked when he saw a man knocked off his moped and apparently killed, with no one batting an eyelid. 'Life don't mean shit over here,' he noted. Moreover, shit was literally floating through the streets, in open sewers. Emerick kept seeing figures wrapped in sheets and bandages. His driver calmly informed him that they were lepers.

Then the group were met with the sobering vision of the studio itself, essentially a sizeable shed, set two streets back from Lagos Lagoon in Wharf Road, in a suburb of the port of Apapa. The studio manager and the tape operator, who Paul was utterly charmed to discover were respectively named Odion and Monday, welcomed the party.

The studio itself, although it boasted top-grade cast-off equipment from other EMI facilities around the world, was in a woeful state. A subsequent search eventually located the microphone collection, stuffed into an old cardboard box. When no sonic screens to isolate the musicians' equipment could be found, they were quickly built to order. Under McCartney's direction, Odion and Monday were sent out to find wood and Perspex. On their return, Paul picked up a saw to give the pair a quick lesson in studio carpentry.

Even more surprisingly, through a soundproofed door at the back of the control room was a noisy pressing plant, housed in a lean-to shack, where Nigerian EMI employees stood ankle-deep in rainwater leaking through a corrugated roof as the smell of plastic filled the air.

Rather than stay in a hotel, the group had booked into a villa complex in Ikeja, on the edge of Lagos and an hour's drive from the studio, with the McCartneys and their three daughters in one cabin and Laine and Emerick in another. The guitarist was amazed when, the morning after their arrival, he drew open the blinds to discover that a travelling African market had set up on their front lawn, selling camels and other native livestock.

The prankster in Laine enjoyed teasing the arachnophobic Emerick by leaving choice selections from the house's dead spider display in the engineer's bed. Sufficiently tormented, the producer decamped to a cheap hotel where he slept in a room overrun by cockroaches. Back at the villa, the McCartney daughters would chase translucent lizards around the exotic gardens in fits of giggles, catching them and collecting them in a large cage that they would proudly display to everyone.

The band and crew soon settled into these alien surroundings. Keen to start every working day with a swim, Paul was given temporary membership of a local country club in return for signing a photo of The Beatles hanging on its bar wall. McCartney's international celebrity soon began to attract invitations – to a moonlit party on a nearby island where everyone was offered a buffet of local delicacies that included slices of oversized African snail; to dinner at the house of Chief Moshood Abiola, future president-elect and then chief executive of the ITT corporation, which was in charge of developing the country's sanitation systems.

Only days into the trip, however, the McCartneys were given a rude reminder of the volatile environment in which they had placed themselves.

Wandering through the supposedly security-patrolled complex back to their own villa from Laine's after a post-studio listening party, they were surprised to see a car draw up beside them. The driver rolled down his window and offered the McCartneys a lift. Paul smiled and told the driver, no thanks, they were happy to walk. The vehicle then motored a further twenty yards up the road and stopped, before its doors flew open and its five passengers jumped out and walked quickly towards Paul and Linda. One – a short, stocky Nigerian, Paul remembers – produced a knife, which he pointed at the singer's throat.

A horrified Linda screamed, 'Don't kill him, he's a musician!' Her husband, sensibly, handed over his wallet, camera and bag – containing cassettes of his new songs – to the robbers.

'We'd been told not to walk around,' says Paul. 'But we were just slightly hippie. Hey, don't worry, feel good and it's alright. So we got mugged. Crazy. All my recordings went and those were all the songs I'd written. The joke is, I'm sure the fellas who took it wouldn't know what it was. They probably recorded over it all.'

As the car sped off, the McCartneys were left stunned. Only when they made it back to their villa did the full realisation of the horror of the incident begin to sink in. Intensifying their shock, the villa was suddenly plunged into darkness. The pair, shaken and paranoid, believed the thugs had followed them home and tampered with the lights, when in reality it was only one of the city's regular power cuts. The couple retreated to bed, pulled the covers over their heads and hoped they would wake in the morning.

The next day, in the studio, the McCartneys were informed by the locals that the situation had in fact been even more dangerous than they'd imagined. A local hood called Crazy Joe, whose story had made it into the pages of *Life* magazine, had recently been publicly executed by the Nigerian police. If they had been black, Paul and Linda were told, they would almost certainly have been killed, since it was now a practice of Nigerian muggers to murder their victims, rather than leave them alive as potential witnesses. It was only because of the colour of their skins that their lives were spared, apparently, since most robbers believed that white people found it impossible to distinguish or accurately describe the features of black criminals.

'Really,' Laine says, 'that's the only reason they didn't kill them.'

Having lost the tapes, McCartney frantically tried to remember the songs he'd written, relying on what he called his 'Beatle training' from the days when he and Lennon, with no access to portable recorders, would have to commit a song to memory. The storming 'Jet', the singalong 'Mrs Vandebilt' and the mantra-like 'Mamunia' all sprang readily to mind, but many of the others had to be reconstructed, as Emerick put it, 'on the fly'. Some verses of 'Band On The Run', for instance, were tweaked to reflect the group's current circumstances, stuck inside the four walls of the small, cell-like studio, faced with grim uncertainty.

True to his upbeat nature, though, McCartney threw himself into the recording process, moving from drums to bass to guitar to the microphone with ease. And Linda's contributions to the music – even if only simple keyboard parts and the gentle harmonies that she, Denny and Paul would use to colour the arrangements – were showing vast improvements from her tentative early days working with her husband. Paul had grown to live with the criticisms of his wife's performances, although they still rankled. 'It was like *oil* off a duck's back,' he says. 'Bit harder to shift.'

If outwardly Paul was projecting utter confidence, there were other signs that inside he remained troubled.

One Friday afternoon, a fortnight into the sessions, while enthusiastically laying down a vocal, he suddenly turned white and started gasping for breath. He stumbled outside to find some air.

At the studio door, in the brutal heat, McCartney collapsed. For the second time in as many weeks, Linda was faced with the terrifying prospect of her husband's life being in danger. 'I laid him on the ground,' she said. 'His eyes were closed and I thought he was dead.'

Geoff Emerick shouted to the studio manager to call an ambulance. Given the parlous state of the Nigerian emergency services, however, it was swiftly decided that it would make more sense to take McCartney to hospital in the manager's car. The star was unceremoniously bundled into the back seat and driven away. Back at the studio, Emerick and Laine half-heartedly continued work, nervously waiting for news.

Later that afternoon, Linda called the studio from the hospital to tell the others that Paul was recovering. For his part, McCartney remembers his return to consciousness as 'floaty' and strangely pleasant. The diagnosis was that the singer had suffered a bronchial spasm caused by excessive smoking. Viewed from another angle, the incident also bore all the hallmarks of a weed-induced panic attack.

In the circumstances, it would be understandable if strong Nigerian weed was heightening the singer's paranoia. On one key night out, it undoubtedly had that effect.

As much as the band could try to block out their disquietingly exotic environment during studio hours, any attempt to cut loose during their downtime only served to remind them of just how far they were from home.

One evening the party decided to visit the Shrine, the open-air club on the outskirts of town owned by Fela Kuti, the self-styled tribal leader of the Nigerian music scene. Only three years before, Kuti had returned to Nigeria from a US tour, freshly politicised, having been inspired by the burgeoning Black Power movement in California and a reading of *The Autobiography of Malcolm X*. Renaming his Koola Lobitos band Africa '70, he had formed the Kalakuta Republic, a communal compound-cum-recording-studio where he could hang out and get high with his entourage, while practising polygamy with an expanding collection of wives.

The musician was already gaining a reputation as something of a folk hero through his championing of Lagos's underclass, not least with his free health clinic set up at the Kalakuta Republic. But at the same time, his brazen spouting of anti-government views in his music and his provocative newspaper advertising columns had found him being singled out as a dangerous radical by the authorities.

Into this charged atmosphere stepped the McCartneys. At the

Shrine, potent spliffs began doing the rounds at their table. Paul suddenly felt adrift in this unfamiliar environment: 'We were a bit over-wasted and I got the screaming paranoias, being in this place on the outskirts of Lagos with absolutely no one we knew.'

Some of Kuti's musicians joined the McCartneys at their table and the mood turned nasty. The ex-Beatle, already uneasy in his altered state, soon found himself being interrogated as to exactly why he'd come to Nigeria to record, the insinuation being that he was there to plunder African sounds. 'It was very heavy,' says Paul. Later Kuti and Africa '70 took to the stage with the band leader in a grass skirt, surrounded by a host of his similarly attired, similarly topless wives. After a lengthy build-up, the group launched into their set of stirring Afrobeat and McCartney's anxiety melted away. In a rush of relief from the 'stress and craziness' of his Lagos escapade, Paul burst into tears.

In the days following the visit to the Shrine, however, Kuti tried to provoke some sense of controversy over the group's presence in Lagos, announcing on a local radio station that McCartney was here only to exploit the Afrobeat sound. A summit between the two musicians was hastily arranged.

Kuti arrived at the EMI studio, glowering bodyguards in tow, and took up a position at the back of the control room. After solemnly listening, arms folded, to some of the new work-in-progress Wings songs, he was satisfied that, the odd conga part aside, they bore no traces of Nigerian influences, and he left reassured.

'I said,' Paul recalls, '"Do us a favour, we do OK as it is, we're not pinching your music."'

'He was trying to get money out of Paul, I suppose,' reasons Denny Laine. 'He wanted a piece of the action.'

Kuti wasn't the only musician to be put out by Paul's visit, either. Firebrand former Cream drummer Ginger Baker, a friend of Kuti's, had one foot in the Nigerian music scene, having spent two years there building a state-of-the-art studio, ARC, near Ikeja Airport, which had been completed and opened only seven months earlier. On learning that the McCartneys planned to use EMI's altogether inferior facility to record rather than his own, Baker felt snubbed. 'I don't know why Ginger would think we were going there to work in his studio,' Laine muses. 'I mean, maybe he thought he could talk us into it or something.'

In the end, ever the diplomat, McCartney agreed to record one song at Baker's studio. 'Just to give him a little bit of a hand-out,' says Laine. The track, 'Picasso's Last Words (Drink to Me)', had been written earlier in the year, in Jamaica, at a dinner party thrown by the McCartneys at their rented house in Montego Bay. In attendance was Dustin Hoffman, who was on the island filming the 1930s-set penal-colony escape epic *Papillon*. After the meal, throwing down a challenge, Hoffman asked McCartney if he could write a song on the spot. The actor produced a magazine with an article about the recent death of Pablo Picasso, whose last words were apparently 'Drink to me, drink to my health, you know I can't drink any more.' Paul picked up a guitar and immediately began fitting a melody to the quote, thrilling Hoffman and his wife.

During the recording at ARC, to show no ill-feeling, Ginger Baker joined in, shaking a coffee can filled with gravel as a percussive accompaniment. Denny Laine, for one, believes that the furore stirred up by Kuti and Baker ultimately served to raise the African musician's profile in the west. 'After that, he came to London with Ginger and they did all sorts of stuff,' he points out. 'At the end of the day, it gave him a lot of publicity. Fela Kuti would never have been as popular as he was if we hadn't gone there and done that album.'

Some hostilities lingered, however, even at the party thrown by the McCartneys to mark the end of their eventful seven-week Nigerian sojourn. During the high-spirited proceedings, EMI's overseas manager casually walked over to Baker and informed him that he was set to fail in his desire to lure artists away from the company's recording set-up. 'We're going to screw you,' he whispered ominously. 'This is EMI territory.'

And so the McCartneys returned to London, triumphant and ultimately unscathed by their African adventure. As a footnote to the tale, however, Paul was further unsettled upon his return to Cavendish Avenue to discover a letter from Len Wood, group director at EMI, urging him to cancel his trip to Nigeria due to an outbreak of cholera in the region.

'I wonder,' says Paul, 'whether I even would've taken my kids there had I known. It was quite a sort of heavy episode, really.'

Four weeks later, on a cold Sunday evening in the last week-end of October 1973, Paul, Linda and Denny stood posing in dark, prisoner-like garb, frozen in the glare of a searching spotlight, against a wall in Osterley Park, west London. Gathered around them, pretending to be clinging together for safety, were chummy Northern chat-show host Michael Parkinson, film stars Christopher Lee and James Coburn, light entertainer Kenny Lynch, boxer John Conteh and the hangdog, deadpan writer and TV wit Clement Freud. 'It was a very odd mix,' says Parkinson. 'God knows how Paul chose those people.'

For the cover of the Lagos album, now entitled *Band On The Run*, the McCartneys – lying one night in bed, where much of their important thinking seemed to get done – had come up with a grand *Sgt. Pepper*-like concept. In passing reference to their drug busts and the fact that they sometimes felt like renegades, they had decided to stage a mock prison break, featuring famous faces of the period. Once the calls had been placed and everyone had agreed a date, this unlikely mob met at an Italian restaurant in Knightsbridge, where they enjoyed a long, boozy lunch.

In a room at the mansion house at Osterley Park, getting changed for the shoot, strong joints were passed around among those partial to a puff of grass. Outside, photographer Clive Arrowsmith arranged the company in their positions and shouted instructions to them from high on a ladder, the spotlight pointing at the subjects being positioned on top of a borrowed Post Office van. 'Not knowing much about photography at the time, technically,' admits Arrowsmith, 'I shot it on daylight film, and it was a tungsten source so everything goes yellow.'

Even this happy accident was to lend something to the iconic image, which was to become almost as famous as the Beatles album cover that inspired it. Released five weeks later, *Band On The Run* was initially slow out of the traps, in commercial terms. Once it had gathered momentum, though, it was to prove unstoppable, becoming the most successful solo album by any of the ex-Beatles, making the US number 1 spot three times.

Whether intentional or not, the themes in the polished, confident-sounding *Band On The Run* were flight and freedom. In 'Bluebird', winged creatures flew to desert islands and coasted on the breeze. In 'Helen Wheels', which appeared only on the US version of the album, the carefree McCartneys cruised the length of the British Isles. 'Mamunia' lifted its misspelled title from the 'safe haven' of the Moroccan hotel where Wings had spent a blissful fortnight. Even the playful nonsense lyric of 'Jet' offered an invitation to soar up and away into the sky.

But it was the episodic title track that best gave an insight into Paul's frame of mind. At the beginning of 'Band On The Run', the mood is one of claustrophobia, of people trapped. Then, once the breakout occurs and the chiming acoustic guitar kicks in, the fugitives sprint into the sunlight, never to return. Maybe, just maybe, Paul had finally managed to escape the long shadow cast by his former group.

Your post-Beatles feud with John was staged very publicly . . .

Yeah. But it's not like nobody else ever goes through that. We went through what everyone else did, y'know. Most people just argue with their family members and ours was done publicly. But I don't really feel it was huge anger. It was more frustration than anger.

7

In La La Land

The rumours first started swirling around in the last days of February 1974. Ringo and Harry Nilsson – nicknamed 'The Beatle across the Water' by the others – were spotted hanging out together at Capricorn Studios, the epicentre of bearded Southern boogie, in Macon, Georgia. It was exactly the sort of out-of-the-way location where you might successfully orchestrate a secret recording session. Soon the chatter turned to overwhelming noise: John, Paul and George were planning to fly out there to join them. The Beatles reunion was on.

It wasn't the first time this kind of tattle had circulated in the four years since the split. Eleven months earlier, a rumour had spread around Los Angeles that Klaus Voorman – Beatle pal since Hamburg, *Revolver* cover artist, bassist with the Plastic Ono Band – was to replace Paul in the reforming group. In truth, the three ex-Beatles plus Voorman were together in the studio hammering out the Lennon-penned 'I'm The Greatest', sung by Ringo on his third and eponymous album, and so the story hadn't been too wide of the mark. John later ruminated that 'Paul would most probably have joined in if he was around, but he wasn't'.

More promisingly, in setting the scene for a reuniting of The Beatles, Allen Klein was now out of the picture. Unsurprisingly, perhaps, his good relations with Lennon, Harrison and Starr had by now been lost in black clouds of bad advice and incrimination. When their management contract with him lapsed on 31 March

1973, Klein, knowing his time was up, announced that he no longer wished to represent them. Then, like a clamp-jawed terrier refusing to drop the bone, he attempted to launch a legal action against all four of the former band members.

Walking into a London radio station to do an interview in December 1973, Paul was approached by a stranger and served a writ informing him that ABKCO was suing him and the other former Beatles for the seemingly arbitrary sum of $20 million. It didn't overly trouble McCartney; he'd never signed the management agreement in the first place.

The buzz surrounding the apparent Macon summit two months later, though entirely misplaced, was lent further credence, however, by the fact that, for a fortnight in New York at the beginning of February, lawyers for both parties had begun examining the details of the dispute between Apple and ABKCO. Frustratingly, any attempts at a settlement broke down, but both Lennon and McCartney individually appeared at the meetings, sparking gossip that they were trying to work out a deal for the future of The Beatles. In Britain, *Melody Maker* went big on the speculation, trumpeting on its cover 'Beatles Get Together!' Teasingly, none of the band's individual publicists or Apple's PR would confirm or deny the story.

Then, on 25 February, Paul put out a press release that appeared to confirm that the group were set to carry on. 'As soon as things are sorted out, we can all get together again and do something,' it tantalisingly stated. 'We've talked about it, but we haven't been able to do anything because this has been going on and on.' Deflatingly, within a fortnight, in an interview with US TV channel ABC conducted at the London offices of MPL, he was talking the reunion down. 'I don't think we'll get together as a band again,' he said. 'I just don't think it'll work actually. It might not be as good.'

It was a real concern. The idea that The Beatles could get back together and just magically pick up from where they'd left off was a naïve one, particularly after the troubled births of both *Let It Be* and *Abbey Road*. 'It wouldn't necessarily have been a great thing,' Paul says. 'What we did with The Beatles was so cool that if we'd started to try and reheat a soufflé . . . that would've spoiled the whole reputation. What would we do? Do some new songs and add a new addendum, a new chapter to the end of the Beatles story? And how long would that go for? And would that get a bit pathetic? And it'd be, like, "Why, boys?"'

Still, a private Beatles reunion of sorts was imminent. In March the McCartneys landed in Los Angeles, a city where in 1974 the weed-refracted hippie idealism of the previous decade had given way to cocaine-shovelling egotism and creative self-indulgence. Its recording studios, clubs and secluded Hollywood hillside properties were riddled with the solipsistic and the drug-damaged. And it was this edgy, unstable environment that greeted Paul. The arch-irony was that for the first few weeks of the near two-month-long holiday in California, he wasn't sure how long he would be allowed to stay in the country, until the legal wrangling over his US visa following the 1973 busts was finally resolved in April.

Paul, according to gossiping music industry tongues, was in town to meet up with John and talk about getting the band back together. This story gained more credibility when Lennon and McCartney were spotted together, chatting and laughing backstage, at the sixteenth annual Grammy Awards at the Hollywood Palladium, where Stevie Wonder scooped Best Album for his peerless *Innervisions* and Roberta Flack walked away with Record of the Year for 'Killing Me Softly With His Song'. John, tempering his hardline attitude towards Paul, considered *Band On The Run* 'a great song and a great album'.

Lennon in 1974, however, was a mess. Behind him, in New

York, his marriage to Yoko Ono lay in ruins, the trigger being his drunken infidelity with a girl at a party on the night of Richard Nixon's re-election on 7 November 1972. Added to this, his career was in freefall. Badly shaken by the brutal reviews for his shonky, poorly selling 1972 political album *Some Time In New York City*, he'd already dismissed its similarly patchy follow-up, *Mind Games*, as 'just an album . . . rock'n'roll at different speeds'. Also hanging over his head was a plagiarism lawsuit from music publisher Morris Levy, who had, rightly, accused him of cribbing the melody and opening lyric for 'Come Together' from Chuck Berry's 'You Can't Catch Me'.

Day to day, further weighing on his mind, he was living under the threat of expulsion from the US by the Nixon administration, which was secretly listening to his phone calls and trailing his cars, and attempting to use a 1968 marijuana drug charge in London as an excuse to turf this worryingly influential peacenik out of the country. The agonies were piling up and it was clear that Lennon was on the brink.

'I just couldn't function,' he later admitted. 'I was so paranoid from them tapping the phone and following me. I was under emotional stress. A manic depression, I would call it.'

His companion in LA was the Lennons' 22-year-old personal assistant, May Pang. In an effort to control her husband's extra-marital behaviour, Yoko had approached the wide-eyed Pang with a view to her becoming her husband's mistress. Pang succumbed when John made a pass at her in a lift. As much in lust as in love with this new girlfriend – eyewitnesses reported that he could barely keep his hands off her – John had effectively replaced Yoko with a model seventeen years her junior.

By this point, Lennon had been in LA for seven months and was in the throes of the wildest period of his life since his days in Hamburg with The Beatles. Two unhinged characters were aiding him in his madness: the demented dervish that was Phil Spector and the spirits-guzzling, drug-ravenous Harry Nilsson. 'We had some moments,' Lennon said of the period in his life that became known as the Lost Weekend. 'But it got a little near the knuckle.'

John Lennon had moved to LA to escape the pressures of being John Lennon. The sprawling city had always been a favourite destination for the singer on Beatles tours, and he believed his problems might evaporate in the Californian sunshine. But his troubles were clearly not behind him. For a start, he was virtually broke, given the tangled mess that was Apple. Staying at his lawyer Harold Seider's small duplex in West Hollywood, he and Pang were living hand to mouth until Capitol Records advanced the singer $10,000 against future royalties.

In all this confusion and uncertainty, Lennon hatched a plan to get Morris Levy off his back and, at the same time, revive his own career. Settling out of court with the publisher, he agreed to record three songs from the catalogue of Levy's Big Seven Music on his next album, proposed to be a set of rock'n'roll standards produced, in typically grandiose fashion, by Spector, the architect of his first three solo albums.

Notoriously temperamental and unpredictable in the studio, Spector owed much of his recent success to Lennon and The Beatles. He was one of the few individuals to inspire awe in Lennon, and their relationship was one of shared admiration. But the producer was at this point going through an acutely strange and manic phase in his life, having recently split from his wife, former Ronettes singer Ronnie Spector, after she claimed he had kept her a virtual prisoner inside their fortress-like LA home.

The uproarious tone of the sessions for the *Rock'N'Roll* album was set on day one, 17 October 1973, at A&M Studios, when Spector – who had packed the live room with 28 musicians, including drummer Jim Keltner, Stones sax player Bobby Keys and guitarist Jesse Ed Davis – turned up late and spent hours painstakingly miking the instruments.

Bored to tears, Lennon and the band broke the seal on a gallon bottle of Smirnoff vodka.

By day two the scene was one of surreal disorder. Spector arrived at A&M, late again, having for no particular reason decided to dress as a doctor, with stethoscope and white lab coat, under which he was surreptitiously packing a pistol. His kick at the time was amyl nitrate, the chief effect of which is a disorientating rush of blood to the head. He would constantly break open and inhale ampoules of it as he directed the musicians. 'John didn't take that,' Pang claims. 'But Phil would come around and put it under your nose anyway.'

Roy Cicala, the owner of Lennon's favourite New York studio, The Record Plant, had flown in to be chief engineer on the *Rock'N'Roll* sessions. 'There was a lot of speed, cocaine, everything going on,' he says. 'Everybody was obnoxious.'

Studio banter between Spector and Lennon became increasingly bizarre and worryingly intense. The producer barked loud, distorted remarks through the musicians' headphones, at one point yelling, 'What's with these fucking horns and birds and seagulls and shit?' Lennon lost his temper and cracked up, shouting, 'Shut up! You fucking . . .' These shenanigans, added to the various other pressures in his life, further affected Lennon's sanity. 'I was trying to hide what I felt in the bottle,' he said. 'I was just insane.'

Matters came to a head one night when a particularly drunken Lennon started freaking out in Cicala's car after being separated from Pang by Spector in the convoy of motors taking them home to the Bel Air house Lennon had borrowed from record producer Lou Adler. Wild and disorientated, the singer went berserk, kicking at the windows, screaming for Pang and, perhaps tellingly, Yoko. Arriving at the house, Spector's bodyguard grabbed Lennon and dragged him to a bedroom where he and the producer tried to restrain the singer by tying him down, further enraging him when he thought he was about to be abused in a weird sex game.

'He got wild because they took his glasses away,' Pang reasons. 'He was as blind as a bat.' Spector and his bodyguard tied him up with neckties. 'He started freaking out,' says Pang, 'because he didn't know what was going on.'

From here on in, the recording sessions became even more warped. Having been thrown out of A&M Studios after a bottle of booze was tipped into the mixing desk, the party continued at The Record Plant West. One day, a loud bang was heard from the control room. Everyone ducked. In the centre of the room stood Spector with a gun in his hand, pointing at the studio ceiling. Pang says, 'John had his fingers in his ears, going, "Phil, if you're gonna shoot me, shoot me. But don't fuck with me ears, man, I need them."' It transpired that Spector had got into an argument with former Beatles roadie Mal Evans and fired a live bullet into the roof. 'It frightened the hell out of us,' says Pang.

In the aftermath, Spector stole the album's tapes and locked them in the basement of his house, claiming to everyone – although it was patently untrue – that they'd been destroyed in a fire at the studio. Only six weeks after they'd begun, the *Rock'N'Roll* sessions collapsed.

Then, into the wreckage, stepped Harry Nilsson. A former bank computer operator turned songwriter for The Monkees, Nilsson and Lennon had been friends since the former impressed The Beatles with a cover of their 'You Can't Do That' on his 1967 album *Pandemonium Shadow Show*, which cleverly incorporated elements of more than a dozen other Fabs songs. On its release, Lennon apparently listened to the album non-stop for 36 hours. During the New York press conference announcing Apple

Records in 1968, both he and McCartney namechecked Nilsson as their favourite new artist. Instantly, Harry was made.

A brilliant if erratic songwriter, whose pinballing humour found him writing lyrics about gang-bangs ('Cuddly Toy') and, incredibly, even his writing desk ('Good Old Desk'), Nilsson enjoyed his greatest successes with his covers of Fred Neil's 'Everybody's Talkin'' from the soundtrack to *Midnight Cowboy* and Badfinger's 'Without You', a transatlantic number 1 in 1972.

Sharing a twisted sense of humour and a penchant for mischief, Nilsson and Lennon were natural buddies. It was perhaps inevitable that the LA-dwelling singer would gravitate towards Lennon. Lennon clearly appreciated Nilsson's edginess and was very likely looking for a male soulmate to fill the hole left by McCartney. For his part, Nilsson's feelings for Lennon ran even deeper: 'I really fell in love with him. He was all those things you wanted somebody to be.'

A visitor to the studio during the frenzied latter stages of the *Rock'N'Roll* sessions, Nilsson claimed to have had a calming influence on the key players, in spite of his own reputation as a prodigious drinker and drugger. 'Suddenly I was the maypole of stability, if you can believe that,' he laughed. 'They were at war . . . and I was a nice little centrepiece they could both dance around for a moment.'

But Roy Cicala, for one, felt that Nilsson was basking in the reflected glory of having a Beatle for a mate. 'Some days I would think that somebody's taking advantage of somebody,' he says. 'The next day I would think, Wow, John is really enjoying it.'

The pair's notoriety was cemented on the evening of Tuesday, 12 March 1974, when, with May Pang, they visited the Troubadour club on Santa Monica Boulevard to watch a performance by New York's folk-tinged, mock-bickering musical comedy duo The Smothers Brothers. The intimate venue was fast becoming Lennon's favourite place to hang out and get wasted in LA. Only weeks before, he'd appeared there in the audience at a show by soul singer Ann Peebles, rat-arsed and with a sanitary towel stuck to his forehead.

He'd asked a scornful waitress, 'Do you know who I am?'

'Yeah,' she'd snapped back. 'An asshole with a Kotex on his head.'

Both Lennon and Nilsson were heavily oiled on their arrival at The Smothers Brothers' show. The pair, along with the teetotal Pang, parked themselves at a table in the VIP area alongside the likes of actor Paul Newman and *Deep Throat* porn star Linda Lovelace. They began necking brandy Alexanders (a sickly cocktail of brandy and milk) and proceeded to loudly heckle the performers, much to everyone's horror.

'Hey, Smothers Brothers,' yelled Lennon at one point. 'Fuck a cow!'

Pang was humiliated. 'The crowd loves it,' Nilsson told her.

'No, they don't,' she replied. 'Do me a favour.'

Then, the Troubadour's manager came over and grabbed Lennon. 'And you just don't grab John,' says Pang. 'It brought him back to the old days. All of a sudden, the tables went flying.'

Swinging punches at the bouncers as they were dragged out of the club and on to the sidewalk, Nilsson and Lennon were photographed by a camera-ready fan looking wild-eyed and out of it. 'The next day John was mortified,' says Pang. 'He sent flowers to everyone.'

Effectively homeless and living off favours, Lennon and Pang moved into a Santa Monica beachside property rented for Nilsson by his label, RCA. The house had been built by Louis B. Mayer and owned in the early 1960s by British film actor Peter Lawford, who lent it to President John F. Kennedy for his trysts with Marilyn Monroe. The first time Nilsson showed Lennon and Pang around the house, he opened the door of the master bedroom the couple were to be sharing and said, 'So this is where they did it, Kennedy and Marilyn.'

The house quickly became the go-to place for over-imbibing thirtysomething rock musicians. Alongside Lennon and Nilsson, Ringo and Keith Moon moved in. Given the lifestyles of the cohabitees, the scene soon resembled one long stag night.

'We lived a normal, reasonable life,' Nilsson later argued. 'We'd wake up in the morning – well, about one o'clock. At first we were very polite. Then, after a while, it was, "Keith, get your nose out of the amyl."'

Ominously, then, with *Rock'N'Roll* on hold, Lennon announced that he was to produce an album for Nilsson. Its title, *Pussycats*, was a jokey swipe at their unruly reputation. 'We called it that to show we were nice guys,' Nilsson said. 'Everyone thinks we're rough-house assholes.'

Quickly the *Pussycats* sessions took a turn for the disastrous, when it became clear to all that Nilsson's formerly flute-like, three-and-a-half octave voice had been reduced to a ravaged croak through his hard living. In truth, Nilsson had ruptured his vocal cords and would frequently disappear from the recordings to lock himself away in the toilet, where, instead of warming up his voice or practising his scales as other singers might do, he was coughing up blood.

At the end of the first day's recording on *Pussycats* at Burbank Studios on Thursday, 28 March 1974, a surprise visitor arrived in the shape of McCartney. The devastation that met his eyes shocked Paul. 'That time in John's life was very wild,' he says.

The drink flowing, the musicians at the studio complex fell into a jam session. That night, for the first time since the tense sessions for *Abbey Road*, Paul and John played and sang together.

'I'm afraid it was a rather *heady* session, shall we say,' admits Paul. 'I ended up getting on drums for some unknown reason. Then we just jammed. But I don't think it was very good.'

It was terrible, as bootlegged tapes, later leaked under the name *A Toot And A Snore In '74*, were to attest. The gathered musicians – Stevie Wonder, who had wandered in from a neighbouring studio, on electric piano, Jesse Ed Davis on guitar, Bobby Keys on sax, Nilsson on vocals, Linda on tentative organ and Pang on token tambourine – sounded woozy and unfocused at their best and utterly lost at their worst.

Lennon didn't sound particularly drunk – apart from a slurred reference to past 'jam *sheshions*' – but was freestyling wildly. 'I fell upon my arse,' he trilled tunelessly. 'And no one seemed to notice. I was wearing my mother's bra. So I say never trust a bugger with your mother.' There was much musical twiddling going on, but nobody seemed to be able to settle on a song.

'Ah, gee, it's been such a long time,' John said, addressing Paul, before bizarrely adding: 'When I look at Jack Lemmon, I'm in love again. I feel him coming all over me.'

Meanwhile, the disconnected riffing and soloing staggered on. The musicians were barely even listening to one another. 'If somebody knows a song that we all know, then please take over,' Lennon bellowed over the racket. 'I've been screaming here for hours. It's gotta be something done round about the '50s or no later than '63 or we ain't gonna know it.'

Eventually, the drunken band slid into a slow funky jam of 'Lucille', Lennon shrieking maniacally and McCartney trying to echo him with a harmony. It was less the remeshing of two great musical minds and more the sound of a pair of drunks shouting at one another over a slightly above-average pub band.

'Where's all that drink they always have in this place?' asked Lennon, sounding like he needed not one more drop. Then he vainly tried to get the group to tune up. 'Someone give me an E,' he said. 'Or a snort.'

Jimmy Iovine, record producer turned Interscope Records boss, then an assistant studio engineer, was a witness to the scene. 'Paul chose to play drums,' he reckons, 'because he was alert enough to say, "This is not how The Beatles are getting back together." He was the one in the room who you could see got it.'

McCartney, uncharacteristically, was taking a back seat, pitching in with the odd vocal interjection. An impassioned Lennon tried singing 'Stand By Me' over a slurry of bum notes, before freaking out at the hapless engineer in the control room: 'Just turn the fucking vocal mike up! McCartney's doing the harmony on the drums, Stevie might get on it there if he's got a mike.' They started up again before Lennon lost it once more. 'I can't hear a fucking thing now!' On their third attempt at 'Stand By Me', an angry Lennon gave up and just played guitar, as Paul scat-sang along and a gruff Nilsson joined in. Wonder, in typically fine voice, started to sing Sam Cooke's 'Cupid' and 'Chain Gang'. Paul offered a half-hearted take on old-time US chain-gang folk song 'Take This Hammer', an old Beatles jamming standby. The band, sounding knackered and clapped-out, finally fell apart.

Lennon offered Wonder a line of cocaine. 'You wanna snort, Steve?' he said. 'A toot? It's goin' round.'

It was an inauspicious event, and, of course, those involved weren't so drunk that they didn't know it. Lennon later vaguely remembered of the blurry night, 'there were fifty other people playing and they were all just watching me and Paul'.

Four days later, early on the Monday afternoon, Paul and Linda and the kids went to visit Lennon at the rented Santa Monica house. Like an overgrown teenager, John was still in bed. To pass the time, Paul sat down at a piano and tinkered around, even playing a medley of Beatles songs, to the lusty vocal accompaniment of Nilsson and Starr. Subconsciously, perhaps, he was awakening something in himself that had lain dormant for the four years since the demise of the group: the thought that he and John might write and perform together once more.

At one point Harry offered Paul a hit of angel dust. McCartney wasn't familiar with the drug, notorious for producing wildly unpredictable effects, from syrupy-headed nodding-out downers to rage-filled hallucinatory delusions.

'What is it?' McCartney asked Nilsson.

'It's elephant tranquilliser,' Harry replied.

'Is it fun?' wondered a doubtful Paul.

Nilsson paused and thought carefully about the question before replying, 'No.'

'Well, you know what, I won't have any,' said McCartney.

In many ways, this incident summed up the dangerous peer pressure that was fuelling the alcoholic and narcotic one-up-manship – the perceived wisdom being that taking anything was better than being straight.

Eventually, John got up. He seemed pleased to see Paul. 'There was a very relaxed atmosphere,' says Pang. 'It wasn't heavy. It was about them just being them.'

At one point, though, Paul gestured to John that he wanted to have a private word with him in another room. Before the McCartneys had left for LA, Yoko Ono had visited them in London, appearing to Paul's eyes shrunken and clad in black like a mourning widow. She'd sadly informed Paul and Linda that John was in Los Angeles with Pang, the reality of the possible finality of their split sinking in.

Paul had asked her, 'Do you still love him? Do you want to get back with him?' Ono said she did. McCartney told her that he planned to visit Lennon while in California, saying, 'I can take a message. What would I have to tell him?' Ono laid out the conditions Lennon would have to meet if he was to return to her, which, given their unconventional relationship, were surprisingly old-fashioned. He'd have to move back to New York. They couldn't live together again immediately. He'd have to woo her, send her flowers, start over again.

In the Santa Monica house, Lennon absorbed all of this information. Before the month was out, he was back in New York. By November, he'd complied with each and every one of Ono's conditions. Only years later did Paul reveal the key role he'd had to play in the couple's eventual reconciliation. That spring in Los Angeles, there had certainly been reunion in the air. It just wasn't to be that of Lennon and McCartney.

As the afternoon slipped away in Santa Monica, the gathering sat by the pool, where a series of Polaroids was taken by Keith Moon's personal assistant, Peter 'Dougal' Butler. Three of these pictures of John and Paul together survived – John in black peaked hat, pale blue denim shirt and darker flared jeans, Paul sporting a wispy mullet and fashionably bushy Zapata moustache, brown patterned shirt and summery white pedal-pushers. The pair are caught by the camera lounging around and shooting the breeze. Neither, of course, was to know that these casual, laidback shots were to be the last taken of Lennon and McCartney together.

It was a peaceful coda to a turbulent time. Not for nothing did Lennon nickname the Los Angeles of 1974 'Lost Arseholes'.

Underlining the general messiness of the LA rock community, three days later Paul and Linda went to visit Beach Boy Brian Wilson – at the time hellishly acid-burned, paranoid and a self-imposed prisoner in his Bel Air home. The McCartneys repeatedly knocked on his front door, waiting for over an hour. There was no response other than the sound of Wilson, hiding from them, softly crying.

When people look back at a lot of your 1970s singles, they're seen as being light, compared to John's stuff and even what George was doing. Does that get on your nerves?

Pfff. Yeah. A bit. But I have to admit, some of it was. I don't give a toss. It was what it was. Yeah, some of my stuff was kinda lightweight, but a lot of it wasn't. The background stuff wasn't. There was enough good stuff to counter all of those accusations. But there's a lot of dubious stuff in there.

Which records do you think were dubious?

I'm not damning myself!

8

Going South

It was time to put the band back together again. Even if it wasn't the one that everyone really wanted him to put back together.

But if Paul was searching for more compliant musicians to help to establish a more stable second incarnation of Wings, he seemed to be looking in all the wrong places.

First, he turned to a diminutive Glaswegian, Jimmy McCulloch, who had been transplanted to London at the age of twelve, rendering his accent a disorientating, vowel-chewing mush of Cockney and west-coast Scottish. McCulloch was only four months past his twentieth birthday when he found himself in a Mercedes van with the McCartneys, heading to Pathé Marconi Studios in Paris to play on a re-recording of Linda's 'Seaside Woman'. Like kids on a school trip, they arsed around on the ferry before driving immediately to the studio, where they all stayed up until eight the following morning. Clearly able to hang, Jimmy was instantly welcomed into the ranks. 'It was a great loon,' said Paul.

McCulloch had been a prodigy looking for a musical home. In thrall to Tommy Steele, The Shadows and, of course, The Beatles, he'd picked up a guitar at the age of ten and instantly proved himself something of a boy wonder. A year later, in cahoots with his drummer brother Jack, he was playing Shadows numbers around the working men's clubs of Glasgow. At thirteen, he formed One in a Million, who cut a failed single for CBS and opened for The Who in Scotland. This cocky, precocious wee individual caught the eye of Pete Townshend when he was helping an old friend, John 'Speedy' Keen, with his nascent group Thunderclap Newman.

Pete asked Jimmy to join the band, completing an odd trio of individuals: McCulloch with his liquid rock-guitar runs, Keen with his yearning hippie vocal and Andy Newman with his clumpy pub piano-playing. In the studio, with Townshend at the desk, his head deep in *Tommy* at the time, McCulloch watched The Who guitarist moulding and manipulating sounds on eight-track tape. Thunderclap Newman's first single, and only hit, 'Something In The Air', released in May 1969 when Jimmy was just fifteen, went to number 1. Success didn't throw Jimmy, but becoming a pin-up did. He wasn't, he protested, into the 'heavy pop angle'. He hated it when girl fans would crowd or crush him, or dangerously wield scissors in an attempt to cut off a lock of his hair.

When the constantly bickering Thunderclap Newman argued themselves into non-existence, McCulloch moved on to the heavy blues circuit. He experienced an accelerated apprenticeship in John Mayall's Bluesbreakers – called up on Thursday, onstage with them in Germany by Sunday. The bandleader threw spontaneous calls for solos in his direction and put Jimmy on the spot in front of a paying audience. He then joined tough Scottish soul rabble Stone the Crows, replacing guitarist Les Harvey, who in May 1972 at Swansea Top Rank had touched an ungrounded microphone with wet hands, zapping him with an electric shock that instantly killed him. The band struggled on with McCulloch for another year before their throaty, Janis Joplin-soundalike singer Maggie Bell walked out on them in Montreux in the summer of 1973.

Disenchanted, McCulloch treaded water for a time in forgettable, short-lived rockers Blue, whose members he found far too straight. 'Not enough guts,' he moaned. 'I'd be all dressed up and ridiculous and they'd all walk on wearing jeans. From the start I was the odd one out. I just didn't fit in.'

The problem was that Jimmy didn't seem to fit in anywhere. When he drifted into McCartney's orbit, McCulloch was thinking about going it alone and making a solo album. 'I'm pretty lazy,' he confessed. 'I don't mind admitting it. It takes a long time to get to know people. So I tend to stay put until something comes along.'

The connection to Wings was made through a mutual friend, roadie Ian Horne. McCulloch was invited by McCartney to hear a mix playback of the *Band On The Run* LP. Then, months after the Paris session, Paul called Jimmy again and asked him to contribute to *McGear*, the album he was producing for his brother Mike at Strawberry Studios in Stockport. 'I agreed to give it a go,' said McCulloch, before admitting that he'd been 'slightly cautious because I'd heard people say he was difficult to work with'. During the sessions, when McCulloch was recording slide overdubs on the resonant, part-metal country-blues guitar known as a Dobro, an impressed Paul walked into the live room and on the spot asked Jimmy to join Wings full-time.

Jimmy was a bit starstruck. 'It was like some kind of a dream,' he mooned. 'Paul was there chatting happily, and I just kept staring at him and thinking to myself, Christ, he used to be a Beatle. And here he is talking to me like I matter.' Ultimately, though, even if he felt awed, McCulloch was far too hard-edged, Scottish and proud to be fazed by the prospect of playing with a Beatle. Jimmy had always been more into John and George anyway, as he perhaps rashly revealed to *NME*. 'Paul as well,' he quickly added. 'I've always admired his voice.'

Before joining the band, McCulloch warned McCartney about his mood swings. Sober, Jimmy was a sweetheart. But once, as was his wont, he started tipping back the spirits and snorting or necking other intoxicants, he turned obnoxious. 'There's a Jekyll and Hyde within me,' he admitted. He explained to his new boss that he 'got a bit funny sometimes'.

'I said, "Don't we all, ducky?"' Paul remembered, 'and left it at that.'

Then there was the problem of finding a drummer. In the last week of April 1974, Wings held auditions at the Albery Theatre in the West End of London, hiring a band of session musos to accompany the candidates while Denny Laine and the McCartneys sat judging them in the stalls.

Among those queuing to try their luck was former Jimi Hendrix Experience drummer Mitch Mitchell, yet to find a decent gig five years after the break-up of the band, and almost four since the death of its leader. Denny Laine remembers that on the day, Mitchell was 'on a head trip . . . maybe he resented the fact that we'd asked him to audition and he wasn't getting the star treatment'.

After lunch, up stepped Geoff Britton, a sturdy blond Londoner who was a member of the UK amateur karate team who had recently triumphed over their Japanese counterparts. Up to this point he had been grinding away on the pub circuit, most notably with greasy 1950s throwback rockers Wild Angels. At the Albery, Britton sat down and settled behind the kit, looking every millimetre the rocker in his leather jacket and worn band T-shirt, and began hammering away with sticks so thick that even the heavy-handed Ginger Baker had deemed them unusable.

Britton sailed through the audition, even when he had to slip into the tricksy shuffle of Duke Ellington's 'Caravan', having served his time in cabaret summer seasons. 'Right up my street,' he gruffly noted. 'I did the business.' Paul liked his soulful,

Linda, Heather and Paul arrive at JFK Airport, NYC, 17 March 1969, five days after their London wedding. Paul: 'She had a child. I was genuinely impressed by the way she handled herself in life.'

Paul and Linda emerge from the High Court in London on 19 February 1971 on the first day of the proceedings to untangle the Beatles' legal affairs. Paul: 'I was having to fight my mates. It was just *fucking awful.*'

© Getty Images/Evening Standard

Allen Klein, the master of casual intimidation, March 1971.

Wings Over Europe soundcheck, Châteauvallon, France, 9 July 1972.
Paul and Denny Seiwell go over keyboard parts with a nervous Linda.
Seiwell: 'She was unhappy and frightened. But she had a lot of chutzpah.'

Paul the bed-headed businessman, behind the desk, 1972.

The McCartneys peer out of the back of a police car, after the Swedish dope bust, Gothenburg, 10 August 1972. Linda to photographer Joe Stevens: 'Just get the pictures.'

Togetherness vibes backstage during Wings Over Europe: L–R: Denny Seiwell, Henry McCullough, Paul, Linda and Denny Laine.

The Wings Mark I front line at the Théatre Antique in Arles, 13 July 1972. L–R: Henry McCullough, Denny Laine and Paul.

The fivesome with the trundling, freakadelic open-topped bus used for Wings Over Europe, July 1972.

1 December 1972, the day 'Hi Hi Hi' was released and instantly banned by the BBC. Paul: 'I think the BBC should be highly praised, preventing the youth from hearing my opinions.'

Outside Campbeltown Sheriff Court, March 1973, trying to keep straight faces, after being fined for growing marijuana in Scotland. Paul: 'We got a load of seeds. We didn't know what they were. We planted them and . . . five of them came up illegal.'

Paul and Henry McCullough onstage at London's Hammersmith Odeon, May 1973, just weeks before their argument that caused the latter to quit. McCullough: 'I was driving off the edge of a cliff.'

'We're not pinching your music': the summit to quell the African-influences 'controversy' stirred by Fela Kuti (right), *Band On The Run*, Lagos, 1973.

The fearless leader of the band. Paul: 'If anyone's gonna make a decision, it should probably be him.'

Dressed up in La La Land. At the 46th Annual Academy Awards, April 1974. 'Live And Let Die' was nominated for Best Original Song, but lost out to Barbra Streisand's 'The Way We Were'.

On the porch of songwriter Curly Putnam Jr's house, Tennessee, July 1974, toasting the end of the troubled preliminary rehearsals with Wings Mark II.

Venus And Mars press shot, May 1975.

The record-trouncing, critics-bowling, all-conquering Wings line-up of 1976:
L–R: Joe English, Linda, Jimmy McCulloch, Paul and Denny Laine.

The outlook returns to cloudy. Back down to a trio, eating fish and chips in the rain, at the *London Town* launch on the Thames, March 1978.

Wings Mark III in Liverpool, aboard the *Royal Iris* ferry, scene of early Beatles gigs, November 1979. L–R: Laurence Juber, Linda, Paul, Steve Holley and Denny Laine. Paul: 'I feel I'm not judged with the same harshness by the people here.'

Take these broken Wings. Paul: 'It was getting a bit boring, to tell the truth. I was getting a bit fed up with *yet another line-up*.'

Full circle: recording *McCartney II* alone, ten years after the solo-recorded *McCartney*, 1979. Paul: 'I think of it as being a nutty professor, holed up in this little laboratory.'

Still smiling amid the crush and chaos, in spite of the potential seven-year jail sentence hanging over his head for carrying nearly half a pound of weed into Japan, January 1980. Paul: 'It was like a mad movie.'

Greeting the British press at the Sussex farm after being deported from Japan, 28 January 1980. Asked whether he was planning to spend time with his family, Paul responded: 'Yeah, if you fellas would leave me alone, that *would* be possible.'

frills-free drumming, and a few days later, the Londoner got the call-back to try out with Wings themselves, being told he was on a shortlist of five.

'So, suddenly I'd gone from no chance to 25 per cent chance,' Britton told *NME*, his arithmetic temporarily failing him. 'Anyway, had this audition, met the boys for the first time. Few days passed, another phone call. Scene is: come for the day, practise with them all, go for dinner. Now we're down to two people. So I'm on trial, right? They are going to suss me out. Everybody is charming to me but nobody gives away a thing. Couple of days go by, and then Paul phones and tells me I've got the gig.'

Britton was thrilled, but there was a nagging worry in a corner of his mind. Wild Angels had recently been caught doing a runner from hotels in Glasgow – 'jibbing', the drummer called it – and, as a result, were due up in court. When McCartney called McCulloch and Britton to invite them on a Wings bonding trip to Nashville in June, the sweating, dithering drummer couldn't confirm until, with some relief, the court verdict handed down was the uniquely Scottish one of 'not proven'.

Wings were a five-piece once again, albeit a markedly disparate one, featuring a former Beatle, his musically naïve American wife, a devoted Brummie, an unhinged Glaswegian and a karate-daft, mouthy Cockney. Worse, it quickly became apparent that certain members of this new group really couldn't stand certain other members.

'He picked the wrong guys,' Britton reckoned in the aftermath. 'The chemistry was doomed.'

Paul's idea was that the trip to Nashville would 'break in' the band. In the end, it very nearly broke up the band.

The new line-up of Wings, plus the McCartney family, flew into Tennessee on 14 June 1974. Even travelling under a cloak of relative secrecy, they were still greeted at the airport by a gang of 40 fans and assorted reporters. Asked about the new drummer, Paul said, 'He has a black belt. I feel with those credentials he'll be able to whip the band into shape.'

Their destination was a farm, set in 133 acres of land, in Lebanon, twenty-odd miles east of downtown Nashville. Its owner was songwriter Curly Putnam Jr, whose country hits included 'Green, Green Grass Of Home' and 'D.I.V.O.R.C.E.'. He had agreed to vacate his home for six weeks in return for the princely rent of $2,000 a week, while he and his wife enjoyed an extended vacation in Hawaii.

At first the McCartneys settled in the main house, with the band living in a neighbouring farmhouse, mirroring the living arrangements at High Park. It quickly became clear, however, that this sense of separation wasn't aiding the group's bonding. Only when the others moved into the big house did the rehearsal sessions in its converted garage become productive.

In their downtime, the group shot basketball hoops, enjoyed barbecues – including one four days in to celebrate Paul's 32nd birthday – and rode motorbikes. McCartney treated himself to a Honda road bike, which he sped around on haphazardly and helmet-less, much to the unease of one of the attendant security guards, who wryly commented, 'The next headline he makes will be about a motorcycle wreck. He doesn't know how to drive that thing.'

Elsewhere, Paul lived out his cowboy fantasies, sauntering around town in mirrored aviator shades and a Stetson. Lebanon, situated in the partly 'dry' Wilson County, had restricted alcohol laws, resulting in moonshining in the surrounding hills. 'Guys came into town in old pick-up trucks and did their whittling with bits of wood,' said Britton. 'It was straight out of a movie.'

As the weeks unfolded, visitors to the farm included Roy

Orbison, who Paul had first met during the early touring days of The Beatles, and veteran Nashville musicians including guitarist Chet Atkins and pianist Floyd Cramer, whose shared credits included Elvis Presley and The Everly Brothers. The McCartneys visited Johnny and June Cash, and were tickled that their daughters instantly began drawling in southern accents, copying the First Couple of Country's son, John.

At the home of music publisher Kevin Killen, Wings' fix-it and gofer during their stay, the host was bemused to find the McCartneys allowing the kids to jump up and down on his new, all-white crushed-velvet couch, their fingers slick with Kentucky Fried Chicken grease. 'They were very lenient parents,' he noted. Ushering them out of the house, while attempting to set his burglar alarm, Killen was horrified to hear the sound of a child bawling. Stella, now nearly three years old, had forgotten her shoes and dashed back inside, straight through a glass door, badly cutting her legs and arms. Linda ran into the house, grabbing towels to stem the blood. Stella was rushed to a hospital at nearby Donelson, where the doctors and nurses kept turning up to peek surreptitiously at her famous father. 'A couple dozen people died at the hospital,' Killen joked to Paul. 'All the doctors were watching you.'

It soon became public knowledge where the band were staying, and fans began congregating around the gates of the farm, requiring off-duty policemen to be positioned at the entrance 24 hours a day. The phones in the farmhouse rang constantly: TV and radio producers inviting Paul to appear on local shows, celebrities calling to say hello or ask favours. The peaking US heart-throb, David Cassidy, repeatedly called McCartney at the Lebanon house. 'The stars all came to Paul for help and advice,' said Britton.

The McCartneys were clearly at ease in Tennessee. They would indulge themselves with leisurely breakfasts of hot biscuits and country ham at the Loveless Motel; they motored to the nearest drive-in movie theatre to catch double features at the end of the day. Linda bought a gobsmacked Paul the double bass used by Bill Black on Elvis Presley's 'Heartbreak Hotel', one of the records that had made a formative impression on the teenaged McCartney back in Liverpool.

One night out involved a visit to the fabled Grand Ole Opry to witness the third annual Grand Master Fiddler Contest. Stepping out of the car with the McCartneys, Kevin Killen noticed that as they approached the theatre, people began to recognise the ex-Beatle and mouth his name in shock. One by one they gravitated towards Paul, forming a crowd. Killen admitted he hadn't reckoned on the extent of McCartney's fame: 'It just didn't dawn on me what an icon he was.' Paul, meanwhile, was unruffled by the attention, having learned how to react to this kind of mob behaviour in his Beatlemania days. 'If you stay calm, you're OK,' he told Killen. 'But if you bolt and run, they'll tear you apart.'

Another evening at Nashville's vaunted Printers Alley, a thoroughfare designed for nightlife, threw up a song. The McCartneys had dinner at the Spanish-galleon-themed country music hangout the Captain's Table, before moving to the Rainbow Room, where they bumped into a pinball-playing Waylon Jennings, who chatted with the rapt Paul about his early days with Buddy Holly. Later, in a boozy haze, McCartney was struck with an idea for a tune, originally to be titled 'Diane', after country singer Diane Gaffney, until Paul was told that she was in a particularly litigious mood and in the process of suing a newspaper reporter who had published an article without her consent.

Possibly distracted, Paul left the Rainbow Room that night without settling his $4.75 bill, resulting in his name being inked into the bar's 'delinquent payments' book.

The next day, Paul was found by Britton sitting on a stoop at the farmhouse, playing guitar, completing the lightly country-flavoured song now called 'Sally G'. Set amid the previous night's shenanigans, McCartney imagined himself falling in love with the titular girl, who serenades him with Hank Snow's 'A Tangled Mind' before breaking his heart. 'That was my imagination, adding to the reality of it,' he says.

Wings recorded the song at SoundShop Studios on Music Row in Nashville, despite the fact that they were essentially on holiday and didn't have work permits. At the same time, they committed to tape the chugging, 'Get Back'-like pop rocker 'Junior's Farm', an upbeat nonsense song written partly in tribute to their time spent lying low on Putnam's estate. On the recording, set to become the next Wings single, Paul sounds positively liberated, introducing McCulloch's melodic, slightly flashy guitar solo with the gleeful exhortation, 'Take me down, Jimmy . . .'

The musicians even found time to record a jaunty, old-time swing instrumental written by Paul's father Jim, entitled 'Walking In The Park With Eloise'. McCartney remembered sitting at the foot of the piano as a ten-year-old while his dad played this self-penned tune and standards such as 'Chicago', thrilled and stimulated by the idea that his father had written an actual song of his own. In conversation at the Lebanon farm with Chet Atkins over dinner, Paul told him about the tune and played it to him. The guitarist suggested they record it, and the result was released under the name The Country Hams in October 1974; a perky, slight indulgence that failed to chart. Jim McCartney, quietly touched, was dismissive of his songwriting effort. 'I said, "You know that song you wrote, Dad?"' Paul remembers. 'He said, "No, I've never written one . . . I made one up."'

These frivolities proved to be entertaining diversions, but ultimately, six weeks in, the band began to grow restless and testy. 'If you're together for six weeks, it's hard work and it begins to tell on you,' reckoned Denny Laine. 'At one point I thought, I don't know what we've come here for, we should be at home gigging.'

Geoff Britton was still trying to come to terms with being in a band with McCartney. During rehearsals, the drummer admits he would catch himself staring at Paul, especially if – as the bandleader had decided to do – they were working up an old Beatles standard such as 'Hey Jude'. 'It seemed like a dream,' said Britton. 'It was beautiful.' Nevertheless, under-prepared for the gig, with his foot encased in plaster due to a karate injury, Geoff was having trouble playing some of the material. 'I was put on the spot a bit,' he said. '"Live And Let Die", stuff like that. I hadn't really delved into the music much. I was goofing off. A poxy kit I didn't like, and I didn't think I was delivering the goods.'

Worse, Britton was failing to gel with the others on a personal level, being a teetotal fitness freak amongst a bunch of stoners. He began to irritate his bandmates, sitting there with his foot in plaster, not smoking or drinking. 'So I'm not quite communicating on a social level,' he said. 'I knew it was gonna take them a bit of time to get off on me as a person, 'cause I'm gonna be a bit weird to them.' In addition, the drummer was growing increasingly garrulous and opinionated: 'I'd get a bit upfront about things. I'd bite my tongue but basically . . . no, I wouldn't.'

One day a major argument broke out in rehearsals. According to Britton, 'Everyone got a bit stoned and then it got heavy.' Jimmy insulted Linda, criticising her playing, and there were tears. Britton turned on McCulloch and the pair nearly came to blows. Paul told the angry Britton that he wanted to 'reassess' the situation. The thunder-faced drummer stomped off to the crew room, determined to quit, asking the roadies for petty cash he could use while he took off and travelled the States. In the end they talked him down, though he was still fuming and ranting, saying, 'I'm not going back in there. I'm either the drummer in the band or I'm not.' The incident punctured Britton's dreamy bubble. 'I couldn't believe all the hassles,' he said. 'We were at each other's throats.'

The next morning, Paul and Linda talked to Geoff, reassuring him that his place in the band was secure. An uneasy peace was established for the next few days. But in Britton's eyes, McCulloch remained the major problem – whether he was accusing Linda of playing the wrong chords or hassling the less fastidious guitarist Denny about his tuning. 'It was very fragile,' said the drummer. 'If he came in wrecked and hungover, everything about him would be negative. If he was on an up, then we'd rock away for hours and it would be absolute magic.'

Britton began to sympathise with McCartney, recognising the difficulty of his position as bandleader and peacemaker, carrying the weight of a monumental reputation. 'He was subject to so many pressures. His whole world was pressing in on him. And in those conditions, well, you are not a normal person.' The drummer felt that, having replaced his formerly teenage buddies in The Beatles with what were effectively session players, McCartney was flanked by yes-men and, as a result, was isolated. 'He didn't seem to have any old friends any more,' he said. 'Paul didn't have anybody around who could tell him when he was out of order or to fuck off. You need that.'

The elephant in the room, as always, was the financial agreement with the band. McCartney was keen to drop the idea of contracts and keep the group arrangement looser, and therefore cheaper, by paying the musicians session by session, performance by performance. The problem, once again, was that no one felt as if they were being offered any kind of monetary security. The original idea had been that everyone would travel to Nashville and sign contracts and seal their commitment to the new Wings.

Now that they were there, and particularly in the light of the intra-band hassles, this was looking far less likely.

The band faced up to McCartney and there was something of a showdown, during which they threatened to walk out. 'It's not like these things hadn't been said before,' Laine pointed out. 'You're walking out. But the next minute you can be walking back.' Somehow, fully employing his powers of persuasion, McCartney managed to talk the band round, convincing them that it would be better if their professional relationship was left non-contracted.

'I've signed so many contracts that got me into trouble,' reasoned Laine, 'I never want to sign anything again. It just didn't seem necessary to me.'

'If you're a real pro and you've got a tour booked,' argued Britton, 'you don't phone up and say, "I'm not going." That's just not on.'

McCulloch, who had been put on a wage for a few months to secure his services after joining the band, similarly decided that he'd rather operate on a freelance basis: 'We'd just go on and get paid for what we do.'

If the personality clashes within Wings Mk II were making Paul doubtful about committing himself to this group – especially legally, given the pain of his Beatles court battles – then Denny Laine was feeling much the same way. 'It was being a bit rushed,' he reckoned. 'I thought, Hang on, let's make sure that this is the right group.' Having served his time as Paul's apprentice, Laine was clearly enjoying the reflected glow of being part of the core of the operation. 'Me and Paul and Linda know exactly where we stand now, and you've got to inject that into the whole group,' he stressed, verbally puffing his chest out.

Jimmy McCulloch was already proving a more gnarly proposition, however, beyond his combative behaviour in the rehearsal room. In the SoundShop session he angrily threw a Coke bottle at the studio's control room window. Then he was arrested for some woefully reckless drunken driving, with Kevin Killen having to sweet-talk the authorities, who politely advised him that it might be better if this wayward Scottish rocker exited the country.

Luckily, the trip was coming to a close. On the day before leaving, the McCartneys met reporters in scorching 90-degree heat at the gates of Putnam's farm. Paul seemed keen to underline his kinship with the Tennesseans, pointing out that he was basically a country boy at heart himself. 'I've got a farm in Scotland,' he said. 'You're not the only people who have farms, y'know. Back in Scotland, we're country people in our own way.'

Still, when Wings landed back in Britain on 17 July, their spirits were low. Britton felt as if he'd blown his big opportunity: 'I said to my wife, "Dream shattered . . . I should've fucking known better."' The music press, meanwhile, picked up on the rumours of discontent within the band, ramping them up, with *NME* wrongly reporting under the headline 'Wings Upheaval' that the band had split permanently: 'The existing line-up of Paul McCartney's Wings appeared this week to have broken up, following what is understood to have been a major internal policy disagreement.' A spokesman for Laine admitted that there had been 'personal difficulties'. The McCartneys' PR, meanwhile, underlined the open arrangement that Paul had agreed with the others. 'Wings members are free to pursue their own musical careers,' read their statement. 'This will enable them to develop working relationships free of contractual ties. Wings will have a fluid concept, which will be adapted to suit current and future projects.'

A vague plan was put in place to compile an album to be named *Cold Cuts*. It would mop up unheard recordings by the previous Wings line-up and introduce the new line-up with the material recorded in Nashville. It wasn't to happen. But Paul talked up the new band in *Melody Maker*, while at the same time admitting that he felt there had been problems in the Denny Seiwell/Henry McCullough version of the group, since no one had dared to talk back to him. He cited 'Mary Had A Little Lamb' as exhibit A.

'No one would say, "No, Paul, that's a mistake,"' he explained, without fully considering what his reaction might have been had the original drummer or guitarist questioned his wisdom in releasing the single at the time. 'It was all a bit ropey,' he added. Further, he accepted that Wings had limitations, in respect to their peers, and recognised how hard it was to put a band together and nurture it. Slightly on the back foot, he claimed they were a purposely loose operation and that they were not attempting to 'be cool and over-reach ourselves and try to be Pink Floyd'.

Instead, Paul reverted to *Let It Be* mode, gathering the band together at Abbey Road in August to record an hour-long TV special, *One Hand Clapping*, that in the light of the ructions to come was to remain unseen for many years. In it, the band turn in slick versions of 'Jet', 'Junior's Farm', rattling rocker 'Soily' and the loping, reggae-ish 'C Moon', sounding tight and strong. They can be heard jamming the breezy if mawkish anti-war pop of Paper Lace's 'Billy Don't Be A Hero', which earlier that year had knocked 'Band On The Run' off the top of the UK singles chart, and which was conspicuously McCartney-flavoured.

Paul was filmed alone at the piano, tinkling his way through an ad lib medley of snatches of cabaret-style songs that he'd constructed with other singers in mind, from the slightly bizarre 'Suicide' – a Sinatra-fashioned ballad written in his teens, and eventually presented to the legendary crooner, who wondered in bewilderment if it was a joke – to the drifty romanticism of 'Let's Love', sung by Peggy Lee and produced by McCartney later that year.

Viewing the *One Hand Clapping* footage, Britton was surprised to discover that, 'seeing us playing, we were a good band'. But as smooth as the actual performances were, the film was revealing in other, less favourable ways: an impish McCulloch exits the room at a close-of-session rendition of 'Bluebird', grinning and muttering that Paul is 'flogging a dead horse'. Later there is an appearance by McCartney's old friend from Liverpool, Howie Casey, five years older than him and a former member of Derry and the Seniors – the first band from the city to play in Hamburg, mapping out the territory for The Beatles. He is seen being conducted, a touch condescendingly, through a reprise of his improvised sax solo for 'Bluebird'. Paul, not a big drinker, had asked Howie if he could get him anything for the session, and the saxophonist had asked for a beer. A roadie was duly dispatched, returning, to the musician's amazement, with a single bottle of beer. 'I'd been working with John Entwistle,' Casey laughs, 'and the place was full of booze, and then we'd go to a club afterwards.'

Elsewhere in *One Hand Clapping*, Laine slurs though his voiceover, sounding staggeringly drunk. Britton unintentionally provides the comedy, bouncing behind his drum kit wearing his karate suit. In one section, he enthusiastically slices and kicks his way through the choreography of a *kata* routine for the benefit of the camera. It is all too easy to see why he was becoming the butt of the others' jokes. Laine would mock the drummer mercilessly, asking him, 'What are you gonna do? Play the drums or chop them in two?'

As one band was falling apart, the legal affairs of another, long dead, were finally being put to rest.

By the latter half of 1974, relations between the former Beatles were decidedly mixed. Paul and John were getting on better than they had done since the split. When Lennon first returned to New

York from LA, and before getting back together with Ono, he shared an apartment with May Pang on East 52nd Street. The McCartneys were regular visitors whenever they were in town. 'We would go out for dinner all the time,' says Pang. Lennon said he and Paul enjoyed 'Beaujolais evenings, reminiscing about the old times'.

The main obstacle in the path of reconciliation was that George didn't want to have anything to do with Paul any more. 'How can we get together if George won't play with Paul?' Ringo asked a quizzing reporter. 'Paul is a fine bass player,' George said, not a little patronisingly, 'but he's a bit overpowering at times. I'd join a band with John Lennon any day, but I couldn't join a band with Paul McCartney.'

Still, by autumn, John was making encouraging noises about The Beatles working together again, saying they'd probably leave it until 1976, when their contract with EMI was due to expire. 'I'd like The Beatles,' he told a journalist, coolly sucking on a cigarette, 'to make a record together again.'

If he did, he had a funny way of showing it. In the second week of December, three of the ex-Beatles were by chance in New York at the same time. A plan was swiftly hatched to meet up for the signing of the recently completed 202-page document that would finally dissolve the band's partnership, freeing up millions in royalties. The papers were to be ceremoniously inked at the Plaza Hotel on Central Park South. On the morning of 19 December 1974, Paul and George arrived at a suite there, to be met with piles of contracts laid out on green baize tables.

Lennon didn't show, on the advice of his astrologer, revealing that the superstitious influence of Ono – she and John having begun the tentative process of reuniting – was back in play. Instead, he sent a balloon to the hotel bearing the enigmatic message 'Listen to this balloon'. Harrison hit the roof. He furiously rang Lennon, only across Central Park visiting Yoko at the

Dakota, and bawled down the line, 'You fucking maniac. You take your fucking dark glasses off and come and look at us, man.'

It didn't work. An untypically huffy Linda later noted, 'The numbers weren't right, the planets weren't right and John wasn't coming. Had we known there was some guy flipping cards on his bed to help him make his decision, we would all have gone over there.'

'It was all quite far out,' said Paul.

George was at the end of his first and only solo tour of the US, which had found him being criticised for his weak vocal performances, and for taking a haphazard, Dylan-like approach to radically rearranging his best-known songs. That night, Paul and Linda attended his show at Madison Square Garden, heavily disguised in shades, Afro wigs and fuzzy fake moustaches, highlighting the sense of the ludicrous in the air.

John, meanwhile, finally signed the dissolution papers releasing the Beatles' money, in Florida, over Christmas, where he was on holiday with Pang and his son Julian. Perhaps fittingly, given the cartoon reality of having been a Beatle, he put pen to paper at Disney World.

The following month, January 1975, Paul invited John down to New Orleans to get involved in the next Wings album. Lennon was seriously toying with the idea and had been sounding out various individuals for their opinions over the previous weeks. He asked Art Garfunkel, who had recently made up with Paul Simon, what he should do about the overtures from '*my* Paul'. Garfunkel told him that he thought Lennon and McCartney should try to forget their personality differences and just make music together. John then wrote to former Beatles publicist Derek Taylor, saying that he was possibly going down to New Orleans 'to see the McCartknees'.

One evening in the East 52nd Street apartment, out of

nowhere, Lennon asked Pang, 'What would you think if I started writing with Paul again?'

She turned to him, open-mouthed, and said, 'Are you kidding? I think it would be terrific.'

Later that night, Lennon disappeared to the Dakota, enticed by Ono who claimed to have discovered a foolproof smoking cure. Whatever happened that night, Pang says that Lennon returned to her changed. The reunion with Paul in Louisiana wasn't ever mentioned again.

The allure of the city's kaleidoscopically funky music scene had drawn Paul to New Orleans. Besides, there were tax advantages to be gained by recording in the US again – he'd be earning 70 cents in the dollar, rather than two pence in the pound. Added to this, McCartney loved the punchy drum sound captured on Labelle's lascivious 1974 hit 'Lady Marmalade', recorded at Allen Toussaint's Sea-Saint Studio, which became the setting for the recording of the next Wings album, *Venus And Mars*.

Ironically, given the fact that McCartney had been attracted to the southern recording facility because of the drum sound, Paul felt Geoff Britton was struggling, both on a playing level and emotionally. The drummer's marriage was in trouble and he had been dreading the trip. 'I was so depressed,' he admitted. 'It should have been the happiest time of my life. But I was miserable and hated it. There was no sincerity in the band, and every day it was a fight for survival, a fight to re-establish yourself.'

Britton noticed that, from the outset in New Orleans, Laine and McCulloch were distant with him, although he wasn't exactly trying to reach out to them with his talk of 'thick Northerners'. 'Well, they were thick Northerners,' he contended. 'There's no hiding facts.' He unequivocally considered Denny 'a bastard'. Jimmy, meanwhile, was 'a cunt'. For his part, Laine thought that Britton was only in it for the money: 'He was always talking about "When I get my big house . . ." The guy was an opportunist. It was a disaster, basically.'

In Paul's measured, diplomatic opinion, 'He wasn't quite like the rest of us. We had a sense of humour in common. He was nearly in with it all. But it's a fine line.'

Two weeks into the sessions, one morning at their hotel in the French Quarter, the McCartneys turned up at Britton's room and told him that they were letting him go. 'I got marched out and that was the end of it,' he says.

'It was horrible because we really wanted it to work,' said Linda. 'It was another depressing period. We had started *Venus And Mars*, but it just wasn't working.'

On many levels, Britton hadn't clicked. In his place came Joe English, a New Yorker blessed with natural swing, recommended by *Venus And Mars* trombone player and arranger Tony Dorsey. The drummer had played with an outfit called the Jam Factory, who had supported Jimi Hendrix and the Allman Brothers, but he had been on the skids for the previous two years. He was playing some sessions on the Macon-centred southern rock circuit, but he was broke and his wife had left with their two kids. It would be some time before it was revealed that English was expertly masking some serious demons of his own.

Floating above their worries, while in New Orleans the McCartneys were determined to enjoy the everlasting party. They took five days off for Mardi Gras and slipped into the crowds dressed as clowns. They threw a party-cum-press-conference on a riverboat, the *Voyager*, and sailed up and down the bayou to the groovesome live R&B sounds of The Meters. The members of Wings turned out, looking resplendent in black top hats. They remained, for the meantime at least, a band projecting the illusion of unity, held together by mirrors and sticky tape.

The mid-1970s seemed to become very intense for you . . .

Well, yeah. But we did what we set out to do. Didn't cave in under the pressure.

9

Lift-offs and Landings

It was just after midnight when the patrol car pulled them over. They had been driving down Santa Monica Boulevard in their silver Lincoln Continental when Paul took a right turn, missing a sign forbidding the manoeuvre and running a red light. As the officer leaned into the car he caught a whiff of grass. Everyone – Paul, Linda and the three kids asleep in the back – was ordered out of the vehicle.

According to the patrolman's report, a search of Linda's purse produced a plastic bag containing seventeen grammes of marijuana, along with a still-smouldering joint fished out from under the passenger seat. Linda and Paul were immediately placed under arrest, before the former – probably fearing ensuing US visa problems – protested that the dope was hers and that it had been her alone, not her husband, smoking the spliff.

Paul insists to this day that the weed was planted by the police. 'They came up with a big bag of stuff that wasn't ours,' he says.

Whatever the truth, the outcome was that Linda was detained for two hours while Paul drove the kids back to their rented house in Coldwater Canyon. He returned to the station where his wife was being held to discover that she had been charged with possession, her bail set at $500. Embarrassed, Paul had to confess that he was only carrying $200. In the middle of the night, he was forced to call former Apple executive director

Peter Brown, who he knew was in town staying at the Beverly Hills Hotel, to borrow the rest.

Worse, there was the threat that a second and more damning charge – contributing to the delinquency of a minor – might be thrown at Linda, since she'd admitted smoking weed while looking after her children. It all added to the couple's mounting feelings of harassment. 'We were being targeted all the time,' Linda groaned. 'Maybe we were asking for it. Maybe we were a bit stupid. But we're not criminals.'

The McCartneys were in Los Angeles enjoying something of a partying lifestyle, living it up at the Beverly Wilshire (where Jo Jo Patrie noted the normally thrifty couple put no limits on the hotel tabs) before moving into the Coldwater Canyon house. There was much to celebrate. Two nights earlier, on 1 March 1975 – before an audience which included the reunited Lennon and Ono, who turned up with a tux-wearing, cocaine-emaciated David Bowie in tow – they had picked up two Grammys for *Band On The Run*. The album had steadily grown to become a towering success: five million copies sold, the best-selling UK album of 1974, named Album of the Year by the previously sniffy *Rolling Stone*, and so on and on.

Wings were in LA putting the finishing touches to the initially troubled *Venus And Mars*, the making of which had become far easier with the introduction of Joe English and the move to California. To toast its completion, the McCartneys decided to throw a costly wrap party for the record aboard the RMS *Queen Mary*, a retired ocean liner docked in the waters off Long Beach. The 200 guests included some of the top players in music and film at the time including Joni Mitchell, Marvin Gaye, Bob Dylan, Cher, Led Zeppelin, Ryan and Tatum O'Neal, Dean Martin and Tony Curtis. Guests were guided into the ship's Grand Saloon along a corridor bearing posters featuring the album's cosmic, cryptic slogan, 'Venus and Mars are alright tonight'. Later a woman, mistaking the planets of the album title as alter egos for the McCartneys, confounded them by walking up to them and saying, 'Hello Venus, hello Mars.'

Surprising everyone, given his recent putdown of McCartney in the press, George Harrison showed up, and he and his estranged bandmate were seen chatting. The party also marked the first time that Paul and Michael Jackson met. Jackson remembered that he and McCartney were introduced and shook hands amongst a large crowd of people, before the latter said, 'You know, I've written a song for you.'

'I was very surprised and thanked him,' a thrilled Jackson recalled. 'And he started singing "Girlfriend" to me.'

Paul didn't make quite such an impression on everyone. As the evening wore on, an utterly soused Dean Martin sat at a table with the McCartneys, repeatedly roaring, 'Who the hell is giving this party? Do I know these people?'

His star in the ascendant once more, Paul began planning a world tour befitting his status. There were signs, however, that he was doing so with some trepidation.

McCartney Productions had recently become the more ambitious MPL Communications, and moved premises from Greek Street in W1 around the corner to a five-storey townhouse at 1 Soho Square. Paul fancied turning its sizeable basement into a club, where he could play lunchtime gigs for office workers and serve up hot dogs, taking him back to the days of the cellar-based Casbah Club in Liverpool. MPL managing director Brian Brolly talked him out of the idea, pointing out that demand for tickets would be unreasonably high and the scheme would prove unworkable. If Paul was trying to shy away from the pressures of a big tour, this wasn't the way to go.

Instead, Wings got their heads down for an intensive rehearsal period lasting four whole months, highlighting just how determined McCartney was to get the band sounding right. There were rumours that the group were to play an outdoor show at Knebworth House in the summer of 1975. Instead, the slot was filled by Pink Floyd, who performed before an audience of 100,000 – too head-spinning a leap for the fledgling second line-up of Wings.

Venus And Mars, however, was a record built for touring. It even opened like a gig, with the gentle acoustic guitar-picking of the title track finding the singer imagining himself in the audience at an arena concert, waiting for the lights to go down. This segued into the thumping 'Rock Show', with its references to Jimmy Page, Madison Square Garden and the Hollywood Bowl and, perhaps tellingly, scoring an entire ounce of dope, far more than the average long-haired punter could afford.

Rather than being Wings' New Orleans-flavoured album, *Venus And Mars* was far more adventurous stylistically, from the floaty Californian FM sound of 'Listen To What The Man Said' and the glassy-eyed hippie balladry of 'Love In Song' to the tap-dancing music-hall frippery of 'You Gave Me The Answer'. The lyrical references took in the lowbrow ('Magneto And Titanium Man', inspired by a comic book found in Jamaica) and the high-minded (sci-fi writer Isaac Asimov influencing the futuristic couplets of 'Venus And Mars – Reprise').

Yet having turned in a credible rock album in tune with the times, McCartney came close to blowing it with an oddball ending. 'Treat Her Gently/ Lonely Old People' was a sensitive, if syrupy ode to old age and dementia, which gave way to a rock-tastic rendering of the theme from cosy UK teatime soap opera *Crossroads*. To Paul, it sounded like a show-stopping Diana-Ross-is-leaving-the-building concert crescendo. To everyone else, it was a touch more cheese than was palatable, even if the soap's producers were subsequently moved to use the Wings version to soundtrack the programme's end credits.

'One of the big things for lonely old people in England is to watch *Crossroads*,' Paul argued, explaining the thinking behind this slightly strange finale. 'That was it, just a joke at the end.' Around the same time, more illuminatingly perhaps, when filling in the 'weight' section of a teen-mag fact file, Paul wrote, '2 stoned'.

Jokey ending notwithstanding, there were high expectations for *Venus And Mars*. Pre-orders alone for the LP exceeded 1.5 million. The cover was just as striking as the one for *Band On The Run*: red and yellow billiard balls, representing the planets of the title, expertly shot by Linda on a low-lit deep-blue baize.

In spending most of their time getting ready for the tour, rarer now were the occasions when the McCartneys would all pile into their new green Rolls-Royce convertible and motor north to High Park. Instead, aside from a summer break in the US when they stayed with the Eastmans in the Hamptons, the family were based for most of the time at Cavendish Avenue in London, where slightly aghast visitors would note that the kids were allowed by their indulgent parents to scribble on the walls.

To the horror of their snooty neighbours, over the years since Linda's arrival the McCartneys' St John's Wood abode had increasingly begun to resemble a city farm. The garden was full of weeds and, on wet days, mud. Alongside a glass-built geodesic 'meditation dome', erected in the late 1960s and containing a large round bed given to Paul by Alice Cooper (who had originally been gifted it by Groucho Marx), it was home to a vegetable patch and a mucky menagerie of animals from dogs and cats to ducks and rabbits. On one occasion Paul left the window of the Roller open and, for a time, the chickens moved in, necessitating a reupholstering job costing £6,000. The family's cockerel would crow the long-suffering neighbours awake at first light. The McCartneys reinstated the stable blocks in the garden, keeping four horses, which, donning hats and jodhpurs, they would ride on Sunday mornings.

All of this made the McCartneys less than popular in their exclusive urban locale. Once an irate neighbour phoned the RSPCA to complain that the dogs were left alone in the house all day when the family were elsewhere. A representative of the animal welfare charity visited, but left satisfied with the assurance that the family's part-nanny, part-housekeeper Rose Martin popped in once a day to make sure they were fine.

Inside, the living-room décor of Cavendish Avenue was millionaire boho with a hint of working-class. There were dark grey and brown carpets, a green armchair and couch – with a rip that the kittens would disappear into – arranged around a low coffee-table covered with a chequered Madras tablecloth. The furniture was cheap or second-hand, and matched with more expensive or antique items: Tiffany lampshades, a clock from the 1851 Great Exhibition, a robot-like sculpture by Scottish artist Eduardo Paolozzi named *Solo*. Dotted around the walls were originals by Magritte and De Kooning.

At the same time, missing their bucolic Scottish retreat, the couple bought an unusual property for £42,000 in Peasmarsh, near Rye, on the Sussex coast. A circular, slightly cramped two-bedroomed cottage with wedge-shaped rooms and over 160 acres of land, it mirrored High Park in being a small house set in an expanse of untamed nature. Its insides were soon filled with the McCartneys' clutter, and the couple shifted half an ark's worth of animals on to the land: horses, sheep, hens, pheasants, even an aviary of budgies. A stream that cascaded over a drop gave the property its name, Waterfall.

Back in London, at the same time, the pressures were piling up. In anticipation of the upcoming tour, a news story in *Melody*

Maker carped, 'Linda McCartney faces her sternest test yet . . .'
On 5 September, Wings performed a dress rehearsal of the tour production at Elstree Studios for an invited audience of guests including Ringo and Harry Nilsson. According to Paul, even after the months of pernickety rehearsal, 'it showed up a lot of holes in the show'.

These were holes that needed to be filled, and quickly. This time around, Wings weren't just a bunch of hippies jumping into a van. This time, there would be no room for mistakes.

'Just what keeps you going?' called out one reporter.

'Drugs!' replied a chipper McCartney.

It was 11 September 1975, the morning after the second date of the British leg of Wings' World Tour, an ambitious jaunt expected to last a year and to sweep through Europe, Australia, Japan and America. To fire up the excitement surrounding it, the band were giving a press conference at the Post House Hotel in Bristol, the city having been the scene of the previous night's show.

As much as Paul was attempting to draw a deep line in the sand between The Beatles and the newly streamlined Wings, he couldn't avoid the inevitable questions.

'Have you seen The Beatles lately?' quizzed another journalist.

'We run into each other and stuff,' said Paul. 'We're just good friends.'

'Is Wings really a logical development from The Beatles?'

'Well, I've always written songs, but with The Beatles we only ever rehearsed for three days at the most. With this band, we rehearse a lot.'

'Will Wings ever become as big as The Beatles?'

'I think it could be, funnily enough.'

'How different is Wings from The Beatles?'

'They scream at our concerts, but they don't scream as much.

People used to come and scream and didn't hear any of the music. Now they can.'

'Do you want to bring back The Beatles?'

'It wasn't within my power to bring back The Beatles. It was a four-way split and we all wanted to do different things. We're all very good friends. John is keeping very quiet at the moment, while unfortunately I'm out working. I like it.'

Later, Linda confessed to one journalist that the ex-Fabs were unsurprisingly sick of being asked over and over and over again about the possibility of them reforming. 'They'll ask about The Beatles forever,' she rightly pointed out. Even onstage, McCartney couldn't escape the relentless interrogation. Midway through the second of two sold-out shows at Hammersmith Odeon in London a week later, one fan shouted, 'What about John Lennon?' Trying to remain cheery and playfully dismissive, Paul responded, 'What about him?'

Nevertheless, the set list for the tour proved that McCartney was confident about his post-Beatles output, comprising as it did mainly songs from *Band On The Run* and *Venus And Mars*. In a nod to his past, however, part-way through, he offered up a crowd-pleasing medley of 'Lady Madonna', 'The Long And Winding Road', 'I've Just Seen A Face', 'Blackbird' and 'Yesterday' – the last two performed solo, on acoustic guitar, literally spotlighting his formidable talents, lest anyone had forgotten. From the outside, Paul projected nothing but self-assurance.

Internally, however, it was another matter. If during a show, from the stage, he could see someone in the audience walking out or even lighting a cigarette, he would fret that he had lost their attention. He hated the fact that, at 33, he was being cast as an old man of rock by the music press or, denting his ego, a throwback to the 1960s. 'I suppose I am from another age,' he ruminated wistfully.

Still, in perhaps the first wave of rock nostalgia, there was enormous demand for tickets for the tour. Fanning the flames of anticipation, in their review of the show, *Melody Maker* deemed it to be 'excellent', going on to say that it would 'awaken Beatlemania across the Atlantic'.

As the tour progressed, this didn't seem like hot air. In Melbourne, 1,500 hardy and determined souls queued for tickets overnight under skies filled with rain, thunder and lightning. Displaying less dedication, the McCartneys slept in for the flight down under on 27 October, forcing a Qantas jet filled with their tetchy fellow passengers to idle on the tarmac for 45 minutes while the family rushed to Heathrow. Hitting him precisely where it hurt, the airline fined Paul $9,000 for holding the plane up – $200 for every minute of the delay.

A cartoon appeared in *The Sun* two days later, sketched by their regular satirist Franklin, depicting a planeload of furious passengers spitting out their Foster's lager, chewing the seats, suffering heart attacks and in one instance pulling out a revolver, as a grinning, laidback Paul, reclining with his hands behind his head, receives the cabin PA announcement, 'We regret having to turn back, cobbers, but Mr McCartney has forgotten his toothbrush . . .'

It had been eleven years since Paul had toured Australia with The Beatles, and once Wings had landed in the country, the response was no less overwhelming. Beatlemaniacal scenes met the McCartneys at Perth Airport, with Paul walking along the front row of fervent fans, shaking hands, while carrying a bemused, four-year-old Stella.

One television reporter touched a recently exposed nerve when he pointed out to McCartney, 'Thirty-three, that's a bit old for rock'n'roll.'

'Ancient . . . ancient,' Paul responded, fiddling with his hair, annoyance clearly bubbling just below the surface.

'Do you think you're past it?' asked the hack.

'I don't know,' Paul replied, visibly ruffled. 'I wouldn't be here if I thought I was. But you come and see the show, and if you like the show, you tell me if I'm over my peak after it, OK?' Before he broke away, he added, 'And if you tell me I am, it's coats off outside, cobber.'

Wings quickly settled in Australia, throwing a 31st-birthday party for Denny Laine on 29 October, cruising around the Perth waters on a hydrofoil. As was fast becoming their routine, they threw a press conference in the city to meet the media. Arriving in a room filled with 200 representatives from newspapers, magazines and TV channels, the group found a figure – in a cheap brown suit, his thinning hair greasily slicked forward, a piece of toilet paper sticking to a shaving cut – apparently asleep in one of their chairs.

It turned out to be Aussie comic creation Norman Gunston (in reality, actor Garry McDonald), who awoke and immediately hijacked the proceedings, turning them into a two-way piss-taking routine between himself and the band. Was Paul planning to open another fruit shop after the failure of Apple? Was there any truth in the rumour that he'd been dead? As a wedded couple in a band, did Linda ever feel like telling her husband that she couldn't perform that night due to a headache? How, indeed, was the marriage going?

'It's alright,' Paul responded, as gales of slightly nervous laughter blew around the room. 'But you're not helping it, Norm.'

McCartney was in a jocular mood throughout the tour. During his solo portion of the set, he took to introducing 'Yesterday' by saying, 'Tell you what, see if you remember this one,' picking the opening chords of his most famous song to thunderous applause before atonally singing, 'Once a jolly swagman' (the opening line of 'Waltzing Matilda'). The audience would howl with laughter, and Paul would pause and begin again.

The news that arrived on 11 November temporarily wiped the smile off his face, however. The Japanese authorities, citing the Scottish marijuana conviction of 1973, were refusing Wings entry to the country. The gigs there had to be scrapped. Paul was initially angered by the ban: the Japanese Embassy in London had already approved his visa. 'They're still old-fashioned out there,' he reasoned. 'The older folks see a great danger in allowing in an alien who has admitted smoking marijuana and they're trying to stamp it out, using all the wrong methods as usual.'

The Melbourne show, having been filmed for Australia, was sent to Japan to be screened as an apology to fans, along with a televised Japanese debate about marijuana. Paul lamented the fact that the McCartneys 'had become martyrs for the cause'. Interviewed in Australia on daytime chat programme *The Mike Walsh Show*, as Linda, Jimmy and Denny lolled around him, looking and sounding lightly refreshed, Paul pointed out that it was a two-year-old charge and that, after arguing their case, the authorities in both Australia and the United States had agreed to let him in. It was the Japanese Minister of Justice alone who had nixed the visit.

'He's no friend o' mine!' joked Paul, in a passable Scottish accent, eyeballing the viewers at home.

'The first chance I get, I'll put him doon,' added Denny Laine.

'You could put him doon, I'll stick the heid on him,' slurred the genuinely Scottish Jimmy McCulloch, looking as if he just might, given the chance.

As a postscript, Paul filmed a message of apology to the Japanese fans. But it was a smirking McCartney who faced the lens to say, 'We're very sorry that we can't come to Japan to play our music to you this time. But if the Minister of Justice says we can't come in, then we can't come in. Don't worry, we'll see you when we come back to your beautiful country . . . *sayonara*.'

He put his hands together and bowed his head, spread them

into a W shape to represent the Wings logo, and then smiled knowingly.

If there was a certain cockiness now evident in the McCartneys' demeanour, it was noticed by others. In New York, Linda's long-time friend, writer Danny Fields, was gobsmacked when the couple visited him, got stoned and then asked to borrow money from him for the cab fare back uptown.

'We don't bother carrying money in New York,' Linda told him. 'We just tell the cab driver who we are, and then we sign autographs for him and he says we should forget what's on the meter.' On this occasion they needed cash for the return journey since, on the way down to Fields's apartment, they'd encountered a driver who hadn't recognised them. 'Sure enough, he wanted money,' Linda moaned. 'I had some coins in my purse. We told him it was a lot of money in New Zealand or something.'

Eight days before Christmas 1975, Paul and Linda turned up unannounced to see John and Yoko at the Dakota. The Lennons were sitting in their bedroom with photographer Bob Gruen when they heard voices directly outside their apartment door. Lennon was instantly freaked, since the arrangement at the building was that any visitors first had to pass by the doormen at the gates and introduce themselves to the concierge, who would then call upstairs.

The Lennons nervously asked Gruen to check who it was. He walked into the hall and unlocked the inner door, leaving the outer door closed. Hearing the sound of voices harmonising, he shouted back to John and Yoko in the bedroom, 'Don't worry, it's just kids in the building singing Christmas carols.' Opening the second door, there before him stood Paul and Linda singing 'We Wish You A Merry Christmas'. The photographer, taken aback, said, 'I think you're looking for the guys in the bedroom . . . come on in.'

As Gruen remembers, 'It was like old friends meeting by surprise and really glad to see each other. We sat around and drank tea.' Paul and Linda griped to a sympathetic John and Yoko about the Japanese dope ban. 'They were talking about what a small thing it was. They were very sorry that they couldn't go to Japan for such a seemingly trivial reason.'

As Lennon and McCartney began to rebuild their friendship properly, in February 1976 a US promoter called Bill Sargent made them an offer that seemed irresistible. He was willing to pay a reformed Beatles $50 million for a one-off show. When, by March, there had been no response, he doubled the offer. At the same time, a US industrialist, Mike Matthews, the head of guitar effects pedal company Electro-Harmonix, offered them $3 million, with an additional cut of pay-per-view TV revenue that would up their share to more than $30 million. Lee Eastman, speaking for McCartney, stated that these offers weren't 'even being considered'.

Privately, Paul asked the other ex-Beatles if they should put out a joint statement turning down the offers. No one would commit to it. Going it alone, McCartney began to contradict himself in the press. One minute he was saying that his response to the offer was a 'positive maybe', the next that any Beatles reunion would only happen 'if we wanted to do something musically, not . . . just for the money'. It came back to that familiar fear that they might desecrate their legacy. Around this time, Paul in London and John in New York had a long chat on the phone. Never once were the offers or the spectre of a reformation even mentioned.

Still, with the Wings tours of Europe and the US looming, The Beatles once again threatened to overshadow everything as Parlophone/EMI reissued all 22 of their UK singles at once, along with a 45 of 'Yesterday'. *Reveille* magazine in Britain reported that this had created a 'Beatles Boom!', particularly among a new generation of teenagers discovering the group for the first time.

At one point, in the UK Top 100, The Beatles occupied 23 places. Accordingly, EMI's profits for the period rose by a third.

But Paul, who had just released the chirpy, critic-challenging 'Silly Love Songs' with Wings, was riled by the idea of having to compete with the ghost of his younger self. 'I wouldn't want "Silly Love Songs" kept off the top by "Love Me Do",' he bristled.

On 18 March 1976 Paul's father Jim died, from a combination of bronchial pneumonia and heart failure, at home in Rembrandt, the house his famous son had bought for him in the village of Gayton on the Wirral, Merseyside. Paul received the news from his stepmother, Angie, in a telephone call to the Royal Garden Hotel in London, where Wings were staying en masse prior to leaving for the European tour.

'I'm sorry, son, it just happened,' said Angie.

'Are you sure?' Paul asked her, shocked.

To the astonishment of outsiders, McCartney didn't attend the cremation, held four days later at Landican Cemetery, near Jim McCartney's home. The idea that a son wouldn't attend his own father's funeral was, of course, unthinkable. In the end, there were two reasons for Paul's decision: first, the media attention would mar the service – Angie said 'it would just be a circus'; second, he couldn't face the emotional trauma of grieving in public. His brother Mike admitted, 'Paul would never face that sort of thing. As Dad would say, "It's just the way you're made, son."'

Instead, Paul threw himself back into work. 'That's just my character. I suppose I coped by remembering him as he was. He used to hate funerals and all of that sort of stuff, so I didn't get involved. I sort of thought, Well, he hated it, so it would be kind of hypocritical to go and do all the weeping and wailing.'

Linda admitted to Danny Fields that going to the funeral would have 'caused problems', but worried that the McCartneys were being criticised for not attending. Paul was later to become estranged from Angie and his stepsister Ruth, who he believed profited from selling memorabilia from his dad's home.

Weirdly, however, even though Lennon was among the first to hear the news and called McCartney to offer his condolences, Paul didn't tell the other members of Wings. The first that Denny Laine knew about it was when Paul was randomly asked in a press conference in Paris whether either of his parents were still alive. McCartney flatly replied, 'No.' Laine was gobsmacked. 'Paul is . . . quite privately shy,' he reasons. 'It's just his personality.'

Meanwhile the group were on a roll, having swiftly completed their fifth album, *Wings At The Speed Of Sound*, released a mere ten months after *Venus And Mars*. The reason for this increased productivity was partly down to the fact that this was the band's first 'democratic' album, opening up the lead vocal performances to all members in overtly trying to prove that Wings was a real band and not merely a construct of session musicians built to prop up McCartney's ego.

In both this open band arrangement and its mellow West Coast characteristics, *Wings At The Speed Of Sound* went some way to emulating the Eagles, then a dominant force in the US charts. The record opened with the literally inviting 'Let 'Em In', in which a languid-voiced Paul acted as welcoming host to an imaginary parade of guests including The Everly Brothers, his brother Mike and his Auntie Gin. Elsewhere, Denny Laine turned in an aching performance on 'The Note You Never Wrote', Joe English was cast as a broken-hearted country singer on the lonesome 'Must Do Something About It', and Linda played it for laughs with the proto-rock'n'roll of 'Cook Of The House', which depicted her getting busy-busy in the kitchen and closed with the sound of chips frying, sounding like applause.

Jimmy McCulloch, meanwhile, in cahoots with former Stone

the Crows drummer/lyricist Colin Allen offered another of their anti-drug songs, mined from the same vein as the cautionary 'Medicine Jar' from *Venus And Mars*. 'Wino Junko' closed the first side of *Wings At The Speed Of Sound* with a lilting melody, finding the 'pill freak' narrator addressing his addictions and even noting that he was unafraid to risk his life for his beloved highs. Even if the words weren't his own, McCulloch might have been advised to listen closer to the song he was singing, since he was increasingly becoming a worrying and unstable element of Wings. At the outset of the European tour, photographer Robert Ellis noted that Jimmy was becoming 'really hard to handle . . . he was constantly paranoid and constantly out of his head'.

This was proved in ludicrous fashion on 26 March 1976 in Paris, where Wings had taken up residence at the swish Hotel George V. After the show at the Pavilion de Paris, the band and entourage, sans McCartneys, sprawled out in the bar, where they began drinking heavily, pulling teen idol David Cassidy into their orbit. At some point the party repaired upstairs, where a fight broke out when a spectacularly leathered McCulloch accused Cassidy of being a 'fag' and took a swing at him. Cassidy went to block McCulloch's punch, accidentally knocking him to the floor. The heated and chaotic scene quickly cooled when it became apparent that McCulloch had injured a finger, fracturing the bone.

The much trumpeted upcoming US tour – due to be the first time McCartney had appeared live in America in a decade, before an expected audience of half a million, yielding an estimated $4 million in profits – was postponed, at great expense, for three weeks, due to McCulloch's drunken antics. Talking to reporters, Jimmy and Paul tried to laugh off the incident. The guitarist fibbed and said he'd broken the finger after slipping on a wet floor when getting out of the bath.

'Yeah,' Paul added darkly. 'We're gonna break his arm next week.'

It's tempting to snip up those solo Beatles LPs and picture maybe 'Jet' on the same album as 'Imagine' and 'My Sweet Lord' . . .

That's right. Could've been alright. Let's do that then and we'll call it The Beatles. It would have been good, I suppose, from that point of view. But we just decided we'd done it. We'd come full circle and enough was enough. It would've been a calculated move to put The Beatles back together, just 'cause some guy offered us millions. Between us, at various moments, one of us would get hot on the idea and the big offer would come in, but, it was, like, Nah. That was one good thing about The Beatles, it just all flowed, it just came shooting out of us. And it was, like, Let's leave it. Let sleeping dogs lie.

10

High over America

Sitting behind a desk, adopting an air of mock-seriousness, Lorne Michaels, producer and occasional presenter of NBC's comedy and music revue *Saturday Night Live*, faced the camera, twelve items into the show's broadcast of 24 April 1976. The starring guests that week included voluptuous film star Raquel Welch and John Sebastian, founder of feelgood 1960s pop band The Lovin' Spoonful, plugging his theme song to high-school sitcom *Welcome Back, Kotter*, set to become the US number 1 the following month. Comedian Chevy Chase had opened the show, in a skit where he presented an award to the best 'political actor', the nominees including presidential candidates Jimmy Carter and Gerald Ford. There had been a spoof ad for a Purina pet food for rats, and John Belushi had turned in his uncomfortably gurning impersonation of British singer Joe Cocker.

Now, in what appeared to be a break in transmission, Michaels looked set to make an important announcement.

'We're being seen by approximately 22 million viewers,' he began. 'But please allow me, if I may, to address myself to four very special people . . . John, Paul, George and Ringo . . . The Beatles. Lately there have been a lot of rumours to the effect that the four of you might be getting back together. That would be great. In my book, The Beatles are the best thing that ever happened to music. It goes deeper than that. You're not just a musical group. You're a part of us. We grew up with you.

'It's for this reason that I'm inviting you to come on our show. Now, we've heard and read a lot about personality and legal conflicts that might prevent you guys from reuniting. That's none of my business. You guys will have to handle that. But it's also been said that no one has yet come up with enough money to satisfy you. Well, if it's money you want, there's no problem here. The National Broadcasting Company authorises *me* to authorise *you* a cheque for $3,000. Here, can you get a close-up of this?'

Michaels held a cheque up to the camera, clearly inked out to The Beatles.

'As you can see,' he went on, 'verifiably, a cheque made out to you, The Beatles, for $3,000. All you have to do is sing three Beatles tunes. "She loves you, yeah yeah yeah" . . . that's $1,000 right there. You know the words and it'll be easy. Like I said, this cheque is made out to The Beatles. You divide it any way you want. If you want to give Ringo less, that's up to you. I'd rather not get involved. I'm sincere about this. If it helps you to reach a decision to reunite, well, it's a worthwhile investment. You have agents. You know where I can be reached. Just think about it, OK?'

Unknown to Michaels, only 22 blocks north of the TV studio at Rockefeller Plaza, Paul and John, together with Linda and Yoko, were sitting up late at the Dakota – watching the show, laughing their asses off and, just for a minute, actually considering his offer.

'Wouldn't it be funny if we went down?' said John. 'We should go down there. We should go down now and just do it.'

The pair toyed with the idea of jumping in a cab and making it to the studio before the end of the 90-minute broadcast. Then, once their laughter had subsided, the cold reality of the prospect set in, and they decided they were too tired. When the show was over, in the small hours of Sunday morning, Paul and Linda left

John and Yoko settling down to watch a screening of the 1960 film adaptation of H.G. Wells' *The Time Machine*.

As jokey as it was, Michaels' offer obviously planted a seed in McCartney's mind. Later that Sunday evening, he returned to the Dakota, this time carrying a guitar. But John, who had been looking after baby Sean all day, was in a very different mood from the previous night, and bluntly snubbed him. There was likely some jealousy at play on Lennon's part – the previous day had seen *Wings At The Speed Of Sound* rise to the top of the US album chart in the first of a seven-week run; he had recently read that Paul, due to Wings' new-found earning power, was worth $25 million and moaned to Yoko that he would never earn that kind of money.

'Please call before you come over,' he snapped at an upset McCartney. 'It's not 1956, and turning up at the door isn't the same any more.'

Later, a contrite John stated, 'I didn't mean it badly.' But the damage was done. Paul turned and left, before flying off in the morning to Dallas to hook up with Wings and begin rehearsals for their American tour. Lennon and McCartney would never see each other again.

Eight nights later, on 3 May, Paul stood side-stage at the Tarrant County Convention Center, Fort Worth, Texas. The venue had been chosen as the best location for the opening night, to ease the band into the tour as far out of the way of the major cultural capitals as was reasonable. It was to be the first time McCartney had performed live in America since the frazzled, road-sick Beatles had retired from touring, just under ten years earlier, before vanishing into the studio. Stepping back into the light, Paul was stunned by the response: fifteen minutes of ovation from the 13,500-strong crowd before Wings had even struck the opening chord.

After months of rehearsals and the preliminary legs of the tour, the Wings Over America show was by this stage a very polished presentation, if still edging towards the softer end of the rock spectrum when held up against the likes of The Who or Led Zeppelin. Nevertheless, it had a suitably dramatic, audience-stirring opener, with McCartney emerging alone from the darkness, lit in red, in a cloud of dry ice, for the gentle 'Venus And Mars' introduction that slammed into 'Rock Show'. The band, long-haired and in fashionable shirts and waistcoats, looked very 1976, with the black-clad, white-scarf-draped singer fronting them on assured, grinning form as, stage left, his wife in her feather-collared dress shifted from Moog to Hammond to Mellotron and heartily sang and clapped along.

One new feature of the live production was a laser display, of which, Paul comically states, he was initially a touch nervous. 'I'd seen lasers at Led Zeppelin's concert at Earls Court [in 1975] and the only thing I knew about them was from the Bond movie where the baddie was about to slice Mr Bond with a laser. So, I literally thought that Robert Plant was being really courageous and endangering his life dancing around in front of these lasers. I was like, "God, that's amazing, what he does for his art, y'know." I fully expected to see Planty sliced up by the end of the show.'

This new, cutting-edge Wings show was a far cry from the shambling UK university tour of four years before. The quintet, with added drama and swing supplied by their four-piece brass section, threw themselves into a set that showcased the strength of Paul's post-Beatles catalogue, from tougher-sounding numbers such as 'Jet' and 'Let Me Roll It' to grandstanding ballads 'Maybe I'm Amazed' and 'My Love', which were complemented, rather than overshadowed, by the selection of Beatles songs reclaimed by McCartney.

For once the critics were, as one, bowled over. 'When the

house lights dimmed,' wrote the reviewer from the *LA Times*, getting caught up in the sense of occasion, 'virtually everyone in the arena stood in anticipation of what was clearly the most notable return to rock concerts since Bob Dylan's 1974 appearance in Chicago. Not only did the two-hour concert demonstrate McCartney's ability to satisfy audiences with his post-Beatles work, it also enabled many in the audience to relive some of the magic of the heralded Beatles era. A double triumph.' The *New York Times* enthused: 'Mr McCartney established himself and his band, Wings, as concert artists in their own right . . . and he did so triumphantly.'

The US tour was run on an enormous scale. Three articulated trucks lugged twelve and a half tons of gear, their roofs stencilled in red with the words 'Wings . . . Over . . . America'. Their drivers communicated via CB radio, as a helicopter rotored overhead, filming the progress of this showy cavalcade. The expanded tour personnel stretched from new guitar tech John Hammel (later to become Paul's personal assistant) and the McCartney brood's nanny Rose Martin to ex-FBI-agent turned security-man Orrin Bartlett, who was employed to oversee a sweep of each venue and grill the staff about potential bomb threats, weapons screening and any strange calls they might have received. In America, the atmosphere felt heightened and possibly more dangerous. According to *Time* magazine, Paul 'worried about snipers'. At the same time, McCartney was being more upfront about his wife's role in his professional organisation. He needed her, he admitted, 'for my confidence'.

The centrepiece of the travelling circus was a rented and customised BAC One-Eleven jet with the obligatory tour logo painted on the fuselage. Inside, the plane was equipped with the usual comforts and distractions of the premier-league touring 1970s rock band – video machine, table-tennis set-up and, hidden behind a curtain at the rear, a mini-discotheque, painted with stars and dotted with fluorescent lights, which was much loved by the McCartney girls. The rest of the interior was kitted out like a lounge, where the band could laze around and be served endless drinks from the corner bar by stewards, before retreating to one of the sectioned-off bedrooms.

Attempting to replicate some sense of familial normality, rather than stay in hotels, the McCartneys had four bases for the American tour: rented houses in Dallas, Chicago, New York and Los Angeles, which they would fly to directly after each show, depending upon where they were in the country. As ideal as the arrangement sounded, the time spent in those lavish houses only served to fuel Linda's homesickness. 'I felt very empty and very lonely,' she admitted.

Her pining was temporarily ameliorated on a day off in Texas in the first week of May, when she spotted a chestnut Appaloosa stallion in a field by the side of the road. Turning off and taking a detour into Lucky Spot Stables, she asked the owner, 'Could we look at that horse out in the field?' He insisted the horse wasn't for sale, but allowed Linda to take it for a ride. Afterwards, and with some persuasion, the owner caved in and agreed to a price. The horse, named Lucky Spot, was shipped to England, where the McCartneys began successfully breeding Appaloosas.

Meanwhile, the tour powered onwards. On the second date, in Houston, Paul was nearly injured by a piece of scaffolding that fell from the elaborate rigging during the set, the metal pole instead hitting tour manager Trevor Jones on the head, an injury that required thirteen stitches. In Detroit, McCartney was ratty onstage, coping with feedback and a pizza-slicing cut on his finger that caused him to mess up the complex guitar-picking of 'Blackbird', and later to lash out at one reporter who had dared to ask the Beatle Question, 'Look, mate, it's 1976, and I don't think most people care about what happened ten years ago.' In Toronto, Ringo and George turned up, sitting in the audience and appreciatively nodding along.

In Boston, Paul and Jimmy McCulloch suffered their first serious bust-up. Closing the main set, Wings jogged to the side of the stage for a breather in preparation for their first encore. Jimmy had left his guitar resting on his amp, volume up, causing it to howl with feedback through the state-of-the-art PA. Then the inexplicably stroppy guitarist announced that he wasn't going back on and swaggered off in the direction of the dressing-room.

McCartney remembers: 'It was like, "*What?*" I mean, I'd never had anyone decide that ever before. So I just ran off and sort of grabbed him.' According to saxophonist Howie Casey, McCartney did more than just 'sort of grab' McCulloch. 'Paul came flying in and smacked him,' he says. The four members of the horn section quickly waded in to separate the pair, with trombonist Tony Dorsey taking it upon himself to hold McCartney back.

'There was violence involved,' Paul concedes. 'I gave him what he understood, really. Now obviously that's not the way you want to operate. But at that moment there was no alternative. He probably would have done the same to me if he'd have been the leader of the band.'

'Jimmy was acting up big-time,' says Casey. 'And it's Paul's show . . . he's the leader, he's the star and all that. You don't do that. But Jimmy had that thing in him.'

'Jimmy was his own man, shall we say,' says Paul, who noted that the guitarist played 'a blinder' following the confrontation. From this point on, McCartney would sometimes take McCulloch aside on the plane for pep-talks meant to steer him away from the self-destructive habits that were intensifying his rollercoaster moods. 'He was always a little dangerous. I did try and warn him a couple of times. Like, what's going to happen when you're 30? You've got your whole life ahead of you. But he liked partying too much and was getting into too many things.'

He wasn't the only one. Wings were far from clean-living and willingly surrendered to the many temptations on offer. In the tour-planning stage, each member of the band was asked what their favourite tipple was and, accordingly, a bottle of whisky or vodka or whatever spirit they preferred would be waiting for them in the dressing-room before soundcheck. The bottles would be immediately cracked open, joints would do the rounds, and some of the more likely suspects might chop out a pre-show line of coke. Unsurprisingly, by the time the gig began, Wings were pretty loaded. Backstage afterwards: more spirits, more spliffs, more lines. It's no surprise that a TV crew who came to the dressing-room of the Chicago Stadium to interview the non-McCartney members found them to be conspicuously wasted.

'There's a lot more going for this band than you actually see,' argued a heavy-lidded Denny Laine, finding it hard to focus.

'It's a question of everybody just putting a lot into it,' Jimmy McCulloch offered vaguely.

Elsewhere, Joe English was on notably chatty if visibly glazed form. 'It's an easy gig, it's a good gig, it's the easiest gig I've had. I mean, it's easy meeting people I'm working with and getting along.' He paused to think about what else to say, before adding, 'Good gig.'

The drummer, it transpired, was something of a dark horse. Howie Casey was the first to notice that, on the UK tour, the genial New Yorker had taken a keen interest in the wares available in British chemists, particularly cough medicines containing active ingredients banned from over-the-counter sale in the States. 'He'd drink bottles of it,' says Casey. 'He'd get out of it on stuff like that. He might have been a little distant at times, but he was alright. Most of the time he seemed on top of it. He was a bloody good drummer.'

Secretly, Joe English was battling a serious drug habit, including heroin addiction. While he never missed a gig, he was prone to becoming utterly zonked and falling unconscious for twenty-four hours at a time before waking up not knowing exactly where he was. He later admitted that there were two or three occasions during his time in Wings when he overdosed on smack. The money he was earning from being in the group was essentially fuelling his addiction and dragging him down.

Whatever state everyone was in, post-show a routine was established where the band immediately left the venue in a fleet of limos and returned to the airport and the waiting BAC One Eleven, before typically hanging around for Paul and Linda, who were always running late or otherwise detained by fans, well-wishers or hangers-on. Then, once the plane's doors were closed, the group and their entourage found themselves in what tour photographer Robert Ellis calls 'a superbubble'.

There was a photograph taken during the 1976 tour, which perfectly illustrated how being a member of the McCartney family must have been, in some ways, completely normal and at the same time utterly surreal. In it, Linda and the four-year-old Stella are seen settling down to dinner in their lounge, the former perched on a sofa while balancing a tray on her lap. Across from them, Paul sits playing a bass guitar as Mary, only six, leans in to listen. It appears to be a fairly typical, cosy, slightly boho picture. Except for the fact that it found the McCartneys aboard their private jet, high in the skies above America.

'That became normal for us,' says Paul. 'In our minds, we were giving the kids a normal upbringing. While at the same time we knew it was not.'

Somehow, the delicate balance that the McCartneys had created between family life and band life seemed to work. Even the more hedonistic tendencies of certain members were successfully hidden from the kids. 'Anyone who was likely to get crazy,' says Paul, 'it would be on their own time, in a hotel room. It would be somewhere where the kids weren't. They were very respectful, and the kids never really saw any kind of hedonistic behaviour.'

'You've got this weird mixture of little kids bounding about the plane and all these hard-arsed musos swilling whisky and smoking fags,' says Howie Casey. 'Maybe we were like uncles. They could be cheeky to us, they could ask us things. It was really nice.' But even if Wings seemed like an egalitarian set-up, from Casey's point of view there was an obvious pecking order. 'We socialised totally with them, but they were the bosses. You knew your place a little bit.'

As much as he wanted to be one of the boys, sometimes the dividing line between McCartney and the others was all too obvious. On the plane, to fritter away the flight times, the musicians would often dig out cards and play a few hands of ten-card brag, gambling with nickels and cents. During one flight, Paul heard the others laughing over a game and asked if he could join in. He was quickly taught the rules and play continued. McCartney nearly won a couple of hands before Casey scooped the pot after showing a game-ending four-of-a-kind. Paul, apparently, 'did his nut' and stormed off in a huff.

'See, that shows something,' Casey reckons. 'It's not the money. It's the *winning*. He's used to winning.'

Another, far more serious incident caused Paul's anger to explode. In flight, inebriated members of the band and entourage would sometimes enter the cockpit and hang out and chat with the laid-back Texan pilots charged with handling the tour plane. On one occasion, trumpeter Steve Howard, holder of a pilot's licence for smaller aircraft, was given a turn at the controls of the jet, acquitting himself admirably. Denny Laine, at the time perhaps worryingly reading a book entitled *Anyone Can Fly*, was also given a go in the pilot's chair. After a few minutes, the real flight crew's attentions having drifted, a call came through from air traffic control warning them that the Wings plane was cruising several thousand feet below its agreed altitude. According to Laine, 'When you take anything off automatic pilot, it goes all over the place for a moment or two.'

Then, during another flight, one member of the miles-high party – reports differ as to the identity of the culprit – sent the plane into a dive, throwing everyone around the cabin. It was at this point that a furious McCartney discovered that drunken members of his group had been taking turns flying the plane, with his wife and children onboard, for some weeks. Never the most comfortable flyer, by all accounts, Paul blew his top. From here on in, everyone in the touring party was banned from the cockpit. 'Which is fair enough,' Howie Casey notes. 'Even though I was pissed, I'd think, No, that's silly.'

Upon realising that his meticulously plotted tour was veering dangerously off-course, Paul called everyone to a meeting and read them the riot act. 'It was a question of, "We've got to keep this on the straight and narrow, we've got to keep this going",' says Robert Ellis. 'Control was the point.'

These days, though, Paul remembers it differently. 'That's the legend,' he says. 'In actual fact, the pilots were on autopilot, and so they let you sit up there and wiggle the joystick a bit, 'cause it's not operational. And when you're pissed, you think you're flying the plane. There's no way I would let that really happen, y'know. You're kidding me? But I wasn't going to be the one to tell them they weren't flying the plane.'

Whatever the truth, as relatively tame as Wings outwardly appeared in terms of 1970s rock groups, with their many and varied excesses, at times McCartney must have felt like he was trying to orchestrate chaos.

'Everything I've done since the Beatles split has been leading up to this show,' Paul told a reporter backstage at Madison Square Garden on 24 May, the start of a sold-out two-night stint at the prestigious, star-making New York venue.

Inside the arena, the mood of the crowd was rising towards hysteria. Word spread – fanned by a quote from McCartney refusing to rule out the possibility – that John Lennon was to make an appearance onstage. Fans crushed at the lip of the stage, while others in the bleachers mindlessly set off flares and fireworks. Arriving onstage, Wings walked tall, to be met with scenes reminiscent of the Beatlemania McCartney must surely have felt had been consigned to the past. Boys ripped off their shirts. Girls sobbed, overwhelmed. Launching into their set, the band rose to the occasion and, well oiled as they were on more than one level, easily surpassed expectations. Even if Lennon was a no-show, for now all talk of Beatles reunions was irrelevant.

On the second night, having insisted on a backstage press ban, Jacqueline Kennedy Onassis showed up with her children, John and Caroline Kennedy, and hung out with the McCartneys in their dressing room, signifying just how far their star had risen. Following the modest early days of Wings, Paul found himself back in the full glare of the media spotlight. 'Yeah, it was interesting,' he says, 'Because we started so small, it was like I wasn't famous. But then, suddenly, all that fame came back. You were suddenly on prime-time news.' A week later, *Time* magazine featured Paul on its cover, in a live shot of the singer rendered in fuchsia and wiggly daubs of blue and green, with the blaringly triumphant headline 'McCartney Comes Back'. Even Linda's confidence seemed to have hit an all-time high. Initially fearing she would be eviscerated by the American press, when asked by a *Rolling Stone* reporter if she had a message for her critics, she replied, 'My answer is always, "Fuck off".'

'A fairly unequivocal answer,' Paul laughs today.

Having through the years graduated up from university bars to theatres to arenas, Wings arrived as a stadium act on 10 June, selling out every last ticket of the 67,110 released for their show at the Seattle Kingdome. Sweetening the satisfaction, this trumped the record set by The Beatles at Shea Stadium by a comfortable 12,000. The Kingdome, opened only three months earlier, was so vast that it had its own internal micro-climate, which was controlled by temperature regulation. Even with the erection of two video screens above the stage, the gigantic venue seemed to dwarf Wings' set-up.

After the soundcheck, Robert Ellis photographed the band standing in the upper tier at the back of the empty stadium. 'It took us half an hour to get from the stage to where the picture was taken and back again,' he says. The Seattle gig was filmed and eventually released as part of the 1980 film *Rockshow*, which revealed the Wings Over America tour in all its victory-lap glory.

'There probably were nerves involved, which I've forgotten now,' says Paul. 'I tend to sort of block them out of memories. I'm sure we were a bit nervous, but by then we'd kind of got a lot of the kinks worked out of the show and felt really good about it. It was very exciting. I remember looking out at the lines of people snaking around the Kingdome. It was really cool to see that. The tour was a special tour, but something as huge as the Kingdome meant we were right back up to the level where I'd left off.'

Into its final furlong, the tour reached California as its partici-pants found themselves close to burn-out. 'The drugs were taking over,' says Robert Ellis. 'I had extreme difficulties keeping myself straight enough to do the work I had to do.' In San Francisco, backstage, the increasingly feral Jo Jo Patrie stole a bunch of front-row complimentary tickets from the tour manager's briefcase before disguising herself to go out to the front of the Cow Palace to sell them. She returned with enough cash to buy an ounce of cocaine, a sizeable amount. This lasted her, Laine and McCulloch for the rest of the tour. But while she didn't dare snort the drug around Paul, who had dabbled with coke in the 1960s and stopped when it 'got too fashionable', Patrie claimed that on one occasion she offered some to Linda during a flight and the two women sneaked into the toilet for a toot.

Diverting to Arizona on 18 June for a show at Tucson's Community Center, a surprise birthday party was thrown for Paul's 34th, which saw him being serenaded by a mariachi band and, blindfolded, bashing a goat-shaped orange piñata with a stick. Then, at a trio of tour-closing shows at the LA Forum beginning three days after, Wings drew a star-stuffed audience that included Diana Ross, Cher, Elton John, Jack Nicholson and Dustin Hoffman.

Outside the venue, a marching band led by someone in a chicken suit parped its way through a version of 'Listen To What The Man Said'. Inside, at the end of a rollicking set, Ringo appeared onstage to present Paul with flowers, while pawing a guitar, as if prompting a spontaneous Beatles reunion. Backstage, the air surrounding McCartney and Starr, perhaps since they were being watched by a roomful of people, was one of slightly forced jollity.

'Well, it wasn't bad,' Ringo said. 'Eight out of ten.'

'Let's see you bloody get up and do it then,' Paul responded in a comedic challenge, mugging nose-to-nose with his former bandmate.

Two nights later the McCartneys threw a party, costing a dizzying $75,000, at the estate that had belonged to silent-movie comedian Harold Lloyd in Benedict Canyon. 'That was a blowout,' says Paul. 'We said afterwards, "That was an exercise in how to spend the entire profits of the tour."' Money was no longer an issue: in seven weeks, the Wings Over America jaunt had grossed $5 million, a mind-boggling amount for the time, and considerably more than anyone had estimated.

This uncharacteristic display of extravagance – more on the level of a society wedding than a showbusiness party – served to attract the usual musical suspects, including the Eagles, The Jacksons and Bob Dylan, but also drew key figures from Hollywood including Henry Fonda, Tony Curtis, Roman Polanski, Steve McQueen and Warren Beatty. Guests were met at the gates of the estate and ferried to the house in a fleet of golf buggies. All partygoers were urged to wear white, since Paul and Linda had arranged for a troupe of Hawaiian artists to wander through the gathering, splashing and spraying people with paint. Everyone took to scribbling their signatures on one another's T-shirts. There was a palm reader, appearances by the Los Angeles Ballet and the Nelson Riddle Orchestra, and even a Busby Berkeley-style waterborne routine performed by faux-starlets in the pool.

Everyone got into the swing, except for Bob Dylan, who by some accounts sat in a tree, musing, for much of the party. Leaving at the end of the evening, he was pursued by Robert Ellis, who had been instructed by McCartney to take shots of all of the guests. Ellis caught up with Dylan in a buggy and began snapping away until the singer peeled away from his friends and leapt on the photographer, demanding to know why he was taking pictures. 'I was going, "I'm Paul's official photographer",' Ellis recalls. 'He says, "I don't want my picture in no magazine."' Back up at the house, many of the revellers leaped into the pool. Those who wandered back down the hill to their parked cars found a single white rose on the dashboard, along with a note: 'Thank you for coming, Paul and Linda.'

'After The Beatles,' Paul reasoned to one journalist in the aftermath, as he came down from the highs of the tour, 'you would have thought it would have been pretty much impossible for me to follow that and to get anything else going. At least, I thought that. This tour has convinced us that we're a group and I think it has convinced audiences too. This wasn't just a one-time trip. This is going to be a working band. We'll be back.'

Success seemed to have restored McCartney's equilibrium, too. 'He's very much back to his old self again,' said Linda, no doubt meaning the peacocking, funny, creative individual she'd first met nearly a decade earlier, before the years of self-crisis and doubt and grind.

It had perhaps also brought back some of his less appealing traits, though. In an interview with US TV presenter Geraldo Rivera on *Good Night America*, Paul came across as smug, evasive and piss-taking. At one point, when McCartney addressed him as 'Freddie', Rivera bravely reached over and gave his face a playful slap.

Back in Europe, inevitably, the comedown kicked in. Paul grew an ill-advised moustache that was less *Sgt. Pepper*, more second-hand car dealer, and Wings mopped up the last remaining dates in Austria, Yugoslavia, Italy and West Germany. In Vienna, the lighting techs bounced laser beams off ancient buildings to dazzling effect. In Zagreb, for the first time, the audience took over from Paul and sang 'Yesterday' on their own, deeply moving its composer. In St Mark's Square in Venice, performing a benefit for Unesco to raise funds to help restore the decaying city, the group provoked mild controversy when it was revealed that – irony of ironies – their heavy equipment trucks had wrecked some centuries-old paving slabs.

At the end of a three-night October run at Wembley Empire

Pool in London, EMI threw a party populated by B-list guests such as singer Kiki Dee, members of art-pop group 10cc and *Old Grey Whistle Test* host Bob Harris. At the end of the night, the guests grew boisterous and pelted one another with cream cakes.

It certainly wasn't hanging around in the Californian sunshine with Henry Fonda and Steve McQueen as hummingbirds flitted in and out of the palm trees. A sense of anticlimax hung in the air, along with uncertainty about the future. Robert Ellis felt that ultimately it was 'an uncomfortable tour. There were changes afoot. Paul was restless about everything.' Despite the undeniable success of the US tour, the photographer says, 'it was always a question of, What's next? Which made it all a bit insecure. There was the sense of the end of an era about it.'

McCartney retreated to the cocoon of the studio, holing up at Abbey Road to sift through the 90 hours of live tapes from the US tour for the triple-vinyl *Wings Over America* album, due in December 1976. Acknowledging the significance of his touring achievement, Paul drove himself hard in the polishing and mixing of the record, becoming a touch obsessive and working fourteen-hour days, seven days a week, for a six-week period. 'Well, it's always intense mixing something when you've got so much stuff to go through,' he points out. 'But it was my baby, and I was very hands-on with it. It was a very personal project, 'cause I knew it had all gone well. I wanted people who hadn't been to the concerts to hear what had gone on.' Before the year was out, Linda fell pregnant again, putting an instant dampener on the notion of any future touring. The couple began to argue about Paul spending so much time in the studio.

Bizarrely, at the same time, spinning off from the sci-fi elements of *Venus And Mars* and reflecting their new-found US celebrity, *Star Trek* creator Gene Roddenberry approached Wings with a view to them playing themselves in his planned sci-fi musical, plotted around an invasion from outer space. As tempting as the offer seemed to the cosmically minded Paul, the project was never to make it past the planning stage, even with McCartney's name attached, since Roddenberry was struggling in his career and unable to convince any of the television or film companies to supply the finance.

With time on his hands, Jimmy McCulloch had formed the tellingly named White Line along with his drummer brother Jack and his friend Dave Clarke. The trio released one single for EMI, the gutsy, harmonising pop rock of 'Call My Name', performed under a shower of silver balloons on ITV music show *Supersonic*, before the record's pressing was mysteriously, according to the band members, halted by EMI.

Hanging around the record company's London offices in Manchester Square one day, McCulloch and Clarke sloped off to a nearby pub, which they found themselves sharing with another recent signing to the label, the Sex Pistols. 'Jim started gobbing off,' says Clarke, 'telling them how crap they were. So this fight started between Jim and I forget which one of them. Me and the bass player of the Sex Pistols [Glen Matlock] managed to drag them apart.'

Clarke says McCulloch had grown cocky during his tenure with McCartney: 'Jim was young and headstrong and had everything that he wanted when he was in Wings, and it's difficult to deal with. I think it went to his head a bit. He could be really charming. But when the drink took over big-time, it was awkward.' It's perhaps no coincidence that, at this point, rumours began to circulate that Eric Stewart, from the recently fractured 10cc, was being groomed to replace Jimmy in Wings.

Wings Over America was released in time for Christmas and, by January 1977, it was sitting at the top of the US chart, completing a remarkable straight run of American number 1 albums that had begun with *Red Rose Speedway*. 'I couldn't believe it,' says Paul. 'I mean, you were always advised not to do double albums, and suddenly there we were doing a triple. That was pretty cool, I must admit.'

In spring, Paul took the opportunity to release a slightly strange project that had been in the can since 1971. Upon the completion of *Ram* six years earlier, McCartney had hired arranger Richard Hewson to put together an instrumental pop-orchestral version of the album, not a million miles away from the easy listening sounds of German bandleader James Last.

The album was finally released in April 1977, under the masquerading name of Percy 'Thrills' Thrillington, an alter ego McCartney had been cultivating for some time. Supposedly a posh society figure, born in Coventry Cathedral in 1939, the fictitious Thrillington back-story had him travelling to Louisiana to study music and to California to learn arranging and conducting, before returning to London to form his own orchestra and apparently becoming friends with McCartney, who helped him secure a record contract. In return, Thrillington had been inspired to pay homage to *Ram*.

To bolster the ruse, since the previous year Paul had been taking out ads in the personal columns of *The Times* and the *Evening Standard*, which found Percy Thrillington announcing his visits to Geneva or Mustique, or excursions to the Torbay Relaxation Centre or the Badminton Horse Trials at Newbury. One would read 'Percy Thrillington wishes to advise friends that he is feeling thoroughly invigorated by the crisp and brisk ski-ing conditions in Gstaad'. Another would make known the fact that 'Percy Thrillington is delighted with the efforts of those concerned with The Yellowplush Gallery to humour his aesthetic needs'.

Letters from readers began to appear in the papers' columns, seeking more information about the witty and mysterious

Thrillington. Of course, the tongue-in-cheek tone of the missives suggested they were probably the work of a prankster. Then a revealing small ad was printed, noting that Mr Thrillington was to be 'taking an extended holiday in South America following the rigours of launching his first record album'. In March 1977 the *Evening Standard* ran an investigative piece, under the head-line 'The Perambulations Of Percy Thrillington', that knowingly followed the trail of clues back to McCartney's PR Tony Brainsby. He denied that Thrillington had been created by Paul as a public-ity stunt.

Upon release, the liner notes of the *Thrillington* album went one further, quoting an EMI press officer as apparently saying, 'Percy Thrillington certainly isn't Paul McCartney as some people seem to think'. In an attempt to throw off the scent, Paul and Linda, travelling around Ireland, found a young farmer in a field and asked him if he fancied doing a spot of paid modelling for them. The bemused youth – 'someone no one could possibly trace' according to the McCartneys – posed for them first in a sweater and then in an evening suit. But, says Paul, 'he never quite looked Percy Thrillington enough', and the session was shelved.

Hearing his songs given such straightforward, light-entertain-ment arrangements must have tickled McCartney, but, beyond being a bit of diverting fun for its creator, it was hard to see the exact point of *Thrillington*. It would be another twelve years before Paul would finally admit in a press conference that he was behind this daft hoax. 'We kept it a secret for a long time, but now the world knows,' he laughed.

On an altogether more serious level, the first months of 1977 saw Apple finally sever all remaining ties with Allen Klein, following a stinging $5 million settlement. McCartney, though, insisted there was still a massive, unexplained hole in the Beatles' earnings. Though he never liked to talk about money, Paul felt moved to point out to the *Daily Express* that with Wings, between 1974 and 1976, he had 'earned more money than I ever earned in all those other so-called boom years'. He said the Fabs had been told that they'd sold somewhere in the region of 300 million records. 'If you compute that,' Paul reckoned, roughly crunching the numbers, 'and say the group should have had 10p a go, then where did that money go?'

Meanwhile, the *Saturday Night Live* joke had run and run. Having had no response from the former Beatles since his spoof reunion appeal, and unaware that John and Paul had watched it live, Lorne Michaels upped his offer to $3,200 and promised to throw some hotel accommodation into the deal. Five months later, he used the ongoing stunt to introduce the first footage of The Rutles, the uncanny, parallel-universe send-up of The Beatles created by Eric Idle of Monty Python and Neil Innes of The Bonzo Dog Doo-Dah Band.

According to the latter, who bumped into an apparently 'edgy' McCartney at a party at George Harrison's house, Paul wasn't entirely enamoured of the clearly affectionate fan-boy parody, featuring Idle's portrayal of him as the wide-eyed showbiz opportunist, Dirk McQuickly, with his knack for writing light, frothy tunes. In truth, the crux of the problem seemed to be that a narked McCartney was being asked his opinion of The Rutles in virtually every interview.

Later, George Harrison, always the most comedy-friendly ex-Beatle, not least in his endorsement and financing of Monty Python, appeared on *Saturday Night Live*. In the opening minutes of the episode, he could be seen muttering to Lorne Michaels in a corridor of the NBC building, asking him if he could have the cheque for $3,000 and being told he could only have his $750 share.

'I've come all this way,' Harrison pretended to protest. 'It's $3,000. That was the deal.'

'How do you think I feel?' spluttered Michaels. 'I feel terrible about it. But it was just one of those mix-ups.'

All frivolities aside, only a year after they'd sat together laughing at the *SNL* appeal, in their increasingly strained and infrequent telephone conversations Paul and John were once more growing painfully estranged. April 1977 found Paul and Linda in New York, staying at the Stanhope Hotel across the park from the Dakota, in town to do some business and catch some Broadway shows. McCartney called Lennon up, even though he felt that, from his former partner's point of view, there was 'so much suspicion'.

Paul remembers he started up the conversation by saying, 'Hey, I'd really like to see you.'

'What for?' Lennon replied. 'What the fuck d'you want, man?'

Paul later confessed that at this stage John still made him nervous, even after all the years and their times of apparent brotherly closeness. 'I actually used to have some very frightening phone calls with him,' McCartney admitted. Paul told John what he'd been up to – eating pizza with the kids, reading them fairy tales.

'You're all pizza and fairy tales,' Lennon retorted bizarrely.

Another time, John raged at Paul in an accent that was becoming more Americanised, and reminiscent of a bald-headed, lollipop-sucking TV detective who was big in 1976.

'Yeah? Yeah? Whadda ya want?' snarled John, answering the call.

McCartney was suddenly sick of this 'vitriolic' Lennon.

'Oh, fuck off, Kojak,' he barked, and slammed the phone down.

Did you feel a sense of vindication after the 1976 tour?

Well, yeah. That really was the kind of pay-off tour. I remember that being what I saw as the turnaround where Wings were now, like, very successful. We had the American tour and 'Silly Love Songs' was a big hit. The great thing happened, which was always a fun thing that used to happen with The Beatles, was you'd put a record out and you'd start playing it live and no one would know it. And it'd be, 'Hold your nerve, boys, we're OK, just keep playing it.' And by the end of that tour, it was the big hit. It was really lovely, that. The nice thing that was happening on that tour, because of the level, was there were a lot of things that were reminiscent of the Beatles days.

Float On

It could hardly have sounded more idyllic. Wings were six weeks into the sessions for their sixth album, in the grey London of February 1977, when Geoff Emerick began regaling them with tales of his recent recording expedition to Hawaii. The seasoned sound engineer started filling their heads with sunshine, just when they were stuck back in the all too familiar environs of Abbey Road, digging themselves into a rut.

Two months later, with McCartney having decided to indulge a rock-star whim, Wings landed in the US Virgin Islands. During the intervening weeks, an apparently simple if potentially troublesome plan had been formulated. In yet another bid to take flight to another location and free up the recording process, the band were to make an album aboard a yacht – its punning working title, *Water Wings*.

The original idea came from Denny Laine, who had a passion for boats. In the early 1970s, he'd lived upon *Searchlight*, a barge moored on the Thames between Shepperton and Chertsey, the vessel later sold to Viv Stanshall of The Bonzo Dog Doo-Dah Band. Recently, he'd treated himself to a 40-foot cabin cruiser he named the *Louis Philippe*, which he kept in the harbour at Rye, near Paul's house, and sailed up and down the English south coast, sometimes with McCartney aboard.

But the real spark of inspiration had come to Laine when he visited Rod Stewart, recording on the Record Plant's floating studio in the Pacific waters off LA. 'I've always loved boats and thought it might be an interesting way to record an album,' said the guitarist, although he wasn't entirely convinced that McCartney would buy into the idea, having had such trouble in Lagos when deciding to go off-road with *Band On The Run*. 'To be honest,' Laine admitted, 'I was surprised when Paul said we should give it a try.' But having just completed the intensive mixing sessions for *Wings Over America* and gone straight into the making of the next studio album, McCartney was looking for a break from the routine. He viewed this Caribbean jaunt as 'an experiment to see if we could work better in a holiday atmosphere'.

An advance party of five techs, including Emerick, John Hammel and assistant engineer Mark Vigars, was sent out to the Virgin Islands at the end of April to oversee the setting-up of the studio. Upon their arrival on St Thomas, they began kitting out a charter yacht named the *Fair Carol* as a waterborne recording facility. It proved not to be the easiest of tasks.

The boat was 100 feet long, but narrow. When its captain saw the amount of equipment the team were hoping to install, he freaked. The heavy mixing desk and washing-machine-proportioned 24-track tape machine were bad enough, before factoring in the weighty amps, the cumbersome Mellotron and so on. In the end, an ergonomic plan was agreed upon, involving the gear being lined up on either side of the boat's lounge-turned-live room and thus equally balanced, in order to avoid difficulties in the water. Carpenters were brought in to build a structure on the open deck to house a control room.

On 30 April 1977, the *Fair Carol* set out for Francis Bay, on the neighbouring island of St John, in anticipation of the arrival of the McCartney family, the band and MPL's Alan Crowder and Brian Brolly. Completing the Wings flotilla was a converted minesweeper called the *Samala*, providing the band and crew with accommodation and catering (simple English grub such as steak and kidney pie), and a trimaran with a huge living space and lower-deck bedrooms, named the *El Toro*, that was to be home to the McCartneys.

The daily routine was a suitably leisurely one: rise around nine, breakfast at ten, followed by a 50-yard commute to the *Fair Carol* in a motorised rubber dinghy. Record until lunchtime, laze around in the afternoon and then work into the evening, until it was time for dinner and cocktails on the *Samala*. Unsurprisingly, this low-gear approach suited Paul: 'I like to record and not have to feel like it's too much work. I hate to think, I'm going to work now . . . I'm going to grind out some music.' Of course, Jimmy McCulloch was much enamoured of this lifestyle that entirely zoned in on music-making and getting high. 'You don't have the gas man coming in or mail that you have to act on,' he pointed out.

The party would anchor the three boats in bays or harbours at St Croix, St John or St Thomas. Then, whenever the mood took their fancy, they would up and sail away to a new location. As time went on, the motor dinghies were abandoned altogether and they'd just jump off one boat and swim to another. In the manner of a rock-star stag party, they had corny white T-shirts made up, bannering their names in black lettering, along with the legend 'M.Y. [motor yacht] *Samala*, Virgin Islands, May 77'. For all involved, this working holiday was an entirely liberating experience. 'No one wore shoes the whole time,' noted visiting photographer Henry Diltz.

'The mornings were really beautiful in the bay,' wrote Alan Crowder in his diary, 'with jumping fish called "Jumping Jacks", laughing seagulls, pelicans and very large birds called frigates.'

Initially, Paul worried about the actual realities of recording on the ocean waves. Day one saw the group take baby steps, reviewing the tapes from Abbey Road and jamming. 'The big problem with recording on a boat,' Paul said, 'was that maybe once we got out there, we might find that salt water had gone through the machines and the equipment, or that they just wouldn't work.' In the end, to his relief, the sessions progressed remarkably smoothly: 'We didn't have any problems with salt water or sharks attacking us.'

They conducted one slightly dippy experiment, attempting to record a jam while the boat was in motion. Of course, given the engine noise, it sounded terrible. 'It was silly and fun, and I don't think it was very good music,' says Paul. But, still, in this environment Wings were stretching out in unexpected ways – instead of hammering out old chestnuts such as 'Lucille' or 'Twenty Flight Rock' in their musical downtime, they might pick their way through Irving Berlin's 'Easter Parade'.

In the afternoons, the McCartney girls would lounge in a hammock, or swing from ropes before freefalling into the blue water. Mary and Stella pestered their father to take turns throwing them over the side of the boat. There was a mini-piano on the *Samala* that Paul played as the girls danced around the cabin. Absent from school once again, the kids were tutored, though in this environment it took a lot of effort to drag them out of the sun in order to concentrate on their studies.

The musicians would idly snorkel in the water, spotting sea urchins and starfish and small, harmless barracudas. One day Denny spied a dolphin's fin moving through the waves and shouted, 'Shark!', terrifying a swimming Joe English. On another occasion, Paul sat on the stern deck of the *Fair Carol* recording an acoustic guitar part as another of the curious creatures circled the boat, surfacing and diving.

Come evening, everyone sat on the deck of the *Samala* drinking rum, the boat twinkling with fairy lights. Bats swooped around in the moonlight, trying to catch flying fish. There was much merriment as the more spirited participants took turns, Paul remembers, 'leaping from top decks into uncharted waters and stuff. I had a couple too many one night and nearly broke something jumping from one boat to another.'

He escaped with a bruised leg and cut knee. But it was clear that Wings weren't entirely seaworthy, and soon there were other mishaps. McCulloch was limping around after sustaining a mysterious injury, while Denny, ever the sailor, took off in a one-man Sunfish sailboat to explore the coves around St John. 'I got lost for five hours,' he admits. Upon his return, he had to be taken to Caneel Bay on the island and treated by a doctor for severe sunburn. Meanwhile, the injury count kept rising: Geoff Emerick managed to electrocute himself in the foot, and Alan Crowder slipped down a set of stairs and broke his heel, returning from hospital hobbling around on a crutch that made him fittingly resemble Long John Silver.

All of the wives and girlfriends except Linda having been excluded from the trip, and left back home in Britain and the States, the musicians were soon talking like a bunch of randy sailors. 'The conversation turns to women every other word,' said Joe English. 'If the word isn't women, it's girls.' A sulky Jo Jo Patrie blamed the ban on an insecure and pregnant Linda. 'I think she was intimidated by the girls perhaps wearing a bikini around Paul,' she huffed. 'Jimmy's girlfriend was the [*Playboy*] Playmate for February 1976, so we would have both gone down there looking pretty terrific.'

To blow off steam, and in a further display of jet-set extravagance, McCartney had an MPL employee fly over from London with a videotape of the 1977 Liverpool v. Manchester United FA Cup Final (United triumphed 2–1). In the moonlit early hours of the morning following the screening, there were races in the dinghies as calls of 'Pursuit, pursuit!' rang out, along with the more fate-tempting enquiry, 'Who's next for the medicos?'

Dropping anchor in the harbour at St John one night, the band cranked up and jammed at full volume. Unknown to them, there was a ban on amplified music in the area after 10 p.m. McCartney remembers discovering that the rules were so strict that even the use of transistor radios was forbidden. And here were Wings, banging away through a PA. 'We had a whole thing going,' he says. 'You could hear it for miles.' The noise quickly attracted the attentions of rangers from the national park which covered 60 per cent of the island. Once aboard the rock-star-annexed fleet, they began snooping around, sticking their noses into ashtrays that inevitably contained joint roaches. In the end, Wings luckily escaped with a $15 fine for disrupting the tropical peace. But as the rangers left, the group defiantly struck up again as they sailed around to the nearby Watermelon Bay.

This kind of behaviour perhaps inevitably drew more in the way of unwanted attention. Soon after, doubtless tipped off by the St John rangers, three US Customs officials made a surprise visit to the boats and, incredibly, left without finding any evidence of soft-drug use. The incident did, however, bring to a head a growing disagreement between McCartney and the captain of the *El Toro*, who had smelled marijuana smoke on the boat on the night the band had arrived, and threatened to report them to the authorities. Now, after this latest development, he turned menacing.

'He was a little sort of heavier than the other captains,' says McCartney. 'He took it a little more seriously. We had an argument with him, and I said, "Y'know, we don't need all this aggro."' The owners of another boat located in the harbour, the *Wanderlust*, had already offered the use of the catamaran to the McCartneys, and so, before they ended up in trouble again, they took this opportunity to literally jump ship. Paul wrote a song about the experience, giving it the title 'Wanderlust' and referring in the lyric to a captain out to make his mark and warning of a bust. The craft seemed 'a symbol of freedom to me . . . breaking away from oppression . . . let's get out of here.'

On 22 May, a letter was sent to Alan Crowder from Peter Baker, the agent who arranged the charter of the boats. It read: 'Dear Alan, As you know the yachts *Fair Carol*, *Samala* and *El Toro* were recently visited by US Customs officials.

'I must emphasise to you and the group that the possession or use of mariahuana [sic] is illegal in the Virgin Islands. And that includes possession or use onboard a boat in territorial waters.

'Please make sure that no drugs, illegal drugs or narcotics of course are taken on board or used on board any of the three yachts now on charter to you and the group. Apart from anything else, illegal actions are specifically excluded by the charter agreement and could give us valid grounds for advising the owner to conclude the charter.'

In a rebellious mood, the band asked photographer Henry Diltz to take a picture of the letter, ornamented with a pack of Bambu rolling papers and the butt of a spliff.

The band returned to the UK re-energised, their heads buzzing with thoughts of other unusual locations they might record in. They talked about putting a studio on a train and travelling across Canada. 'Next year, darling,' Paul jested, 'I was thinking of hiring a string of cable cars in the Bavarian Alps.'

Back home, however, the music scene was changing, with the dawning of punk having made the soft rock of bands like Wings sound outdated virtually overnight. McCartney, perhaps to his credit, stuck to his guns musically, even if he recognised it might find him being labelled a dinosaur. 'The hard nuts of the music business, the critics, are gonna hate me because I'm not writing about acne,' he moaned. Still, this extreme shift in musical fashion, he stressed, now made The Beatles seem as if they were from another age entirely, even if it had only been seven years since they'd broken up. No one, he harshly argued, could 'think of The Beatles as a current group, no matter which way you looked at it'.

In private, Paul and Linda joked about going punk, giving themselves the suitably snotty nicknames Noxious Fumes and Vile Lin. Writer and broadcaster Paul Gambaccini, visiting the recording sessions in the Virgin Islands, had been surprised to hear Linda singing The Damned's 'Neat Neat Neat' to herself one day aboard the *Fair Carol*. It turned out that Heather, now fourteen, was into punk. Paul – no stranger to the compelling powers of primal rock'n'roll after the days of his youth in Hamburg – noticed a remarkable transformation in his daughter after she had gone to see The Stranglers. 'She came back a changed person, over the moon, just loved it,' he said.

At Abbey Road, on his return from the Caribbean, McCartney even knocked off a comedy punk song, as a jokey gift to Heather, entitled 'Boil Crisis'. He revealed to one journalist the opening lines of the piss-taking lyric: 'One night in the life of a kid named Sid, he scored with a broad in a pyramid.' McCartney realised, of course, that he couldn't put the song out, no matter how tongue-in-cheek it was intended to be. 'If I release it,' he rightly pointed out, 'people will only slag me off.' Instead, his typically whimsical, typically eccentric response was to go in entirely the opposite direction, with a song in the traditional Scottish folk style extolling the beauty of the south-western tip of the Kintyre peninsula.

Summer 1977 found the McCartneys spending a lot of their time back in Scotland. This arrangement didn't please either Jimmy McCulloch or Jo Jo Patrie, though Denny Laine and Joe English seemed happy enough to rough it in the countryside. The barn at Low Ranachan had by now been professionally converted into a rehearsal and recording studio and basic living quarters for the musicians. McCulloch sneeringly nicknamed it The Bunker. Patrie turned her nose up at the small cottage she was given to share with Denny and their two kids, Laine and Heidi, with its cement walls and bare furnishings comprising, as she saw it, 'a couple of old chairs and some ragged, pee-stained mattresses'.

Those who couldn't take to rural life found the existence in Scotland hard going. In a surreal protest, the bored, stoned roadies drew the image of a television on their cottage wall and pretended to watch it. Stuck out there on the farm, Jimmy McCulloch, his drinking and drugging beginning to intensify, started to crack up. Jo Jo Patrie later wildly stated that this led to the guitarist sneaking into the High Park cottage in the middle of the night and pointing a gun at the McCartneys while they slept, before suffering a breakdown and attempting to shoot himself. No one else, though, has ever backed up her story.

The truth appears to have been far less melodramatic, and a touch more daft. Revealing the depth of their devotion to their chickens, left home alone in London, the McCartneys arranged to have their brood driven in a taxi from St John's Wood to Argyll, at a cost of over £100. Then, one evening on the farm after a binge, a drink-maddened Jimmy took a couple of dozen of the eggs produced by the hens, carefully collected each day by Linda and Paul, and angrily splattered them on the interior walls of the roadies' cottage.

As trivial as this might have appeared to outsiders, it was seen by the McCartneys as a final act of abuse. Linda cried when she saw the mess. Paul, for the last time, went wild at Jimmy, grabbing him by his skinny neck and telling him to get the fuck off his farm. 'It got a bit fraught up in Scotland,' McCartney later admitted, with no little amount of understatement.

One morning not long after, Paul took a call from Steve Marriott, the increasingly wayward singer and guitarist of the Small Faces, who was putting the band back together. McCartney remembers that Marriott said, 'Oh, hi mate. Er, me and Jimmy have been up all night and he's decided he wants to leave your group and join mine.' Feeling miffed, but stuck for an answer, Paul replied, 'Hey, good luck to you guys, I hope it works out,' knowing in his own mind that it wouldn't. Then McCulloch came to the phone and said, 'Look, thanks a lot. See you around.'

When the rift went public, both Paul and Jimmy offered anodyne quotes to the press. 'It is a pity he's leaving,' said McCartney, 'but problems have been building up for quite a while now and so the rest of us are happy to carry on without him.'

'I enjoyed playing with Wings and I learned a lot from Paul,' remarked a butter-wouldn't-melt McCulloch. 'But I felt it was time for a change and the ideal change for me was the Small Faces. They're old friends of mine whose music I've always enjoyed.'

Only later would either publicly reveal his true feelings about the whole messy affair. 'I don't think anyone was too upset about the parting,' said Jimmy. 'We had some very good times together. Although Linda doesn't know much about music, she's a really nice chick.'

For McCartney, the break-up had been a long time coming. In hindsight, there had been two unspoken options: either the group could have struggled through the making of another record, suffering the likely agonies and arguments, or McCulloch would have had to knuckle down and do what McCartney asked of him. 'Jimmy decided to leave,' Paul said to one reporter. Then he added, sounding a touch self-serving, 'Luckily, he'd done all the required stuff on the album that we wanted him to do, so it worked out quite well for us.'

Behind this front, Paul was becoming increasingly infuriated by his inability to maintain a lasting line-up of Wings. Having tried to loosen up and allow the musicians more creative freedom, he was now attempting to shield the carefully tended normality of his family life from the rock-piggery happening only a short distance away on his farm. As ever, he painted a face on the situation. Asked about the various trials of keeping a group together, he vaguely reasoned, 'You get all sorts of weird little problems that you can't do much about.'

Along with the ever reliable Denny Laine, McCartney got his head back down into songwriting. The chorus for the soon-to-be-ubiquitous 'Mull Of Kintyre' had been kicking around since 1975. In the mornings on the farm, Denny would wander over from his cottage to High Park to have breakfast with the McCartneys. One day this unhurried routine slipped into the afternoon, when Paul suggested that they climb up the hill with a bottle of whisky and a couple of acoustic guitars. There the pair shared ideas for the verses of 'Mull Of Kintyre' and completed the misty-eyed anthem.

Realising that it needed a suitably rousing climax, McCartney invited Tony Wilson, the leader of the local Campbeltown Pipe Band, up to the farm to play him the freshly written song and ask him if he could score an arrangement for bagpipes. At first, the two sat in the small kitchen at High Park working through the tune, before Wilson suggested that they perhaps step outside since the bagpipes were piercingly loud. It quickly became clear that the song naturally suited the sound of the ancient drone. A plan was made to add an accompaniment of massed pipes and drums to the upcoming recording.

When Wilson broke the news to the other pipers at the band's next meeting at the local church hall, it met with a mixed response. Some of them were thrilled by the notion; others felt that they were selling out their traditionalism by agreeing to play on a pop single. The youngest member, Jimmy McGeachy, only fifteen, at first suspected it was a wind-up, even though he often spotted the McCartneys in the town. 'You'd see Paul walking about in his welly boots,' he remembers. 'Mary and Stella, you'd see them with Linda. And Heather was there quite a bit, 'cause she used to hang about with the young farmers set. She would take the mickey out of us, about the Bay City Rollers and all that. She was an early punk, the first time we'd seen a spiky haircut. It was all happening down in London, so for us boys on the west coast of Scotland, it was the first time we'd seen somebody come up from London who looked pretty cool.'

In the early evening of Tuesday, 9 August 1977, the members of the Campbeltown Pipe Band – by day joiners and electricians, farmers and schoolboys – all piled into a minibus, wearing their full kilted regalia, and headed up to the McCartneys' estate. Waiting for them at Low Ranachan were Paul, Linda, Denny Laine, Joe English (whose drumming contribution was in this instance redundant), Geoff Emerick, John Hammel and, most welcomingly, tour manager Trevor Jones with a wheelbarrow full of cans of McEwan's Export. Clearly well rehearsed, the pipers' stirring contribution was nailed in one take, and the beer flowed. The drums were added next, recorded al fresco beside the barn. Listening to a playback in the studio, the now merry local musicians suggested that the song was a definite single, one that would likely appeal to expat Scots the world over.

Paul wasn't so sure about 'Mull Of Kintyre'. Photographer Robert Ellis remembers McCartney playing an acetate of the single – counterbalanced with the relatively rocking 'Girls School' – to him and various members of ELO in London soon after. 'He was going, "Ooh, which is the A-side, what do you think?" I was going, "Well, what are you talking about? It's 'Mull Of Kintyre', isn't it?" He was saying, "Oh, I don't know. I think it's a bit too twee and sugary." Of course, the vote round the room was quite clearly for "Mull Of Kintyre". But he still wasn't convinced. He was definitely not that secure about that song.' In the end, hedging his bets, McCartney released 'Mull Of Kintyre/Girls School' as a double A-side on 11 November 1977, the same week that the iconoclastic, game-changing *Never Mind The Bollocks, Here's The Sex Pistols* was sitting at number 1 in the UK albums chart. The cover of the single revealed another truth: Wings were once again reduced to a trio, after the departure of Joe English. The official reason given was that the American drummer had found it hard to acclimatise to life in Britain. But, still hiding his addictions, English was suffering from a lot more than homesickness. He later admitted that his life was a wreck and that in his heart he knew he had to leave the situation. In addition, in a now all too familiar complaint, he said he was becoming dispirited with his lack of creative input within the band. English returned to the States and duly became a born-again Christian, enduring more years of drug problems before finally becoming clean due to his renewed faith.

Meanwhile, it was a heavily pregnant Linda who added her harmonies to 'Mull Of Kintyre'. Secretly, the McCartneys were hoping that their fourth child would be a boy, and to Paul one strange omen suggested as much. For the past few months he had taken to wearing an old tweed coat that he had thriftily picked up second-hand at Oxfam. Reaching into a pocket one day, he pulled out a baby bootie that, spooking him, was blue. 'It was like a *Twilight Zone* moment,' he marvelled. On 12 September 1977, James Louis McCartney was born at the Avenue Clinic in St John's Wood in London.

A month later, a promo clip for 'Mull Of Kintyre' was filmed, featuring McCartney perched on a wooden fence gate strumming his acoustic guitar, as in the background Linda emerged carrying baby James in a shawl. McCartney was joined by Denny, and the pair strolled towards Saddell beach, where in the distance the Campbeltown pipers could be seen striking up and stridently marching over the sands. In the final scenes, locals gathered around a towering bonfire on the beach at night, singing along with the closing refrain.

It was a cosy picture that was bound to vex the punk-fed critics. But, once released, 'Mull Of Kintyre' assumed a life entirely of its own, selling half a million copies within three weeks of its release and hitting number 1 in December for the start of a nine-week run. It seemed to reach out to the kind of record buyers who never really bought records, while confirming McCartney's fears that the song would cement his image as a comfy, middle-aged balladeer. At the same time, the single's inexorable success far surpassed any expectations he might have had for it, which clearly tickled him. It was the monumental hit record that he never anticipated or, deep in his rocker heart, necessarily wanted. 'The song touched me,' he said, 'but I wasn't sure it was everyone's cup of tea.'

As demand ramped up, other video performances of 'Mull Of Kintyre' were filmed: one featuring the three members of the band sitting on a grassy mound in a wobbly-looking pastoral studio set at Elstree; another for the Christmas TV special of comedian and impressionist Mike Yarwood, where they were arranged on high stools, a carpet of dry ice billowing around their feet, as the Campbeltown pipers filed in from behind. In a sketch later in the show, Yarwood, dressed as Chunky Punky – a spiky-haired and safety-pin-wearing incarnation of then Chancellor of the Exchequer Denis Healey – visited the McCartneys in their pretend living-room. Paul was seen quickly stuffing a wad of banknotes under the lid of a piano, playing up his stingy image, forever the beloved light entertainer.

Some members of the Campbeltown Pipe Band, meanwhile, were becoming disgruntled about where exactly the humongous profits from the song were going. They aired their grievances in the papers, moaning that they'd only been paid flat session fees for their arguably crucial contribution to the record. This wasn't entirely true. After recording the song, Jimmy McGeachy remembers, the musicians were given 'an envelope with some cash in it, ready to get spread around. We thought, Oh, this is alright.' They were given £30 each for the recording session itself, plus another £300 each for their appearance in the video, with around £300 each following in royalties. 'To me, it wasn't an issue,' says McGeachy. 'Some of the older guys . . . it was a bit of a hindsight thing that some of them thought about it.'

Wings' performance of 'Mull Of Kintyre' on *Mike Yarwood in Persons* was, staggeringly, watched by more than 21 million people, almost 40 per cent of the British population. 'From there on,' says Denny, '*whoosh*, up it went.' For those who had perhaps let The Beatles slip to the back of their minds, Paul McCartney was once again a household name.

When the millionth copy of the single, containing a hidden certificate, was bought by a fan named David Ackroyd, EMI gave him a gold disc. But the Campbeltown pipers had been wrong about the support of the expatriates in one key territory – the record flopped in America, where bewildered DJs focused on 'Girls School', which struggled to number 33 in the *Billboard* chart. Back home, however, 'Mull Of Kintyre' was to top 2.5 million sales, nudging past The Beatles' 'She Loves You' and, for a time, becoming the biggest-selling UK single ever. Effectively, in terms of his sales power, McCartney had lapped himself.

It was to be a commercial blip, however. The singles subsequently pulled from the album recorded in the Virgin Islands, now entitled *London Town*, showed diminishing returns in Britain: the gliding synth pop of 'With A Little Luck' made it to number 5, while the stomping, mock-pissed-off rocker 'I've Had Enough' faltered just outside the Top 40.

There were signs that Paul was touchy about the completed *London Town*. Playing the record to Tony Bramwell, who had worked for The Beatles at both Brian Epstein's NEMS and Apple, McCartney casually canvassed his opinion. 'Well, it'll be alright when it's finished,' said Bramwell. At this, McCartney lost the plot, apparently shouting at his former associate, 'What the fuck do you know? I fucking brought you down from Liverpool.'

After a run of years characterised by self-assurance and valida-tion, doubt was beginning to creep back into Paul's mind. 'We didn't seem to be writing any real hard rockers,' he admitted in the wake of the album's release. 'Next time around we'll go for a bit more sweat.'

This mood of uncertainty was reflected by the press launch of *London Town*, held on a miserable, wet and windy day in March 1978, on a boat sailing up and down the Thames. The McCartneys and Laine were hustled around by photographers, before they tried to adopt a cheerful demeanour while eating fish and chips from newspapers in the rain. It was another boat, but this time in a very different climate. After the splash of sun, the outlook had returned to cloudy.

Making *McCartney II*, back on your own again. Was this a conscious move away from Wings?

Y'know, it was really 'cause synthesizers and sequencers came in and I was intrigued. Since leaving The Beatles, I've done that, working on my own thing. Which I always think of as sort of being a nutty professor. You're just holed up in this little laboratory, experimenting with sounds.

12

Take These Broken Wings

There were signs that McCartney was growing tired, and more specifically tired of Wings. 'It was getting a bit boring, to tell the truth,' he was later to admit. 'I was getting a bit fed up with *yet another line-up*.' But, of course, given his determined work ethic, at times bordering on the obsessive, he found himself putting together yet another line-up.

Amusingly, he first met the guitarist who was to replace Jimmy McCulloch in Wings in a toilet at CTS Studios in Wembley, during the marathon mixing sessions for *Wings Over America*. Laurence Juber was a 24-year-old session musician who was hawking his skills around London. His recent gigs had included various TV shows and the qualifying rounds for the Eurovision Song Contest. It was Herbie Flowers, the bassist responsible for the elastic low-end riff on Lou Reed's 'Walk On The Wild Side', who introduced him to Paul over the urinals. The pair awkwardly shook hands in the Gents and weren't to see one another again for eighteen months.

Juber subsequently met Denny Laine when he played a version of The Moody Blues' 'Go Now' in the house band on the David Essex TV show, impressing Laine by perfectly mimicking the guitar solo from the live Wings version of the song. Six months later, he got a call from Laine asking him if he'd like to come for a jam in the basement of the MPL offices.

The guitarist, who didn't own a Wings record, borrowed a

couple of their albums from his brother in order to swot up. 'I can't say that I had been a huge fan of the band,' he confesses, 'because at that point I was busy trying to be a hot-shot studio guitar player.' When Juber arrived at the audition, Paul introduced him to Chris Thomas, the producer who had started his engineering career with The Beatles at Abbey Road on *The White Album* and gone on to work with Pink Floyd and, most recently and intriguingly, the Sex Pistols. Having laughed at the idea of punking up his sound, Paul was now clearly serious about wanting to toughen up the band. Thomas was someone from McCartney's past who might help guide him into the uncertain post-punk future. Juber picked up on this, even as he was being offered the gig: 'There was a sense that there was a desire to take things more in a rock direction.'

The calm, polite, softly spoken guitarist, born in the east end of London and a graduate of the music course at Goldsmiths College, where he'd even studied lute, was the polar opposite of the tempestuous Jimmy McCulloch. This very likely endeared him to the worn-out Paul and Linda, along with the fact that he was a strict vegetarian, which interested the couple, at the time nearing the end of their long transition into forever forgoing meat.

At the same time, a new drummer arrived on the scene, also via Denny. Steve Holley had recently played with Elton John, so he wasn't unnerved by the idea of working with a famous face. Introduced to Laine by a mutual friend, he turned up at a house-warming party at Denny's place and within minutes was sitting behind a drum kit jamming with Paul and Linda. 'I just sat down and started playing,' he says. 'I think they saw an easy way to get a replacement drummer, as opposed to going through a long audition process.'

The new Wings fell together quickly and painlessly. But it was the first time McCartney had been backed by essentially jobbing musicians, for hire for anyone from Cleo Laine to Kiki Dee, who perhaps lacked the musical character of his former bandmates, however turbulent his relationships with them had been. Later, Paul admitted as much. 'Even though they were good players,' he said, 'my enthusiasm had peaked.'

This Mk III version of the group first convened in June 1978 at the Scottish barn studio, now named Spirit of Ranachan. Unlike several of their predecessors, Juber and Holley weren't at all sniffy about being asked to live and work in such a far-flung and relatively unrefined environment. The drummer, who acknowledges that he was still fairly green at the time, says, 'I didn't really know how anything worked in the music business at that level, so for me it was a complete surprise.' The guitarist, who had a little more experience, notes, 'There were some creature comforts there, but nonetheless it was a converted barn.'

The pair were clearly just thrilled to be working with McCartney. There were early indications, however, that things weren't quite right. One evening at the barn, Linda confided to Holley that she really didn't want to be in the band any more. 'All I truly want,' she told the drummer, 'is to be here with my family.' Denny, meanwhile, could suddenly pull rank in unpleasant ways. Holley says that he'd written the heavy, loping guitar riff for what became 'Old Siam, Sir' in rehearsals one day, before Denny picked up on it, aped it, and claimed it as his own when Paul arrived. An argument, verging on a fist-fight, broke out between Laine and Holley, which had to calmed by McCartney, who, perhaps through loyalty, sided with Denny.

Holley was given a strong indication of the level of dedication required from him now that he was a member of Wings when, out of the blue, he was called by Jimmy McCulloch, asking him to play on his first solo album. Not knowing exactly what the deal was now regarding his extracurricular playing, not least with someone who had split from McCartney not so long ago, the drummer asked Alan Crowder at MPL how he thought this information might go down with Paul. 'I remember it not being well received,' Holley remembers. 'He said to me, "You'd be out of your mind to do that."'

As the making of the album moved south to England, Paul and Linda began looking for a place to work that was an easy commute from their home at Peasmarsh, rather than forcing them to schlep up to London every day. Lympne Castle in Kent seemed to provide the answer, continuing their ritual of recording in unusual locations while being within an easy drive of their home. A medieval castle with arched Gothic windows and spiralling stone staircases, it brought a sense of otherness to the proceedings. 'It had battlements and even a ghost,' says Juber. The band set up in the ballroom, snaking their cables up the medieval stairwells to the drawing-room turned control room upstairs.

Paul threw everything into the record that was to become the maligned *Back To The Egg*, recording dozens of songs that ranged from rattling new wave-ish rockers like 'Spin It On' (which still sounded too smoothed out to be truly edgy) and the power-popping, Squeeze-echoing 'Getting Closer' to the old-timey crooner swing of 'Baby's Request'. There were weird – and not in a good way – collages of spoken word by Lympne Castle owners Mr and Mrs Margary, who quoted obscure literary texts over funky grooves ('Reception') or faux-classical arrangements ('The Broadcast'). There was too much material, and yet not enough of it to gel into a cohesive album.

For their part, the two new musicians might have started to sense that Paul was a touch jaded about the whole affair. 'Jaded is a loaded word,' points out Juber. 'But you have Paul's work ethic, which is just to keep working. The goal was productivity.'

'If he was jaded,' Holley argues, 'well, how could you not be? He'd achieved so much. There was a disappointment that was evident in a lot of areas.'

It was coming to the end of the 1970s, and just like the low, fuggy mood that had surrounded the close of the previous decade, there was a feeling that, for McCartney and his generation of 1960s musicians who had survived the subsequent years, a familiar kind of hangover was beginning to kick in.

This became all too dramatically evident at the beginning of September 1978, in the wake of what had been established as the annual Buddy Holly week, inaugurated by McCartney three years earlier. For Paul, this yearly occurrence worked on two levels – he was able to pay tribute to one of his formative musical heroes and, since he'd bought Holly's song catalogue back in 1971 as an investment at the urging of Lee Eastman, he was able subtly to promote his business interests.

The first event, in September 1976, after Wings had returned from their US tour, saw producer Norman Petty ceremonially present McCartney with the cuff-links Buddy Holly had been wearing on his fatal flight in 1959. In 1977, the late singer's former backing band The Crickets reunited for a performance. This year would be marked by the British premiere of the Gary Busey-starring biopic *The Buddy Holly Story* at the Odeon cinema in Leicester Square. The guests, including David Frost, Carl Perkins, Eric Clapton, members of Roxy Music, and Keith Moon, wearing a black leather jacket and Wings T-shirt, were treated to dinner beforehand at the voguish Covent Garden restaurant Peppermint Park.

Moon, who was sober at this point, but who had been snorting cocaine earlier in the evening, looked both wired and weary, and older than his 32 years. He fell ill during the screening and left. Along with his girlfriend Annette Walter-Lax, he returned to the

Curzon Place flat in Mayfair that he was borrowing from Harry Nilsson. Four years earlier, the flat had been the scene of the death from heart failure of Mama Cass of The Mamas and the Papas.

The Who's drummer, after scarfing down a sedative called Heminevrin to take the edge off his alcohol withdrawal, fell asleep in bed in front of the TV while watching the Vincent Price horror flick *The Abominable Dr Phibes*. In the morning, Moon woke and ate a breakfast of steak and eggs made by Walter-Lax after an argument during which he had told her to 'fuck off'. He popped more pills, watched the rest of the film and nodded out. At 3.40 p.m. on the afternoon of 7 September, his girlfriend woke to find him dead.

Less than four weeks after his death, Keith Moon was the ghost at the scene of McCartney's next grand venture. As if a cocky display by Paul and his contemporaries to celebrate the fact that they'd survived the tumultuous 1970s, Rockestra found McCartney conducting his musician mates as they made a big noise. On 3 October, at Abbey Road, he assembled this mock-orchestra of premier-league bassists, guitarists, keyboard-players and drummers to create the 'Rockestra Theme'.

Those who accepted the invitation and made up the numbers included musicians who had come up alongside McCartney (Hank Marvin, Pete Townshend), those who had followed (Gary Brooker of Procol Harum, David Gilmour of Pink Floyd, John Bonham and John Paul Jones of Led Zeppelin) and even a sole representative of the new-wave community (bassist Bruce Thomas of Elvis Costello's band The Attractions). Among the no-shows were Jimmy Page (although a roadie did set up his amp ready for his arrival), Jeff Beck (who didn't like the idea that he had no control over the final track) and Eric Clapton. 'He didn't feel like it,' Paul commented tersely on the non-appearance of Clapton.

The resulting, largely instrumental track, a chugging, bluesy rocker aspiring to the grand movements of big-band swing, was nailed in five takes, sounding like it was perhaps more fun to play than to hear. There was certainly no shortage of high-jinks on the day, including, according to Jo Jo Patrie, a line of coked-up rock stars queuing up to use the men's room. Even with the spectre of Keith Moon haunting the proceedings, the party went on. The comedown, however, was to be a long one. Two years later, John Bonham, too, was to die, choking on his own vomit after a heavy drinking binge.

Denny Laine's own indulgences were worsening, though he still found time to get married, on a yacht in Boston harbour on 5 November, to Jo Jo. The bride in particular was a bit put out that the McCartneys didn't show for the ceremony, only weeks later sending the happy couple a silk bedding set, unwrapped, in a shopping bag, with no card. There was clearly still no love lost between the McCartneys and the untameable former groupie.

Paul and Linda were, at the same time, being surprisingly profligate in other respects. In preparing the cover for the forthcoming hits compilation album *Wings Greatest*, a design team was flown to the Swiss Alps to shoot a figurine of a burlesque dancer – with her arms outstretched, as if ready to take to the air – positioned in the snow. It became something of a ridiculous endeavour: a snowdrift was artificially created, shots were taken from a helicopter. Ultimately, the image used might have been captured in any decent photographic studio back in London for far less than the $8,000 it cost to create the sleeve of *Wings Greatest*. 'It really did not need that degree of money and time and effort spent on it,' reckoned photographer Robert Ellis. 'It was a complete and utter obscenity.'

The spending didn't stop there. Becoming irked by the fact that he was frequently unable to book his spiritual recording home at Abbey Road, with entire months at the facility having been blocked out by EMI's new darling, Kate Bush, McCartney, at great expense, turned the basement at MPL into a facsimile of the studio, pointedly naming it Replica. The making of *Back To The Egg* continued there, running over into the first weeks of 1979. It was becoming clear, though, that Denny Laine, never one for spending days and weeks poring over takes and mixes, was growing weary of the endless recording. 'I'm desperate to be on tour,' he said. 'I get twitchy sitting around in a studio. I'm quite sure we'll be touring soon, otherwise I honestly feel that I wouldn't be able to stay in Wings.'

McCartney still drove himself relentlessly onwards. 'It was hard to get Paul not to work,' says Laurence Juber. 'I remember being in Replica studios when he had a lousy cold and he was still at it. It took a lot for Paul to call the session off and say, "I just don't feel up to it."' In many ways, McCartney was striving for the breakthrough that never came. Even when he'd bagged the Latin-tinged dance-floor groove of the naggingly catchy 'Goodnight Tonight', an obvious single, Paul had reservations about the track. Still searching for a likely hit, at the close of one fruitless session at Replica he threw down a challenge to the other members of Wings: come up with a song over the weekend, and we'll consider it for the next single. Obviously, for the other musicians, this was a potentially lucrative opportunity. Separately, Juber, Holley, Laine and even Linda got their heads into writing mode over the weekend, only for Paul to arrive at the studio on Monday and trump them all with 'Daytime Nighttime Suffering', a song he'd written himself over the previous two days. It was as if, missing the games of creative one-upmanship he'd enjoyed playing with Lennon, McCartney was manufacturing a false sense of rivalry.

Indecision set in again, this time over whether 'Goodnight Tonight' or 'Daytime Nighttime Suffering' – mixed and remixed nearly 50 times – should be the A-side, with Paul doubting the firm opinion of the others that the former was the clearly superior song. 'We sat around for years – well, it seemed like years – discussing it,' McCartney said. 'The normal soul-searching you go through. And we decided, No, it isn't right, we won't put it out. And about a week later, I played the record again. I thought, That's crazy, we've made it . . . why not put it out?'

As the tracks for *Back To The Egg* were being completed, McCartney turned to David Bowie, himself nearing the end of a peerlessly inspired 1970s, to ask for his opinion of the new songs. Chris Thomas recalled that Bowie sat there saying, 'Like this . . . not that . . . this is good . . . keep this . . . not that one', doubtless relishing the novelty of being required to critique an ex-Beatle. His art-rock-slanted views were perhaps not to be trusted, however. Bowie, mischievously, suggested that the abstract, minute-and-a-half-long 'The Broadcast' should be Paul's next single.

Instead, Wings released 'Goodnight Tonight', complete with a video shot at London's Hammersmith Palais, featuring the band sporting 1930s garb – black suits and dickie bows, their hair slicked back with gel. Fooling around on the stage during the long day, the group ran through rock'n'roll standards including the enduring 'Twenty Flight Rock', McCartney's acid test for any band. But this was a more vanilla and conservative outfit in many ways, lacking the wildness of spirit that Jimmy McCulloch, Henry McCullough or even Geoff Britton had brought to the party. Holley, unable to find the make-up artist at the end of the shoot, was even nervous about being forced to drive home with his hair pinned and greased, wearing thick foundation. 'I just thought, I hope to God I don't get stopped,' he says.

McCartney had just signed a new US record deal, fuelling the procrastination over the first single to be released by the new if not entirely improved Wings. His contract with Capitol having lapsed, he moved over to Columbia, cutting himself a money-hoovering deal that made him the highest-paid recording artist in the world, with a $2 million advance on his future albums and an unparalleled 22 per cent royalty, at least four per cent more than any of his rivals had secured. The president of the company, Walter Yetnikoff, even threw in a clause that allowed Paul and Linda the use of the company's private jet.

Paul was a prestige signing for the record label. When he first visited Columbia's offices in New York for a grip-and-grin meeting with its employees, some of them shook with nerves, as if they were being granted an audience with the Queen. Still, there were those at the company who felt that the deal was over the top. Later, one anonymous employee was to say, 'It was too much money for an artist who was obviously past his prime. We knew we would have to really work our asses off to try to earn some of that money back.'

At the same time as business was booming for McCartney, Allen Klein was being jailed in New York. Found guilty of tax evasion, he was given a two-year sentence, of which he would only have to serve two months. Commenting at the time, Paul tried not to sound too pleased. 'I feel sorry for him now,' he said. 'But I was caught in his net once, and that panicked me. I really wanted to do everything to get him. I was contemplating going to where he lives and walking outside his house with placards. I was really crazy at that time.'

With the villain of the piece in jail, the ex-Beatles seemed to be in a more playful mood. At the 19 May 1979 wedding celebration thrown by Eric Clapton at his home in Surrey to toast his marriage to Patti Boyd – notably, of course, George Harrison's first wife, the two friends having reached some kind of peace in the aftermath of the difficult affair – the former bandmates were practically on frolicsome form. Paul described Ringo and George as 'two old flames' as he called them to the stage in the marquee pitched on the lawn of the estate, and along with Clapton they drunkenly hammered through some old rock'n'roll standards and even a few Beatles numbers, including 'Sgt. Pepper's Lonely Hearts Club Band' and 'Get Back'. 'The music was terrible, absolute rubbish,' said Denny Laine, who watched this impromptu and over-refreshed three-quarters Beatles reunion from the audience of party-goers. 'It's lucky nobody made a tape.'

Back To The Egg was launched with a surreal press call held in the hallowed Studio Two at Abbey Road, its interior decked out as if it were the inside of a giant frying-pan. Journalists sat at tables under parasols made to resemble enormous fried eggs. Asked about his future intentions, Paul, unsurprisingly, said he was planning to take this new line-up of the band on the road.

The marketing budget for the album, underwritten by Columbia, was far higher than for any of the previous Wings albums. The band returned to Lympne Castle to shoot a number of expensive promo videos, including one for the ballad 'Winter Rose', which the production team decided needed a snowy setting, requiring them to spray gallons of white foam over two areas of the grounds. 'They'd promised the Margarys, the owners of the castle, that it wouldn't damage any of the grass or foliage,' Steve Holley remembers. 'But then it washed away and it had turned everything brown.'

A minute-long TV ad, screened during prime-time, announced *Back To The Egg* as 'a timeless rock'n'roll flight through twelve superbly produced new songs on an album that really is perfection'. It was certainly an album made by a perfectionist, even if he was one unable to wholly trust his creative instincts.

Upon its release in May, 'Goodnight Tonight' reached a respectable number 5 in both the UK and the US. The album followed, peaking at six in Britain and, disappointingly, eight in America. *Back To The Egg* sold more than a million copies in the US, a respectable figure in the middle of the economic recession of 1979, but this didn't quite satisfy McCartney's investors at Columbia. Part of the problem was that – in a practice that harked back to the 1960s, when it was thought that not putting a single on its parent LP offered value for money – Paul had argued against including 'Goodnight Tonight' on the album. But times had moved on and, particularly in the US, every album release needed a radio hit, or two, to push sales. By not featuring the hit single on the album, opined one record executive, Paul had shot himself in the foot, particularly when the follow-ups released from *Back To The Egg* in the States – the chiming, upbeat 'Getting Closer' and the tailored-for-FM-radio Philly soul homage 'Arrow Through Me' – failed to even puncture the Top Twenty.

Acknowledging its relatively poor sales, Paul joked that it was less a concept album and more a 'bomb-cept' album.

Unperturbed, and flush with the proceeds of the Columbia deal, that summer the McCartneys bought the property neighbouring their Sussex home, Lower Gate Farm, for £250,000, planning at some point in the future to knock down its semi-derelict farmhouse, perched on a hill, and build in its place a house designed by Paul. The plan was purposely modest. A five-bedroomed house, which provided each of the kids with their own room, it was not overly expansive. The couple hated the idea of living in some huge, posh country home where the children might be 'rattling around in the east wing, and you never see them'.

They reinstated the property's original name, Blossom Wood Farm. Within its 159 acres there were stables, a windmill building that Paul earmarked for a recording studio and an old cottage that Linda turned into a pottery studio. Linda took a hippieish, Mother Nature's daughter approach to owning so much green space. 'I was lent all this for a little while,' she told her friend Danny Fields. 'And I have to take good care of it, so I can give it back just the way it is.'

July found Paul alone, in his studios in Sussex and Scotland, messing around with the tracks for what was to become his second solo album, *McCartney II*. Without Wings, he began experimenting with synthesizers and sequencers, recapturing the freedom he'd enjoyed when making the first record. Once again he found himself at play, balancing a snare drum on the rim of a toilet and whacking it with a stick to see what kind of resonant sound it made.

Almost all of the songs were entirely improvised, beginning with the bubbling synths of 'Front Parlour' and the bouncy falsetto dub reggae of 'Check My Machine'. 'Temporary Secretary' was a letter song, in the style of 'Paperback Writer', directed at the head of the Alfred Marks Recruitment Agency, requiring the services of the typist of the title, delivered in a cartoon American accent over a clubby beat. It was frivolous and liberating stuff. 'Check My Machine' and the hypnotic electronic track 'Secret Friend' – which weren't to make the original cut of the album, surfacing only on subsequent reissues – were long and unhurried. Other songs weren't quite so forward-looking and experimental, however, with 'On The Way' and 'Nobody Knows' essentially being bluesy rock knock-offs.

There was a real maturity evident elsewhere, though, Paul having just turned 37. 'Waterfalls', inspired by the natural feature at the Sussex estate, found McCartney plaintively fretting about the safety of his loved ones. 'One Of These Days' might have been lifted from *The White Album* and captured Paul peering into the future with a certain serenity, writing in the becalmed hours after a visit from an acquaintance who was devoted to Hare Krishna.

The making of *McCartney II*, in isolation and in secret, was a real indication of the fact that Paul was tiring of the complications of working with other musicians. It was ten years since he'd last done the same, hiding himself away in Cavendish Avenue during the dark days of the end of The Beatles. It was a closing of the circle.

Then, on 27 September 1979, Jimmy McCulloch died. In the two years since leaving Wings, the guitarist had continued his drinking and drugging around London, moving into a posh Maida Vale flat and ripping through the not insubstantial royalties that had followed his time with the band. The reformed Small Faces had, as McCartney predicted, been a short-lived enterprise. Jimmy had subsequently played in Wild Horses with similarly hard-edged, hard-living former Thin Lizzy guitarist Brian Robertson, and an outfit called The Dukes, signed to Warner Brothers.

McCulloch had gone AWOL for a couple of days in September, failing to show up at a rehearsal with The Dukes at Dingwalls nightclub in Camden. Phone calls to him went unanswered. Worried, his brother Jack made his way over to the flat in Maida Vale. When there was no reply to his knocks, and he noticed a strange, unpleasant smell emanating from inside, he took his shoulder to the door and burst it open.

Jimmy was discovered sitting up in an armchair, with a burned-out spliff between his fingers, clearly dead. He was 26. There was some evidence that someone had been with him and absconded, likely scared. Cannabis, morphine and alcohol were found in the guitarist's blood, but other than the joint roach, no drugs were found in the flat. The police concluded that the place had been tidied up in a hurry. The door-chain had been broken by someone other than Jack.

Deputy coroner Dr Paul Knapman concluded, 'There are certainly some odd circumstances and, because of this, I think an open verdict is the proper one.' Jack McCulloch was quoted as saying, almost threateningly, 'I'm sure somebody was in that apartment when my brother died and I'd like to find out who it was.' The exact circumstances of Jimmy's death remain a mystery.

'I was shocked . . . it was crazy,' says Dave Clarke, McCulloch's former partner in White Line. 'But I have to say there was always that thought at the back of your mind. Knowing Jim as I did and his personality . . . it wasn't something that I thought *couldn't* possibly happen. I never saw him near any heroin. I think it probably came later. It was all uppers and drinking and grass.'

It was perhaps no surprise that Paul, who, of course, couldn't bear funerals, didn't attend McCulloch's wake. But neither did Denny Laine. 'I was pissed off with Jimmy over lots of things and I'd kind of fallen out with him,' he admitted. 'I know it sounds funny to say, but when somebody dies you can still be angry with them.' Paul said of Jimmy's death, 'In the end, he was just too dangerous for his own good.'

That autumn, the sales of Wings albums topped 100 million. At the same time, the people behind the *Guinness Book of Records* presented McCartney with an award to mark his landmark achievements, naming him the most successful recording artist of all time. The gong handed to him was a disc made of rhodium, a substance twice as expensive as platinum. The organisers had originally wanted to cast it in osmium, before discovering that the rarer metal was highly toxic.

Still, this elevated status appeared to do little to firm up McCartney's sagging self-belief. In once again trying to step away from his fame and downsize his ambitions, Paul had suggested that the new Wings, still untested live, should go out on a low-key tour of small British clubs, to refine their set and get closer to their audiences. The notion perhaps revealed McCartney's inner doubts about the band. 'At the moment, we don't want a great big tour of the world with everything it entails,' Paul announced in the pages of the Wings newsletter *Club Sandwich*, 'so it looks as though we'll just be turning up with our guitars and plugging them in wherever they want to listen to us'.

In the end, promoter Harvey Goldsmith managed to up the scale, talking Paul into nineteen theatre dates. As it transpired, throughout the jaunt, Paul and Linda were there with the band, but somehow apart. Whenever possible, they would drive home after the shows to Sussex or London.

McCartney had promised to launch his next tour back on hometown turf in Liverpool. Demand for tickets overwhelmed the box office of the Royal Court Theatre, forcing the line to be closed on more than a thousand fans who had queued outside overnight in the late autumn cold. These were scenes that were being repeated up and down the country.

Standing waiting to go on stage at the Royal Court on 23 November, the first night of Wings' British tour, saxophonist Howie Casey was amazed to see just how nervous McCartney was. Paul turned to him, minutes before showtime, and said, 'Oh God, I hope this goes well.' Casey, taken aback, replied, 'Paul, this is like the Second Coming. You're gonna go down well just walking on the stage.'

The Royal Court, which Paul had frequented as a kid, was at the time struggling financially. McCartney had donated £5,000 to the cause, which was seen by its organisers as 'a great boost to the theatre', while attracting some criticism from local government. One of the city's Labour councillors carped, 'I don't see why Paul McCartney should be singled out for special praise. The Beatles could have given a million and not missed it. They made their millions and we've not seen them since.' He was a lone voice, and one that failed to be heard in the clamour caused by Paul's arrival back in Liverpool. 'I feel I'm not judged with the same harshness by the people here as elsewhere,' McCartney said.

On the afternoon of the opening night in the city, Paul played a free matinee show for pupils from his former school, the Liverpool Institute, organised by his former geography teacher and now headmaster, Bertram Parker, nicknamed Blip. He remembered Paul as 'a bright and cheerful lad who did a reasonable amount of work', before recalling with a smile that the last time he'd seen McCartney, in his pre-fame days, it had been when he repaid a small debt to the teacher's wife. 'A sixpence that he'd borrowed to go to the cinema,' Parker grinned. That afternoon, rocketing the headmaster's cool, Paul started the show by saying, 'Hello, Blip, nice to see you.'

The media trailed after McCartney the whole day: the *Liverpool Echo* joined him for a trip on the Mersey on the *Royal Iris* ferry, the setting of some early Beatles performances; a camera crew from BBC tea-time magazine show *Nationwide* captured his every move for a twenty-minute documentary. Before the evening show, in a news item on local radio, one reporter frothed up the atmosphere in the city. 'Theatre staff are predicting the greatest explosion since the Merseybeat mania of the 1960s and the police are taking no chances,' he babbled. 'They're prepared to draft in extra men at the first signs of the hysteria McCartney attracted during the heyday of The Beatles.'

In truth, despite the roaring responses, Paul felt the band was under-rehearsed, the performances phoned-in. *Rolling Stone* reviewer Mick Brown could tell that the singer's heart wasn't in it. 'Everything seemed designed to take the spotlight off Paul McCartney and spread it among the rest of Wings,' he noted. 'The impression given was not that of a deity with a box of thunderbolts, but a band onstage for the hell of it.' Howie Casey says he felt that, from his vantage point at the back of the stage, something had changed in the Wings set-up beyond the shake-up in personnel. They had turned even less rock'n'roll, effectively becoming a showband in some ways. 'They gave us black suits and it became almost formal,' he says.

In Steve Holley's view, despite the impression given to its audiences, McCartney hated the 1979 tour. After one underwhelming show in Brighton, Paul told the drummer backstage he thought it 'stank'. Finding themselves back trying to juggle touring and family life again heaped more pressure on the McCartneys' relationship. 'It caused a lot of trouble between us,' said Paul. 'We both work at it and have a laugh or have an argument,' said Linda. 'But we always end up in the laugh.'

In Edinburgh, part-way through the gig, the power failed, and, in the semi-darkness, the band turned into troupers and rallied the crowd. Denny performed a jokey striptease and unveiled some acrobatic skills; Linda and the horn section roused everyone into a singalong of 'When The Saints Go Marching In'. Outside Manchester Apollo, fights broke out in the streets between desperate fans and greedy ticket touts. On the last night in Glasgow, Wings turned out in kilts and brought the Campbeltown Pipe Band on for a roof-lifting 'Mull Of Kintyre'. 'We did the encore and everybody went ballistic,' says Jimmy McGeachy. Performing the rubbery funk of 'Coming Up', a song solo-recorded during the *McCartney II* sessions, Paul zoomed in on one particularly enthusiastic audience member. 'This kid was bopping away,' he recalled. 'I thought, Oh, this is a hit.' Luckily, the show was being recorded by a mobile studio unit that night, and this B-side live version was to be favoured by DJs in the US over Paul's solo A-side version, reaching number 1.

Rising up the British charts during this time was McCartney's first attempt at a festive record, 'Wonderful Christmastime', a bright, synthy concoction put together alone in the summer and destined to become a perennial. In the slightly muted aftermath of the British tour, he sat down with promoter Bill Graham to plot a US jaunt, due to follow a trip to Japan early the next year. Knowing how Linda might feel about this, it was possibly no coincidence that he presented his wife with a marriage-sweetening, grand-gesturing gift of a ranch in Arizona, a property she'd visited and adored back in her university days in the south-western state.

Wings closed out the year with a show at Hammersmith Odeon in London on 29 December, set up following a plea from the UN's secretary general Kurt Waldheim to reunite The Beatles for a benefit to raise funds for the victims of war in Kampuchea. The fact that this was always going to be highly unlikely did nothing to dampen the raging press speculation that, finally, nearly ten years on, the four were to reform. In fact, calls were indeed placed to Ringo and George, who agreed to appear, though not as part of The Beatles. John, in New York, wasn't interested. Then, when the papers got wind of Harrison and Starr's agreement to participate, the two pulled out. And so it was left to McCartney to tell Waldheim that Wings would play the show.

It was a long, rambling night, and flat in its execution. Denny Laine was drunk, but not as spectacularly as Pete Townshend, who turned up for a live gathering of the Rockestra and proceeded to fuzz his way through 'Let It Be'. The assembled cast – among them Robert Plant, John Bonham, ex-Faces bassist Ronnie Lane and James Honeyman-Scott of The Pretenders – all agreed to wear the requisite uniform for the evening, a silver suit and top hat. The Who's guitarist, though, noisily refused to dress up, shouting, 'I'm not wearing that fucking shit.'

'Pete was breathing Rémy Martin fumes down my neck,' Laurence Juber remembers. 'I put the top hat on him at one point and he took it off and threw it into the audience.'

The final Wings show of this difficult year proved both an anti-climax and an inauspicious end to the decade. 'There was a growing sense from Paul that it was getting to the endgame of the band,' says Juber.

No one was to know that the group had just played their last gig.

Japan, 1980: what was going through your mind?

How the hell did that happen? But it did. Then it became just a film, y'know. A slow-motion film of Japan. The inside view of Tokyo. An insider's view! Jesus! It was just unbelievable.

13

Stuck Inside These Four Walls

Later, he was to wonder if it had been some strange act of self-sabotage.

It was almost as if I *wanted* to get busted, he thought to himself.

The first days of January 1980 saw Wings regroup at Hog Hill Mill Studios, McCartney's newly completed facility at his Sussex estate. Maybe it was something to do with rehearsing at home. Maybe the dawning of the new year, and decade, only served to remind him of his waning passion for the band. But for Wings, rehearsing for merely a week in preparation for a major tour, the pall of lethargy was all too obvious.

'We hadn't really rehearsed enough,' Paul admitted. 'For the previous Wings tour we rehearsed a lot.'

Steve Holley didn't think the band were ready for the upcoming Japanese tour, either. 'I didn't feel at my best when we set off,' says the drummer. 'I remember the rehearsals being less than satisfactory. They hadn't yielded enough security for Paul. So when we left, there was a cloud hanging over it.'

Paul and Linda flew with the four kids on Concorde to New York on Saturday 12 January, booking into the Stanhope on Central Park. Once there, through an east coast connection, they bought half a pound of grass. Legend would later have it that McCartney then phoned Lennon at the Dakota, the call taken by Ono, to say he could come over with some 'dynamite weed'. The offer was declined, but, in the aftermath, the rumour spread that Yoko – incensed that the McCartneys planned to stay in the Lennons' favourite suite at the Okura Hotel in Tokyo – tipped off a cousin who worked in Japanese Customs that McCartney was coming in carrying a hefty bag of dope. Ono would dismiss the accusation, saying drugs hadn't been mentioned in the conversation and she didn't even have a cousin who worked at the airport.

Puncturing another hole in this conspiracy theory, of course, is the fact that no one could have imagined Paul would ever have been stupid enough to try to smuggle dope into Japan, the country that just over four years earlier had banned him for his drug conviction.

But, leaving for Japan, he couldn't bring himself to flush the stuff down the toilet. It was to be the dumbest thing he'd ever done in his life. 'I was,' he says, 'an idiot.'

Paul hadn't set foot in Japan since 1966 with The Beatles. Having had his visa turned down nine years later, forcing the cancellation of the 1975 tour, he was now to be allowed back into the country for eleven concert dates over eighteen days, the authorities having taken into consideration McCartney's popularity with Japanese fans.

Straight off the plane, 16 January 1980, Paul – with Linda and the kids and Laurence Juber, who had joined them on the flight from New York – grinned and capered around for the photographers and reporters. Once the storm of flashbulbs died down, the party moved through to an immigration holding area, where they spent two hours going through paperwork with officials. 'It was tedious, to be honest,' says the guitarist.

From there, they made their way with their luggage through to Customs. Blue-uniformed, white-gloved Japanese officers began opening bags at random, performing standard spot checks, pulling an item or two, though not everything, from each. One unzipped a beige canvas suitcase. Inside, lying on top, was Paul's folded jacket. The official reached inside it and pulled out the clear plastic bag of grass.

Paul, recalls Juber, standing next to him, 'turned kind of white'. The officer, visibly stunned and embarrassed, almost made to cover up the bag of weed again with the coat. Then he quickly realised that he couldn't possibly ignore what he had just seen. He duly alerted his superior and Paul was hurriedly ushered into a back room.

Juber was dumbstruck. Alan Crowder from MPL had warned the band that, prior to entering Japan, they had to take every precaution to ensure they weren't carrying a crumb of dope. They were to vacuum their pockets, scrub their fingernails. Now, because of the foolishness of the boss, a stony-faced Japanese Customs man was handing him a screwdriver and ordering him to remove the panels from his guitars, to search for any other stashed packages.

'All of us had been warned, whatever you do, don't take stuff into Japan,' says McCartney. 'And there it was. The look on the Customs man's face when he pulled a bag of pot out of my suitcase was priceless. I mean, it was just like a sort of mad movie.'

But however much Paul felt as if he was outside himself, looking in, this was really happening.

When it was all over and done with, no one could ever work out why such a stupid thing had been allowed to occur. There were those who said it revealed the superstar bubble that McCartney floated around in. Paul, on some level, felt he was above the law, a hangover from the Beatles' sense of diplomatic immunity. 'I think of my kind of drug involvement as harmless,' he later said, 'so I walked straight into Japan after a fourteen-hour flight, thinking, It's not that bad. Most people taking that kind of thing into the country would give it to the roadies.

That just shows that I wasn't really thinking about it. I was taking *my* opinion of it instead of the legal opinion.'

Maybe his rebellious side told him he could get away with it. Even if he was caught, he was likely thinking, his power could effectively snuff any legal difficulties, just as it had done in the past. 'I'm still not quite sure how it all happened, to tell you the truth,' he offers now.

This time around, though, his fame and wealth couldn't protect him. In order to secure the visa, McCartney had signed an affidavit declaring that he no longer smoked marijuana. The Minister of Justice had rubber-stamped the application and approved the visit. Now the singer seemed to be making a fool of Japanese law. In losing face, the authorities decided that an example had to be made of McCartney. He was arrested and handcuffed, and filmed leaving the airport amid a scrum of police and reporters. Outside the fans were screaming, like it was Beatlemania all over again. 'But instead of going to a gig,' says Paul, 'I was going to a cell.'

McCartney was taken to Kojimachi police station in central Tokyo and questioned for an hour. 'I made a confession,' he says, 'and apologised for breaking Japanese law.' The promoter, Seijiro Udo, issued a statement saying a decision about the shows would be made imminently. Some phone calls having been made, the announcement followed, saying the tour was off. One hundred thousand tickets had been sold, making for a possible loss of 100 million yen, or nearly £200,000.

Denny Laine and Steve Holley, who had flown in first class from London on TWA with the crew and management an hour earlier, were parked on a bus outside the airport, wondering what was causing the delay. Alan Crowder came to tell them there had been a 'slight problem' with the McCartneys' flight. After a period of waiting, the band were driven to the Okura Hotel. Exhausted after the eighteen-hour trip, the drummer went to bed and was woken by a call from Linda, telling him that Paul had been arrested. 'I actually thought she was just playing a trick on us,' he says. Emerging from the lift downstairs in the lobby, Holley was met with the sight of a mob of journalists. He spotted the crew in the bar, sitting with their heads down, looking dejected. 'I went, Oh no.'

Meanwhile, Howie Casey and the rest of the brass section were sitting in a room at the Okura, drinking wine and smoking cigars, in celebration of the fact that they'd had their wages raised to $1,000 a gig for the Japanese tour. 'So we're mid-cigar and half a bottle of wine gone,' says the saxophonist, 'and Alan comes in and says, "Have you heard the news? Paul's been arrested." We're going, "Fuck off, Alan, don't take the piss." And of course, it was true.' Casey and the others were baffled at the risk McCartney had taken, everyone having been quietly advised prior to the trip that marijuana could be freely bought through contacts at the US Army bases in the country. 'They could have got it no problem,' he points out.

Holley says the band were quickly made to feel as if they were persona non grata in the country. To fox the press, the tour party faked their exit from the hotel, making a big show of leaving via the front door before nipping around the back to a waiting van that would take them to the train station and on to Kyoto, where they could sit out the fuss.

Transferred after questioning to the Metropolitan Jail, and stripped of his personal effects, including his wedding ring, Paul was now prisoner number 22. He was appointed a public defender, Tasuku Matsuo, who soberly informed him that two Japanese men had recently been sentenced to three years after being caught with only half the amount of marijuana found in McCartney's suitcase. The truth was that he could be facing anything up to seven years in prison.

Linda was at the Okura, with the kids, waiting for news. 'It's a strain,' she told reporters. 'I wouldn't mind if we knew what was happening and knew he was getting out.' Sick with worry, sinister fantasies began to creep into her mind about what was now happening to her husband. 'I was thinking they might be torturing him.'

She was eventually allowed into the prison to see Paul, on the other side of a metal grille, having been told that she couldn't bring the kids. Her husband didn't tell her that he could be looking at a seven-year sentence. 'If I'd known what Paul was really facing,' she said, 'I'd have fallen apart.' At the same time, her father Lee Eastman in New York, apparently furious, said his son-in-law was in 'a hell of a mess' and dispatched John Eastman to Japan.

Stuck in his cell, McCartney was quietly terrified: 'It was scary for the first couple of days, I must say. I felt worse for what I'd landed the family in. If I'd just been some single guy, I'd have sort of thought, You're a total nutter and you deserve to get nicked. But it was more the impact it would have on them that was really doing my head in. And also, unless you're an old lag, you don't know the scene. So it takes you a few days to sort of see what's going on.'

The first night, he couldn't sleep, and a blinding headache set in. His biggest fear was being raped. 'So,' he says, 'I slept with my back to the wall.'

Each morning, the lights in his eight-by-four-foot cell would come on at dawn. McCartney, as he had been instructed to, would then roll up his tatami mat, designed for the Japanese stature and so too short for him. He then had to sit cross-legged and wait for cell inspection. Throughout this process, he still felt oddly detached. 'I kept thinking I was watching a war film. They shouted out "22" in Japanese and I had to shout back, "Hai".' Pushed through the door was a breakfast of three bread rolls with miso soup, which in the future he would never be able to face again. Supper was a bowl of rice. The lights went out at eight.

On the second day, with Matsuo at his side, Paul was interrogated in English for six hours by the police at Kojimachi. He insisted that the marijuana had been for his personal use and he continued to take a pro-dope stance, arguing that it was less toxic than alcohol. 'I tried to tell them ciggies were worse,' he says. 'They wouldn't listen, of course, because many of the police there chain-smoke.' The line of questioning often seemed bizarre to him. 'They wanted to know everything. I had to go through my whole life story – school, father's name, income, even my medal from the Queen.'

As he attempted to leave the station, around 200 fans chanting 'Free Paul' blocked the exit. The police pulled McCartney back into the building. Officials were still refusing to say whether he would be deported or face trial. In the press, one well-known Japanese music journalist, Ichiro Fukuda, was damning of the singer, saying, 'For a man like McCartney to violate the law means he has no respect for Japan.' There was even a media ban imposed that prohibited the playing of any of his records. But encouragingly, perhaps, the Minister of Justice made a statement saying Paul 'had not legally landed when he was seized'.

On the third day, prosecutors asked the Tokyo District Court to allow them a further ten days to question McCartney. It was clear that they were determined to continue to take a tough line, particularly in light of the fact that the news had made front pages the world over, effectively becoming an international incident. When Paul put in a request to be allowed a guitar in his cell, it was flatly denied.

He was visited by the British consul, Donald Warren-Knott.

They talked for fifteen minutes, the UK official apparently cheerful, but ultimately powerless. An official statement was put out by the press office at the detention centre: 'He slept well in jail, but he is concerned about his wife Linda and four children.'

'Linda wasn't going to go back to England,' Paul points out. 'I was looking at the kids being brought up in Japan.'

On the other side of the world, several days after McCartney had been jailed, a clearly distressed 29-year-old fan named Kenneth Lambert arrived at Miami International Airport, walked up to one of the desks and hysterically demanded a ticket to Japan in order to, as he put it, 'free Paul'. Being unable to produce either any money or ID, he began arguing wildly with the airline clerk, before pulling a genuine-looking toy gun from his pocket. A policeman shot him dead on the spot.

Across the country, Laurence Juber landed in Los Angeles and exited the airport to find bootleggers hawking unofficial T-shirts commemorating Wings' tour of Japan, with the word 'cancelled' slashed across them. 'It was a big deal,' he points out. The band had lingered on in the Far East until 19 January, three days after Paul's arrest, only leaving, slightly dazed, when it became clear that there was no chance of the tour being rescheduled.

As part of their deal, all of the members of Wings had been given a round-the-world first-class air ticket allowing them unlimited stops en route back to London. Denny Laine flew to the MIDEM music industry conference in Cannes to cut a deal for a solo album. This annoyed McCartney, riled by the thought that his guitarist was sunning himself in the French Riviera, while he was locked in his cell, facing a highly uncertain future. A slightly aimless Steve Holley travelled to Australia to visit family. 'I thought, Well I'll go there and I'll hang out and I'll see what happens,' he says. 'I just didn't really know what to do. It wasn't clear.'

Back inside the Metropolitan Jail, as letters and telegrams flooded in, Paul felt his spirits begin to lift. 'Well, I'd seen *Bridge on the River Kwai*,' he says. 'I knew what you had to do when you were a prisoner of war. You had to laugh a lot and keep cheery, 'cause that's all you had. So I did a lot of that.' One of his jailers, Yasuji Ariga, was quoted as saying, 'He is very polite and has made a good impression on the guards.'

On 22 January, Linda visited her husband for the second time, taking him some sci-fi novels, a cheese sandwich and some fruit, and staying for half an hour. 'He looks incredibly well,' she said, upon leaving. 'He was managing to smile and crack jokes. In fact, he was laughing so much he even got me laughing, and, believe me, I haven't been able to do much laughing during the last week.'

As the days passed, and he realised that the jail wasn't quite as dangerous as he'd imagined it might be, McCartney began banging on the walls and communicating with other prisoners, who would shout back vaguely British references: 'Maggie Thatcher!', 'Bell's whisky!' He responded by making 'the worst jokes in the world . . . but they helped to relieve the tension'. He began a dialogue with the prisoner next door, who could speak a bit of English and who, similarly, was inside for smuggling dope. 'I became quite matey with the chap,' he says. 'We sang and laughed together as if we had been mates for ages.'

He was allowed two cigarettes a day, smoked outside during the daily exercise period. Given the option of a private bath, he decided to show solidarity by agreeing to wash in the communal bath with his fellow inmates. 'I wasn't shy,' he says. 'You're not as proud in jail. It knocks it all out of you.' As grinning guards looked on, he sang the prison work song 'Take This Hammer' and the perky 1920s hit 'When The Red, Red Robin (Comes Bob, Bob, Bobbin' Along)'. 'Their favourite, though, was "Yesterday",' he points out.

Naked among a group of convicts, here he found himself finally performing in Japan, if not in a way he might ever have imagined.

He initiated a game that he called See Who Can Touch The Ceiling, knowing that, at five feet ten inches, 'with my great western height', it was no contest. One of the larger, more imposing prisoners, tattooed with the image of a samurai warrior all over his back and talking through another who could interpret, asked McCartney why he was in the prison. When he replied, 'Marijuana', the heavy looked at him with a frown and indicated through the other that he was sure to get seven years. 'He was just trying to frighten me,' Paul reckons. 'I said, "No, no, no . . . ten." And they were all over on the floor in a heap, laughing at that.'

Elsewhere, the other three former Beatles reacted to Paul's imprisonment in different ways. George and his new wife Olivia sent a telegram saying: 'Thinking of you all with love. Keep your spirits high. Nice to have you back home again soon.' Cornered by reporters in the south of France, Ringo sounded simultaneously judgemental and sympathetic, telling them, 'It's the risk you take when you're involved with drugs. He's just been unlucky.'

John, meanwhile, told his photographer friend Bob Gruen that Paul couldn't have predicted, as an ex-Beatle, that he would have had his bag properly searched. Like everyone else, though, Lennon was wondering, 'Why would he carry pot when he finally was allowed in?' His personal assistant Fred Seaman later claimed that John sent him to fetch all the newspapers so that he could pore over all the reports, and would sit watching TV for hours trying to catch every bulletin detailing McCartney's progress.

'You know, it serves Paul right,' he told Seaman. 'Paul wanted to show the world that he's still a bit of bad boy.' At the same time, without knowing it, he agreed with McCartney's assessment that on some level he'd knowingly invited trouble. 'I think subconsciously,' said Lennon, 'he wanted to get busted.'

By 24 January the details in the Japanese press were being exaggerated, with one claiming that the marijuana McCartney had been caught with was worth £700,000, or just under £100,000 an ounce. In truth, Customs representatives had estimated that the 219 grammes they had confiscated from the singer had a street value of 600,000 yen, or just over £1,000. At the hotel, Linda was asked by a journalist how long she planned to stay in the country. She firmly told them, 'I'm prepared to stay in Japan for as long as it takes.'

It didn't take long. The next day, the charges were suddenly dropped – the result of the pressure put on the authorities by Eastman and Matsuo, added to the fact that Paul was contrite and obviously not a drug smuggler. Moreover, the whole messy affair was becoming an embarrassment to the Japanese, who clearly couldn't decide how to deal with the problem and wanted it swiftly resolved. Technically, they decided that, because McCartney's visa was taken away from him the minute he was arrested, he was now an illegal alien who should be deported. The statement from the Japanese police read: 'Charges were not brought against Mr McCartney because he had brought in the marijuana solely for his own use and already he has been punished enough'. After ten days in a cell, Paul was released. 'We were so lucky,' said Matsuo.

At the airport, booked on the first available flight out of the country, which happened to be the 12.30 p.m. Japan Airlines to Amsterdam, a sheepish if jocular Paul grabbed a guitar and serenaded the press with a brief snatch of 'Yesterday', the song carrying a very different resonance in the circumstances. The day before, Paul's troubles had been all too evident. Now, his mood was one of acute relief.

On the plane, Paul was tearfully reunited with Linda and the kids. Booked on the same flight, however, was a pack of opportunistic journalists, and in the air the couple were continually hassled for quotes. 'I'll never come back to Japan again,' Linda promised. 'It's my first trip and my last.'

Paul was depressed about the fact that when his belongings were returned to him, his wedding ring was missing. 'That made me very, very low,' he admitted. In its place he now wore a curled paper-clip, saying, 'It's the sort of gesture that Linda and I will look back on rather romantically.'

Clearly emotional, he said to the *Daily Express*, 'This is the longest I've ever been away from my family in ten years. I don't want a separation like it again.' He told another reporter, 'I've been a fool. What I did was incredibly dumb. I was really scared, thinking I might be imprisoned for so long and now I have made my mind up *never* to touch the stuff again. From now on, all I'm going to smoke is straightforward fags and no more pot.'

It was a long, exhausting flight, with a stop to refuel in Anchorage, Alaska. After finally touching down in the Netherlands, the McCartneys were flown by private jet to Lydd Airport in Kent. From there they were driven home, disappearing up the driveway of their Sussex estate.

Even in jail, Paul had still been thinking about work. 'In the clink I had time to think,' he said. Further marking the distance he felt from Wings, he resolved to finish the tapes he'd recorded alone the previous summer and release them as the solo LP *McCartney II*.

At the same time, in an act of catharsis, he wrote a private memoir he called *Japanese Jailbird*, penned in longhand over ten days and stretching to 20,000 words. 'I wrote it all down,' he said. 'I sort of thought, God, this is like writing an essay for school. I can't do it. I'm frightened of the piece of paper. But I knew I had to write it down to remember the incident. I forced myself to write it.' Ultimately he decided against publishing it, reasoning that it would only drag this unfortunate episode in his life back into the public mind. Instead he bought a printer and produced one paperback-sized copy that he could fit into his pocket.

The next time Laurence Juber saw McCartney, he says, the singer was 'a little chagrined . . . but also, kind of, "Well, that was an interesting experience."' The whole sorry matter had also proved costly. In the final tally, McCartney lost nearly half a million pounds: £200,000 to refund the promoter, who had threatened to sue, with an additional £100,000 in legal bills, plus the living costs of the stranded family, band and crew, which totalled around £10,000 a day.

In the 26 January edition of *The Sun*, a headline quote from McCartney declared 'I'll Never Smoke Pot Again'. From here on in, he would certainly change his tune in terms of his public advocacy of marijuana use.

He met the press at the gates of Blossom Wood Farm. 'I'd prefer to forget this incident right now,' he told them. Asked whether he was now planning to get back to 'the English way of life' and spend time with his family, Paul tetchily responded, 'Yeah, if you fellas would leave me alone, that *would* be possible.'

The last thing Paul wanted to do, it seemed, was to get back rehearsing with the group. 'It sucked the momentum out of Wings,' says Juber. This was partly as a result of a sudden rift between McCartney and the long-serving Denny Laine, who in the wake of the debacle had returned to the UK and spent most of his time at Rock City Studios in Shepperton, recording his own solo album. Indicating his ambivalent feelings about the drama, Laine called it *Japanese Tears*, after the opening song which found him comforting a Wings fan distraught about the cancelled tour. Throughout, it transpired, the band had still been paid their weekly wage retainers, but had each lost out in the region of £50,000 in tour profits. Laine admitted he was miffed: 'I felt I was entitled to an explanation, but I never got one. He felt very sorry for himself when he came out of prison but he didn't seem to understand he'd upset a lot of people.'

McCartney next resurfaced on 30 January, when he filmed a pre-recorded tribute for a forthcoming edition of the TV show *This is Your Life*, dedicated to George Martin. Later, he talked to Paul Gambaccini for *Rolling Stone*, saying that his Japanese arrest had reminded him of when, as a kid, he would get on a train in Liverpool with a second-class ticket and sneak into a first-class compartment. 'And I *always* got caught,' he stressed.

It was clear that Paul's freewheeling years were over. 'I suppose I was treated this way because I am Paul McCartney,' he reflected, not acknowledging the fact that anyone who had tried to smuggle half a pound of dope through Japanese Customs would have been treated the same way, and, moreover, that his fame had saved him from a long prison sentence. 'It's not bad for you to be humiliated at times,' he reckoned. 'It's sort of cleansing.' At the same time, this new-found notoriety upped his cool, *Rolling Stone* naming him 'the world's most famous pot smoker'.

Looking back now, he refuses even to entertain thoughts of whether or not he could have endured a seven-year stretch in a Japanese prison.

'I'd prefer to not even let that question go round my brain,' he sighs. 'I've put it away and it's over with now.'

What effect did John dying have on you personally?

It was just a huge loss. As it was to all his mates and, in actual fact, to the rest of the world. It was a combination of the fact that he wasn't coming back, the circumstances in which he'd died, the whole futility of it all. I don't know if you ever get over those things.

14

The Wake-up Call

Linda was coming up the driveway of the Sussex farm, returning from the school run, when Paul emerged from the house. As soon as she saw his face she knew something was wrong. He was sobbing; he looked desperate. She'd never seen him in this state before.

It was the morning of Tuesday, 9 December 1980. 'He told me what had happened,' she remembered, 'and then we were both crying.'

For all their carping and sniping, bitterness and petty disgruntlement, Paul and John had been getting on better. Their relationship had progressed via a series of infrequent telephone calls that had become warmer than their scattered bursts of sharp words in the media might have suggested. During the small-talk and trivia of one conversation, early in 1980, McCartney casually asked Lennon whether he was writing songs. 'Just out of my curiosity,' Paul explained. 'He told me he was finished doing that.'

In May, *McCartney II* was released, intended as a double but, perhaps sensibly, edited down to a single album. Exploring new possibilities in video technology, Paul shot a promo for 'Coming Up', in which he played all the parts of a group named, with a nod to new wave, The Plastic Macs. Lennon would later point out that it was an ideal fantasy scenario for McCartney, since he'd essentially always wanted to be a one-man band.

For the clip, Paul dived into the dressing-up box to play out various rock archetypes: the hairy Neanderthal drummer, the spaced-out hippie guitarist, the four members of a greaser horn section. On keyboards, he mimicked the discomfitingly expressionless Ron Mael of Sparks; on second guitar, the grinning, thick-horn-rimmed Hank Marvin of The Shadows. On bass, most surprisingly, in collarless jacket and mop-top, pumping away at his old violin-shaped Höfner, he reinhabited the character of Beatle Paul, with all the woos and cutesy hair-tosses.

It was a stranger experience than he might have anticipated. 'I almost chickened out,' he admitted. 'But once I put on the old uniform, I thought, Ah well, it's a laugh, what the hell.' On the body of the bass he found taped an old Beatles set-list from their final 1966 tour that he'd forgotten was there, instantly zapping him back fourteen years. As he walked on to the set dressed as Beatle Paul, the mood among the studio technicians instantly turned buzzy; some suddenly asked him for his autograph. He found it 'a very kind of weird, exciting feeling really. I felt like I was at a TV show twenty years ago. It felt exactly the same.'

Only in the days after did he realise that, for him, it had been an exorcism of sorts. 'I'd actually gone and broken the whole voodoo of The Beatles,' he said, ''cause I'd been him again and it didn't feel bad.'

Lennon was being driven by Fred Seaman through Cold Spring Harbor, Long Island, when he first heard 'Coming Up' on the radio. 'Fuck a pig, it's Paul,' he exclaimed, before turning up the volume and nodding along. 'Not bad,' he decided at the song's conclusion. He asked Seaman to buy him a copy of *McCartney II* and set up a new stereo system in his bedroom specifically so he could listen to it. The next day, 'Coming Up' was still rattling around John's head. 'It's driving me crackers,' he told Seaman, before venturing the opinion that even if its parent album was patchy, at least Paul was back trying to do something eclectic and experimental.

While Lennon had apparently retired and disappeared, McCartney maintained his public profile and began to pile up the awards: he was named Outstanding Music Personality at the British Rock and Pop Awards, won Best Instrumental for 'Rockestra Theme' at the Grammys, and was presented with an Ivor Novello award by Yul Brynner, the star of *The Magnificent Seven* and *The King and I*. Even Linda was picking up some belated recognition, with Argentinian director Oscar Grillo's animation for her single 'Seaside Woman', released three years earlier, bagging the Palme d'Or for Best Short Film at Cannes. The McCartneys slipped into the cinema unannounced and watched the screening, quietly touched by the unexpected applause it prompted.

In France, McCartney held a press launch of sorts for *McCartney II*, handing out free LPs to journalists. He was asked by one if there was ever the chance of new Lennon/McCartney material. 'Well, I wouldn't say there would be, actually,' he replied, explaining that John had told him he had no interest in making music. 'Most of us do our jobs to arrive at a point where we no longer have to do our jobs,' he reasoned, 'and we can put our feet up and enjoy life for a change. I think John's probably reached that point.'

Secretly, in fact, John was writing again, his dormant competitive rivalry with Paul awakened after hearing *McCartney II*. In Bermuda, over the summer, the songs began to pour out of him. First came the eerily prophetic reggae of 'Borrowed Time', to be followed by the narky, fame-rejecting 'I Don't Wanna Face It' and the serene, absence-explaining 'Watching The Wheels'. If the passing of time had softened his edges, there was real self-awareness and maturity surfacing in his music, beyond the sloganeering and abstract aphorisms of the past. It was his last creative surge.

Meanwhile, Paul was still on the campaign trail. In June he shot the strange fantasy video for 'Waterfalls', in which he appeared oddly straight, his hair trimmed like a banker's, sporting beige cords and Fair Isle waistcoat, backdropped by multi-coloured fountains of water and at one point sharing the set with an eight-foot polar bear named Olaf. Revealingly, because of the Cannes success of 'Seaside Woman', Linda was on the promotional treadmill too. She informed *Woman's Own* that she and Paul were yet to make wills. Elsewhere, she told the *Daily Mirror* that the couple saved money by cutting one another's hair.

In the meantime, Paul talked to Southern Television's weekday local news programme *Day by Day*, the interviewer taking an unsettlingly prescient line of questioning in the light of what was to come, asking the singer about the problems of being an ageing rock star. No one could escape growing older, said McCartney.

'Except people like Buddy Holly and Elvis Presley,' the presenter pointed out, before hastily adding, 'Hopefully nothing like that will happen to you.'

'Sorry, what do you mean by that?' Paul interjected sharply.

'I mean they were stopped in their prime by death, right?' the presenter blundered on. 'For that reason they will always be remembered. In a sense, they're immortalised.'

'Oh yeah, I know,' Paul replied, before turning gently facetious. 'I mean, I'd rather stick around and get old than, like, be terrific and famous and die young. *Myself*, y'know. Some people like going out in a blaze of glory. I'm not one of them.'

From there, the interviewer segued into the obligatory Beatles reunion question. There was currently no chance of it, according to Paul. 'No, no, no,' he said. 'I don't think John would ever be interested in getting the group back together again.'

For his part, around the same time, in the press John dismissed the notion of a Beatles reunion as 'an illusion'. As ever, Lennon's feelings towards McCartney were highly erratic. He confessed he'd liked 'Coming Up', but thought Paul 'sounded like he was depressed' on 'Waterfalls'. 'I don't follow Wings,' he curtly told *Newsweek*. 'I don't give a shit what Wings are doing.' The journalist then apparently quoted Paul saying that, in his opinion, Lennon had gone to ground because he had done everything else in his life 'apart from be himself'. At this, Lennon exploded. 'What the hell does that mean?' he roared, accusing Paul of knowing nothing about his life during his house-husband years. 'He was as curious as everybody else was. It's ten years since I really communicated with him. I know as much about him as he knows about me, which is *zilch*.'

It wasn't entirely true, since the pair would still sometimes call one another up. On 9 October, John's 40th birthday, Lennon and McCartney talked for the last time on the phone. John had just completed most of his return album, *Double Fantasy*. Paul called in the evening and the pair – Lennon perhaps regretting his most recent caustic comments – discussed how they were always being baited to put one another down in the press.

'Do they play me against you like they play you against me?' John wondered.

'Yeah, they do,' said Paul.

In June, six months after their last rehearsals, Wings got back together for two weeks in the abandoned concert hall at Finston Manor, Tenterton, Kent. It was a lacklustre affair that found them jamming a heap of songs for possible inclusion on an album called *Hot Hits, Cold Cuts,* to be part old singles, part new tunes. It was never to be released. Instead, most of the new McCartney material was tested out in a rudimentary fashion before being squirrelled away by Paul for use on his future solo albums. Denny Laine, bored, announced he was going out on tour on his own.

Meanwhile, Paul decided to return to cartoon land, entering AIR Studios in central London and reuniting with George Martin, for the first time since 'Live And Let Die', to begin work on the soundtrack for a planned animation centred on the check-trousered *Daily Express* comic-strip character Rupert Bear. Songs worked on included *Ram* outtake 'Sunshine Sometime' and others with the kid-friendly, slightly stoned-sounding titles 'Tippi Tippi Toes' and 'Flying Horses'. Paul even revived 'The Castle Of The King Of The Birds', an ornate piano piece first tinkered around with in January 1969, during the Beatles' *Let It Be* sessions in Twickenham.

In the gaps, McCartney half-heartedly started work on a Wings album at home in Hog Hill Mill Studios. The sessions were due to relocate in the new year to George Martin's newly completed AIR studio on the Caribbean island of Montserrat. With the old Beatles producer back on the team, rumours perhaps inevitably began to percolate that John was due to join Paul there in the early months of 1981.

Not one ever to stray too far from a TV camera during this period, Paul, sitting next to Linda, made a high-profile appearance on the coast-to-coast US breakfast show *Good Morning America*, relayed live from their Sussex home. During the interview, as the power failed and the lights continually cut in and out, the McCartneys said much to host David Hartman but revealed little beyond trivialities.

Did they celebrate Thanksgiving? Yes, they did, due to Linda being American, but as vegetarians, they had a 'macaroni turkey'. Who was 'Yesterday' written about? 'Your wife,' quipped Paul, ribbing the host. Had Linda idolised Paul before she met him? No, she actually preferred John. 'No accounting for taste,' McCartney tutted. 'These women. I mean, what can you do, Dave?' How, in the face of his status as a top-flight rock star, did the family manage to maintain a reasonably normal lifestyle? 'We've got a ridiculously small house with four kids in two bedrooms, would you believe?' Paul volunteered, referring to the circular Waterfall house where the six were still living as they waited for McCartney's plans for the new-build to be approved. 'So by doing things like that, just not living with a big style, it seems to naturally keep pretty close and intimate.'

It was 27 November, only twelve days before the looming tragedy. The interviewer turned to the subject of Lennon's apparently lingering resentment of McCartney. Recognising the fact that John might be up and watching at home in New York, Paul's response was cautious, and at the same time untypically frank.

'After all of that stuff that has gone down over the years,' he said, 'I actually kinda keep a bit quiet now. 'Cause, I mean, anything I say, he gets resentful of. So I dunno, really, it's just a weird one. I don't quite know why he thinks like that. I mean, what do you do about that?'

On 8 December, his final day, Lennon, doing an interview for RKO Radio, performed a public volte-face as regards McCartney, recognising him, along with Ono, as being the major creative collaborator of his life. 'There's only been two artists I've ever worked with for more than a one-night stand, as it were,' he said. 'That's Paul McCartney and Yoko. I think that's a pretty damn good choice. As a talent scout, I've done pretty damn well.'

Later there would be some comfort found in the fact that his final words on Paul were ones of positivity, approaching some kind of love.

The call came in just before nine on the morning of the ninth. Steve Shrimpton from MPL phoned Paul in Sussex to break the horrific news that John had been murdered in New York, just under five hours earlier; shot by a deranged fan on the street outside the Dakota, before taking his last, stumbling steps into the concierge's office. The details, at this point, remained sketchy.

The news had first flashed up on Reuters at 4.55 a.m. UK time. Five minutes later, grave announcements were made in the 5 a.m. radio bulletins.

Neither of the McCartneys could ever quite remember the words Paul used when breaking the news to Linda. 'I just sort of see the image,' Linda said later. 'It's like a picture . . . a snapshot. Soul's camera.'

McCartney, distraught, phoned his brother Mike. 'Paul was too distressed to talk properly,' he recalled. 'He just said, "Keep sending the good vibes down from Liverpool", to help him through the day.'

Paul didn't know what to do with himself. Dazed, and due to be recording in AIR London with George Martin that day, he made the decision to go ahead with the session. At 11.30 a.m. he was driven out of the gates of Blossom Wood Farm, telling the waiting reporters 'I just can't take it in at the moment.' Later he would try to explain why he'd thought it was appropriate to travel to the studio: 'I was in shock. We all went to work that day . . . to not be sitting at home, is the truth.'

Upon arrival at AIR, McCartney and George Martin, as the latter remembered, 'fell on each other's shoulders, and we poured ourselves tea and whisky and sat around and drank and talked and talked.' Clearly, for Paul, there was some security to be found in being with his and Lennon's one-time father figure. 'We grieved for John all day,' said Martin, 'and it helped.'

Denny Laine was there, and naturally had wondered whether McCartney would show up at all. A physically shaken Paul told him, 'I just don't know what to think.' Always utterly thrown by death, he was in a state of emotional paralysis. 'Even at the best of times,' said Denny, 'he wasn't really too articulate when it came to expressing how he felt about things.' As ever, McCartney turned to his music.

Everyone attempted to do some work on a track, the appropriately titled 'Rainclouds', the lyric of which found the singer pleading for the dark formations above his head to be blown away. Of course, little progress was made with the recording. Paddy Moloney of traditional Irish folk group The Chieftains had flown in from Dublin that day to add uilleann pipes to the song. Paul said to him that Lennon's death was 'tragic and useless and didn't make sense', while looking utterly stunned.

'There was a kind of unspoken sadness,' Moloney said. 'It was subtle, and there wasn't any crying or moping about. I don't think it had really sunk in yet. I don't think at the end of the session that it had really penetrated either . . . that John was dead, gone forever.'

At the end of one attempt at a take, McCartney and Laine were standing beside an enormous floor-to-ceiling window overlooking Oxford Circus when a green lorry painted with the words Lennon's Furnishings passed by below.

'Oh God, look at that,' said Denny, before noticing McCartney's eyes were filling with tears.

'I'll tell you one thing, man,' Paul confided in him. 'I'll never fall out with *anyone* again in my life for that amount of time and face the possibility of them dying before I get a chance to square it with them.'

Later in the afternoon, he called Yoko in New York. McCartney remembers that Ono 'was crying and cut-up and had no idea why anyone should want to do this.' She told him how warmly John had often talked about him in private. 'It was almost as if she sensed that I was wondering whether the relationship had snapped.' Later, he would look back on his last conversation with Lennon and realise 'we were still the best of mates'.

Leaving the studio at the end of the day, McCartney offered short responses to the questions of the journalists who had been standing all day on the pavement in Oxford Street. He said that he'd been in the studio 'just listening to stuff . . . I just didn't want to sit at home.' One, inanely, asked why. 'I just didn't feel like it,' Paul responded, obviously irritated. As he made to leave, his final comment to the reporters was: 'It's a drag, isn't it?'

'I probably should've said, "It's the world's most unholiest . . . worst-ever drag . . . in the universe",' he says now. 'Y'know, that might have explained what I was thinking a bit better. But I just sort of said, "It's a drag." And that came out very flippant. It wasn't flippant. And anyone who saw me on that day knows it wasn't.'

The words would haunt McCartney for years. More than flippant, in the light of the deep shock and open grief that was spreading around the world, his lasting comment in reaction to the death of Lennon was seen as offhand, uncaring and even callous. When this brief but provocative statement began to filter out, Paul was instantly damned by the media. 'I felt every inch for him,' said George Martin. 'He was unwise, but he was off his guard.'

Paul tried to put out the media fire by issuing his own statement: 'I have hidden myself in my work today. But it keeps flashing into my mind. I feel shattered, angry and very sad.' He acknowledged that John had often been rude about him in the press, but said that 'I secretly admired him for it. There was no question that we weren't friends. I really loved the guy.' He concluded by saying that his late friend would be remembered in future years as an international statesman, whose 'Give Peace A Chance' had helped to hasten the end of the Vietnam war. 'He often looked a loony to many people. He made enemies, but he was fantastic. He was a warm man who cared a lot.'

Later that night, back at home in Sussex, the McCartneys and the kids sat and, like the rest of the world, watched the news reports on TV. As music industry pundits began to turn up onscreen, offering their in-depth analysis, Paul began to feel his anger rising. 'I thought it was well tasteless,' he said. 'Jesus Christ, ready with the answers, aren't we? Aren't we just ready with a summary?' Ultimately, of course, he was enraged by the fact that these journalists were being relatively eloquent in their tributes to Lennon, when he had been awkward and inarticulate. 'They were the ones who came off good because they said suitably meaningful things,' he sadly points out. 'I was the idiot who said, "It's a drag."'

He raged against the now identified killer, if impotently and still somehow inexpressibly: 'I remember screaming that Mark Chapman was the jerk of all jerks. I felt so robbed and emotional. It was crazy. It was anger. It was fear. It was madness. It was the world coming to an end.'

Finally, behind closed doors, he allowed himself to break down. 'I wept like a baby,' he says. 'It was a heavy personal blow.'

These days you pay tribute to both John and George in your live shows. What goes through your mind when you play those songs? Are you aware of the heightened emotion in the crowd?

You're not as aware of it as the people in the audience are. But you're aware of a feeling. The nice thing is it's a common feeling, 'cause it's you and them feeling it. Obviously when I do 'Here Today' or 'Something', I'm thinking of John or George. There's an inherent emotion in those songs. The music just touches a raw nerve.

15

End of the Road

The day after the world learned of the death of John Lennon, there was a pheasant shoot in the forest near Blossom Wood Farm. Linda was forced to go outside, locate the hunters and have a quiet word that, in the circumstances, the sound of gunfire was the last thing the McCartneys wanted to hear.

Paul was in a fogged state of disbelief. The next time he left the farm, it was for the MPL Christmas lunch in London where, understandably, it was hard to rouse the festive spirit. 'There was a lot of sadness there,' says Laurence Juber. 'It was overshadowed by not only the fact that Paul had lost his musical soulmate, but also there was a certain kind of threat to the fact that, if somebody could assassinate John, they could also do the same to Paul.'

The fear of being next was never far away. 'Paul,' said Linda, 'was in so much pain', and he found it hard to shake the dread that he or a member of the family might be targeted. It was an anxiety he shared, naturally, with the other two surviving Beatles. 'That was a question that was whipping around the three of us,' McCartney admitted. 'Like, are you next?'

Inevitably, perhaps, there were bizarre threats coming in from unhinged individuals. There was one report that a stalker carrying a knife had been caught attempting to break on to the McCartneys' estate. From here on in, Paul and the family were always accompanied by security guards. Laurence Juber dropped by AIR London in January 1981 to find the singer's every move being shadowed by heavies. 'Somebody had been making death threats in New York,' he remembers. 'It was scary.'

Linda explained to her friend, Danny Fields, that the family were forced to maintain a low profile, more for the sake of the children than anything else. 'There were some nuts,' she told him, 'but we had to take them seriously. We have so much more security around us now. Our lives have really changed.'

As time wore on, however, Paul realised that – having never allowed his fame to hamper or hinder him in the past, in taking a determinedly ordinary approach to his everyday life – living behind a wall of security was not for him.

'There are crazy people everywhere,' he reasoned. 'I was really worried for a few weeks afterwards. But I couldn't really live like that. My attitude is to try and push it out of my mind.'

As planned, on 1 February 1981, the McCartneys flew to Montserrat to continue work on the next album, with Denny Laine, but notably without Laurence Juber and Steve Holley, indicating that Wings were once again reduced to their core trio, at least for studio purposes. Back at the helm was George Martin, the thinking being that the producer's old-fashioned record-making values would ensure tighter quality control over the material. There had been moments of inspiration on *Back To The Egg*, while *McCartney II* had worked as a creatively liberating experience. But still, Paul rightly acknowledged that there had been something lacking in his most recent albums.

While the previous trips to far-flung destinations had allowed him a window of escape, in the light of Lennon's murder there was to be no such relief on Montserrat. Constantly shadowing him on the island were the paparazzi, tailing him in cars and on scooters. It was the first time he'd experienced this kind of behaviour – to be expected perhaps in London, Paris or New York – in what was essentially a holiday setting, and it riled him. He tried to ram them with his hired Jeep, calling them 'monsters'.

Over the coming weeks, a parade of invited musicians arrived at the Caribbean studio. A fortnight in, Ringo showed up with his new girlfriend and soon-to-be wife, actress Barbara Bach, adding his rolling drum parts to McCartney's future single, the sunny 'Take It Away'. Following him five days later was rockabilly musician Carl Perkins, a hero to the nascent Beatles, who traded lines with Paul in the skiffle swing of 'Get It'. The American, like others before him, was impressed by the McCartneys' apparent normality and familial closeness. 'We tried the jet set, Carl, and it's plastic,' Paul told him. Next flew in Stevie Wonder, to make a cameo appearance on the synthy funk of 'What's That You're Doing' and duet with McCartney on the race-blurring 'Ebony And Ivory'. As time passed, it was clear that the record was becoming less a Wings album and more of a solo outing, exploring the burgeoning 1980s trend for major-name collaborations.

Not surprisingly, then, Denny Laine felt increasingly sidelined and undervalued. His dwindling creative influence aside, he was annoyed that once again Jo Jo hadn't been allowed to come on the excursion. At the same time, he was stewing over his perceived lack of financial reward for his contribution to McCartney's output over the previous ten years. He flew home, peeved and disillusioned.

When the sessions returned to AIR in London, one day early in March, Laine simply didn't turn up. Trevor Jones and then John Hammel both placed calls to his house, with the guitarist refusing to come to the phone. Then Paul rang and spoke to Jo Jo, who told him, with no little satisfaction, that Denny had 'asked me to give you and everyone else the message' that he wasn't coming back. After a decade of loyal service, Laine was quitting.

'It was obvious we wouldn't tour again,' Denny said at the

time, by way of explanation. 'But touring is the purpose of being in the business as far as I'm concerned.' Laine knew, of course, that essentially McCartney was making another solo album and Wings probably wouldn't survive. In truth, he jumped before he was pushed.

'It would've been Wings, plus all these other names,' he said of the record that was to become *Tug Of War*. 'But it became his album because I left and there was no Wings any more.'

In private, though, George Martin had been encouraging McCartney to drop the façade of the band and release the album under his own name. 'The idea of working with Wings again . . . in truth, it would have just been limiting, I thought,' said Paul. 'And George agreed. I slightly blamed it on him a bit. Only a bit though.'

In the last week of April, the Associated Press agency got wind of the split and issued the following story.

'Ex-Beatle Paul McCartney, who formed the group Wings after The Beatles split up in 1970, is now facing problems with his band. Denny Laine, the band's drummer [*sic*] since it was formed in 1971, quit suddenly on Tuesday in a disagreement over McCartney's decision to halt the group's public appearances temporarily. The departure left only two members of the group, McCartney and his wife Linda. "There is no row," said Laine's manager Brian Adams. "But Denny likes to tour and Paul has decided that Wings will not make any tour plans for the future."

'Laine, 36, decided to quit the group during a recent recording session in the West Indies, where the next Wings album was made. McCartney halted public appearances because he had received several death threats since the murder in New York of fellow ex-Beatle John Lennon on Dec 8. A McCartney spokesman denied the report, adding that Wings would still exist.'

This official denial was merely a delaying tactic, of course. Steve Holley, having read of the break-up in the *Evening Standard*, phoned McCartney to ask him if it was true that the band was over.

'Uh, yeah, I've been meaning to call you,' Paul said.

'It was just horrible the way it went out,' says Holley. 'Even though every fibre of my body was telling me that it was going to happen, it was awful.'

For Juber, there was a sense of missed opportunity. The guitarist feels that if the bust in Japan had never happened, then the group would have gone on to tour America successfully in the summer of 1980, establishing *Back To The Egg* as a major as opposed to minor album. 'Then,' he reasons, 'Wings would have gone out with a bang, rather than a whimper.'

Denny, rehearsing with his new band at Rock City Studios in Shepperton, talked to the press to confirm that the schism had been created by McCartney's refusal to tour. One prying reporter, exploiting the apparent fall-out, asked Laine if, as the gossip suggested, Paul was a difficult man to work with. 'Well, I've had my moments,' the guitarist offered, as if leaving much unsaid.

The key problem, as Laine saw it, was that McCartney was too famous to tour on a relatively normal level, without the accompanying hoopla his presence attracted. 'Because of who he is,' he says today, 'that was one of the drawbacks really. I was ready to go out and do my own thing.'

In truth, it was only half the story. During this period, Laine was suffering from various problems in his personal life. At a Mayfair nightclub he was involved in a tussle with Jock McDonald, singer with punk band the Bollock Brothers, the matter resolved without charges being brought. Following that, he crashed his Ferrari into a fence. 'I don't seem to be having much luck lately,' he noted at the time. Then, far more seriously, Jo Jo Laine suffered a drug overdose at the couple's home in Laleham, Surrey, after her father – shot and paralysed two years before by her schizophrenic brother – died in America. She was rushed to hospital, where she made a full recovery.

The couple's marriage had already been in trouble, exacerbated by Jo Jo being left behind in England while her husband was in the Caribbean. At the time, Laine blamed the McCartneys: 'Paul and Linda's refusal to allow Jo Jo on Montserrat went a long way to destroying my marriage.' Upon Denny's return from the *Tug Of War* sessions, Jo Jo confessed that she had been unfaithful to him with John Townley, a singer signed to EMI. 'I'd always denied any affairs I'd had,' she said, 'but this one I was open about.'

The feud between McCartney and Laine was to go public, the former pointing out that the latter had quit the group, saying that he missed playing live, and yet hadn't been on the road since leaving. 'But that was my problem,' says Denny. 'It was hard for me to go out and play live after Wings, like it was hard for him to play live after The Beatles. It's very difficult when you've been in a big band. I couldn't go out doing Moody Blues material. You want to move forward.'

Only much later, in the face of ongoing accusations of his financial tightness, did McCartney address Laine's money grumbles about his time in Wings, saying that there were receipts in the MPL office for over a million pounds paid to the guitarist down the years. 'Now, you tell me a guy in any group who got that for the period we were together,' Paul argued. 'If you think I sound mean after that, I've got to disagree with you. I mean, these people like Denny Laine, "He didn't pay us enough". Well, what I think is, Yeah, well, I did. I know exactly what I paid him. It's a million.'

From the perspective of one unnamed former Wings employee, Denny was paid more than the other group members to act as

Paul's second-in-command, keeping the band on an even keel, particularly when sailing through stormier waters: 'He was the go-between. But he didn't really share the McCartney family circle. Denny was his own man, and unfortunately Jo Jo didn't see eye to eye with Linda.'

Later, living in Spain, Denny fell in with a couple of journalists who offered to write a biography of him. He says the pair absconded to London and filleted their interview transcripts for the juiciest details before selling them to *The Sun* without his knowledge or approval. The revelations were of the lurid and druggy variety – Paul and Linda spent over £1,000 a week on weed, smoking joints 'the way ordinary people smoke cigarettes'; they smuggled dope through an airport in the hood of toddler James's coat; Paul's head was so clouded by the stuff that, due to chronic indecision, his albums took forever to make.

Worse, perhaps, Laine claimed that in all of his time with McCartney, he got no closer to knowing the real and 'complex' Paul. 'Even though I've written countless songs with him and we've been stoned together hundreds of times,' he was quoted as saying, 'I still don't feel I am very close to him. He is the best person I've met in all my life at hiding his feelings.'

In the wake of the apparent exposé, the McCartneys largely kept schtum, although Linda was to venture the opinion that 'so much of it is rubbish. I thought Denny came off badly. I could see some girlfriend or an ex-chauffeur writing such rubbish, but a musician?'

Looking back today, Denny insists, 'We never fell out. Nothing like that. But it certainly looked like we did.'

In the final reckoning, Wings had proved to be a long and difficult endeavour. 'To me,' Paul said, 'there was always a feeling of letdown, because The Beatles had been so big that anything I did had to compare directly with them.' Linda, controversially, given her own musical struggles, declared that none of the members of the group, across all of the line-ups, had ever been accomplished enough to work with an increasingly frustrated McCartney, who was forced to carry their weight. 'They were good,' she said, 'but not great.'

The death of Lennon, meanwhile, had caused the remaining ex-Beatles to turn reflective about their relationships with one another. In a reunion of sorts, McCartney and Starr were to come together to play on Harrison's playful Lennon reminiscence 'All Those Years Ago', the first time all three had appeared together on record in more than ten years. Parts of *Tug Of War* revealed more of Paul's own feelings about John. The title track concerned itself with the push and pull of competitive relationships, while the highly emotional, 'Yesterday'-echoing 'Here Today' was clearly directed at his lost friend.

One verse recalled an event in September 1964, during the first Beatles US tour, when their flight to Jacksonville, Florida, was diverted to Key West in order to avoid the destructive path of Hurricane Dora. Grounded, and with a rare evening off, Paul and John sat up all night and got drunk and bared their souls to one another, ending up in tears. McCartney said that while writing the ballad he imagined a cloud parting in the sky above his head and Lennon blowing a raspberry at him. 'This is what the song is, y'know,' he said. 'I'm sort of saying, "Even though you blow that raspberry, I really did know you."'

'Songwriting is like psychiatry,' he went on, possibly disclosing more about his creative urge than he had ever done before. 'You sit down and dredge up something that's deep inside and bring it out front. And I just had to really say, "I love you, John." I think being able to say things like that in songs can keep you sane.'

After the shock of Lennon's passing, and the sobering lesson of Japan, the McCartneys' hunger for travelling the world as a merry band was gone. Ten years in, particularly for Paul, the desire for constant forward motion had finally subsided. 'We just thought,' he said, 'we've done it now.' In reality, of course, post-Tokyo, there was every likelihood that securing visas for many territories was set to be a long, involved and painful process, and possibly one it was best to avoid.

Mission accomplished, more or less, the couple returned to their now semi-permanent base in Sussex. There Paul could record, free from pressure or worry, at his studio, while Linda wandered around on the farm, tending the horses, taking pictures. If the McCartneys were hankering for a quieter, more self-sufficient life, here was their chance. After all, he was still only 38, his wife 39.

'Really, I try to lead a pretty normal life,' he said, repeating a familiar refrain, before revealing a certain truth. 'The only abnormality is being Paul McCartney.'

In just over ten years, he had come full circle. Here he was, doing it all over again: splitting with his band, making a record by himself, disappearing with his family.

In the summer of 1981, the ramshackle cottage on the hill at Blossom Wood Farm was torn down to make way for the building of the new house, plotted, as everything was, to McCartney's design.

It would be another eight years before he would tour again. For Paul, for now, it was the end of the road.

Epilogue

Almost 30 years later, in his office at MPL in London, Paul was talking about Linda. Following her death from breast cancer, aged 56, on 17 April 1998 at the ranch in Arizona, McCartney was obviously devastated. He laid low for close to a year, before emerging creatively re-energised and seemingly ever more determined to make some of his best music since the 1970s.

In 2007, with *Memory Almost Full*, it appeared as though he had paid coded tribute to Linda, a perhaps over-studious fan having worked out that its name could be reshuffled into an anagram that read: 'For my soulmate LLM', the initials standing for Linda Louise McCartney. In truth, the title came from a message that flashed up on McCartney's phone, which he felt held a certain poetic quality, particularly in his advancing years.

'It's such a clever anagram,' he said. 'At first, I thought, Maybe I won't tell anyone I didn't know it was there, just let 'em guess, y'know. It was very weird. I found out about it on the anniversary of Linda's passing when my eldest daughter told me about it. She said, "Thanks for that dedication, Dad, that's great." I said, "What d'you mean, babe?" She said, "The anagram." I thought, What's she talking about? She told me and I said, "God, that's pretty spooky." She said, "I'll tell you what's spooky, is you didn't know about it. It would be pretty spooky anyway that you could get that anagram out of it. But the fact that you didn't even know about it . . ."'

He paused mid-sentence as suddenly, outside, there was a loud bang that sounded like a gunshot.

When a second explosive crack quickly followed, McCartney was up on his feet and over to the window. 'Murder in Soho!' he exclaimed. 'Shock horror!'

'It's probably just a car backfiring,' I said as I joined him to look down over Soho Square, seeing nothing.

'Probably is,' he said, distracted, if not visibly nervous.

'I'll protect you, Paul,' I joked, pretending to fling myself in front of him. 'I'll take the bullet.'

He laughed and turned to his publicist Stuart Bell, sitting in a corner of the room. 'Oh alright,' McCartney grinned. 'OK, then. You heard that, Stu.'

'Actually, I won't,' I added. 'I'm just being nice.'

'"Yeah, you can take it, Paul,"' he said, putting imaginary words in my mouth. '"Go on then . . ."'

We sat back down and McCartney picked up his conversational thread.

When he talked about Linda, he was in turns protective of her memory and wistful about what might have appeared to be minor recollections.

In the early 1990s a bootlegged tape had done the rounds, featuring her vocal cruelly isolated from the mixing desk at a live show as she sang along to 'Hey Jude' and failed to hit the notes. 'It was dreadful,' he admitted. 'She'd sort of go, "Oh, Jesus Christ", when she heard it. And it was mean, whoever did it. You couldn't get it back. It was one of these things, where she'd be [*clapping above his head*] the crowd leader in the band. But, y'know, you just had to take all that stuff.'

At the same time he remembered their frequent drives in their Mercedes up to AIR London from Sussex, where they would phone ahead to a Chinese restaurant en route and order veggie spring rolls to collect. 'Great memories of that,' he nodded. As trivial as this perhaps seemed, it held a certain poignancy: for all his wealth and fame and power, Paul, of course, couldn't bring back Linda and relive the simpler pleasures the couple enjoyed.

The mock-gunfire incident had maybe served to illustrate a point that I was now a bit nervous about bringing up. When he didn't tour for most of the 1980s, some people assumed it was because he was scared to appear in public after Lennon's murder. Was there any truth in that?

'No, y'know,' he said, dismissively. 'We've said already, people speculate about anything. They always credit me with motives that I haven't even dreamed of. It's kind of interesting really, the way they sort of *perceive* my life and analyse it for me. I just find it very strange. 'Cause they're hardly ever right. In that case, I never thought about touring much. People used to say to me, "Oh, it's ten years since you've toured." I'd go, "*Is it?*" What was I doing? I dunno. Bringing up kids, writing some songs, going on holiday. I just know that I haven't done it for a little while. That's all that was really. I don't know why. Maybe I didn't fancy it.'

'But, understandably,' I added, 'after the circumstances of John's death . . .'

'That's the least likely explanation,' he said, cutting in before I could finish the sentence. 'I didn't give up touring 'cause I was scared to. It wasn't that. It was just 'cause I didn't fancy it. I can't remember, to tell you the truth. I didn't have a band, probably. I think that was the reason, if you think about it. I mean, it's pretty straightforward really. Why didn't he tour? 'Cause he hasn't got a band.'

'You can always find a band though, can't you, Paul?' I pointed out.

'You can,' he replied, a touch abruptly. 'If you can be bothered. But I don't suppose I could be bothered.'

He accepted that, over time, he had been forced to recognise that he could never find a replacement for Lennon as a songwriting partner, having tried to form subsequent creative partnerships with both Eric Stewart of 10cc and Elvis Costello.

'I think the inevitable thing that I realised,' he said, 'and that I sort of knew all along, was that John was an impossible act to follow. He and I were just so sort of natural and read each other and did such good work . . . he said modestly.'

'I think you can cut yourself some slack there,' I offered.

'But to pick up that ball and run with it is very difficult for anyone,' he continued. 'So I did a little bit of collaboration, but obviously none of it could match up to working with John, which was just the magic mix. We just fell into it. We were kids, we learned how to do it together. We read each other, y'know. I knew where he was going, he knew where I was going. We corrected each other and directed each other. So that was the thing. What John brought to the collaboration was unique. And I think what I brought to the collaboration was unique. We just happened to hit it.'

It was clear McCartney had no regrets about some of the weirder choices and stranger records he made in the 1970s. Ultimately, he just shrugged them off.

'I think the more sophisticated people or the more hardcore rock'n'roll fans were going, "*What* is he *on*? I'll have some of those drugs",' he laughed. 'I mean, people still do think of it like that. "What was it, man? There must have been some special . . . substance he had to make him to do that." But really, y'know, I don't embarrass myself by stepping out of the box. I almost don't notice myself doing it.'

We returned to the idea that he really has no grasp of how people perceive him, which in many ways, is a blessing. 'I get some feedback,' he said. 'And some people'll talk about my composing history and might be very flattering. Then some people will just sort of say, "I think a lot of what he's done's rubbish." So . . . I don't know. I hear these opinions and I just carry on regardless. I'm not gonna let any of that stuff affect me, 'cause I just do what I think is right at a given time. And it may or may not be right. But I don't care if it's wrong. 'Cause it's what I have to do. It's what I *fancy* doing.'

He has always been, he stressed, a man without a career plan. 'I don't think of myself as someone with a *career*,' he said, as if the word brought a nasty taste to his mouth. 'I just think of myself as someone who likes to have a go at various things. I'm certainly not one of these people who's really clever and goes, "Well, I can't do that because that will ruin my image." I don't even know what my image is. I'm making it up as I go along.'

If McCartney spent the 1970s trying to outrun the ghost of his Beatles past, it proved to be an impossible task. Over the years he was slowly to come to terms with his legacy, introducing more and more Beatles songs into his live repertoire, while gently kicking against the virtual canonisation of John Lennon.

Sometimes the latter seemed petty and pointless, such as when, on his 2002 live album *Back In The US*, he controversially reversed the Lennon/McCartney credits on many Beatles songs to reflect the fact that he had made a greater contribution to the composition, consequently provoking the ire of Yoko Ono. Nevertheless, in settling scores and tidying up the truth, he was, in effect, keeping his and John's rivalry alive, much as Lennon would surely have done had he lived.

I asked him if he believed, post-Beatles, that he'd had the respect he deserved?

'I dunno, man,' he said. 'I think on and off, yeah. Sometimes

I think, Yes I have, sometimes, I haven't. But I don't necessarily think I deserve anything. I'm not one of those people, "How dare you? Do you know who I am?" It's like, Hey man, if you don't dig it, fine by me. You don't have to like me. But if you do, I'd probably prefer it. Like anyone.

'But I would never say I've not had the respect I deserve. It's too pompous to say that. If I do something right and someone likes it, cool. And I'm always trying to get it right. It doesn't always come off. But it won't have a large bearing on my next attempt.

'My *career* is certainly not carefully considered,' he stated breezily. 'And I think that's probably quite obvious.'

Looking back, he said, for him his time in the 1970s represented achievement.

'Achieving the impossible, really,' he emphasised, before remembering the words of those critics who rejected the idea that he would ever create anything that could be held up against the golden light of The Beatles. 'It had always been, "You can't do that, that's not gonna be possible." I *slightly* believed that and thought, Yeah, but I want to be in music, so I'm gonna have to do *something*, and this is my best shot.

'But, y'know, it was doubtful. So the idea of actually achieving that impossible target, by *Band On The Run* and by the tour of 1976, was great. It was very gratifying, and the other thing was, I'd taken along my missus, who had no stage experience whatsoever, but who had agreed to accompany me on this adventure. And it was a wacky thing. But, come on, man, we were hippies.

'So it was nice that even against all odds and all of the trials we went through – and there were a few – that suddenly we found that we'd done it . . . we'd cracked it.'

I wondered how he felt the period had changed him.

'I suppose it taught me to be a bit independent,' he said.

'Calmed me down a bit. 'Cause it was kind of frightening leaving The Beatles, I think, for all of us, to some degree. So to just come out of that period was a good thing. I survived.'

We were done and began to say our goodbyes.

'Escort this man from the building,' McCartney instructed one of his assistants with a smile, shaking my hand firmly. Five minutes later, we bumped into one another again two floors down in the MPL reception area, Paul struggling to open the front door while wrestling with an unwieldy pile of papers.

As we stepped on to the pavement together, McCartney heading for a black people-carrier with smoked windows, he paused to reconsider everything we'd talked about.

'Hope I don't end up coming off like the world's greatest nutter,' he grinned. 'And if I do, then that'll be good for my image.' A mischievous glint could suddenly be detected in those world-famous eyes. 'Give them something to think about.'

And with those parting words left hanging in the air, Paul McCartney, former hippie renegade turned knight of the realm, walked away, leaving the past behind him.

Selected Discography

ALBUMS

PAUL McCARTNEY

McCartney
UK: Apple PCS 7102, 17 April 1970
US: Apple STAO 3363, 20 April 1970
Reissued: Commercial Marketing B004WJRF6C, 13 June 2011
The Lovely Linda/That Would Be Something/Valentine Day/Every Night/
    Hot As Sun/Glasses/Junk/Man We Was Lonely/Oo You/Momma Miss
    America/Teddy Boy/Singalong Junk/Maybe I'm Amazed/Kreen-Akore

McCartney II
UK: Parlophone PCTC258, 16 May 1980
US: Columbia FC-36511, 22 May 1980
Reissued: Commercial Marketing B004WJREMW, 13 June 2011
Coming Up/Temporary Secretary/On The Way/Waterfalls/Nobody Knows/
    Front Parlour/Summer's Day Song/Frozen Jap/Bogey Music/Darkroom/
    One Of These Days

Tug Of War
UK: Parlophone PCTC259, 26 April 1982
US: Columbia TC37462, 26 April 1982
Reissued: Parlophone B000005RT9 9 August 1993
Tug Of War/Take It Away/Somebody Who Cares/What's That You're Doing/
    Here Today/Ballroom Dancing/The Pound Is Sinking/Wanderlust/Get It/
    Be What You See (Link)/Dress Me Up As A Robber/Ebony And Ivory

PAUL AND LINDA McCARTNEY

Ram

UK: Apple PAS 10003, 21 May 1971

US: Apple SMAS 3375, 17 May 1971

Reissued: Commercial Marketing B007L96VCY, 21 May 2012

Too Many People/3 Legs/Ram On/Dear Boy/Uncle Albert-Admiral Halsey/ Smile Away/Heart Of The Country/Monkberry Moon Delight/Eat At Home/Long Haired Lady/Ram On/The Back Seat Of My Car

PAUL McCARTNEY AND WINGS

Red Rose Speedway

UK: Apple PCTC251, 4 May 1973

US: Apple SMAL3409, 30 April 1973

Reissued: Parlophone B000000721M, 7 June 1993

Big Barn Bed/My Love/Get On The Right Thing/One More Kiss/Little Lamb Dragonfly/Single Pigeon/When The Night/Loup (1st Indian On The Moon)/Medley: Hold Me Tight, Lazy Dynamite, Hands Of Love, Power Cut

Band On The Run

UK: Apple PAS10007, 7 December 1973

US: Apple SO3415, 5 December 1973

Reissued: COMMERCIAL MARKETING B003XX2O8C, 1 November 2010

Band On The Run/Jet/Bluebird/Mrs Vandebilt/Let Me Roll It/Mamunia/ No Words/Picasso's Last Words (Drink To Me)/Nineteen Hundred And Eighty Five

WINGS

Wild Life

UK: Apple PCS 7142, 3 December 1971

US: Apple SW 3386, 7 December 1971

Reissued: Parlophone B000005RPU, 7 June 1993

Mumbo/Bip Bop/Love Is Strange/Wild Life/Some People Never Know/I Am Your Singer/Bip Bop Link*/Tomorrow/Dear Friend/Mumbo Link*

*Reissues only

Venus And Mars

UK: Capitol PCTC 254, 30 May 1975

US: Capitol SMAS 11419, 27 May 1975

Reissued: Parlophone B000007210, 7 June 1993

Venus And Mars/Rock Show/Love In Song/You Gave Me The Answer/
Magneto And Titanium Man/Letting Go/Venus And Mars Reprise/Spirits
Of Ancient Egypt/Medicine Jar/Call Me Back Again/Listen To What The
Man Said/Treat Her Gently/Lonely Old People/Crossroads Theme

Wings At The Speed Of Sound

UK: Parlophone PAS10010, 26 March 1976

US: Capitol SW11525, 25 March 1976

Reissued: Parlophone B000007221C, 7 June 1993

Let 'Em In/The Note You Never Wrote/She's My Baby/Beware My Love/
Wino Junko/Silly Love Songs/Cook Of The House/Time To Hide/Must
Do Something About It/San Ferry Anne/Warm And Beautiful

Wings Over America

UK: Parlophone PCSP 720, 10 December 1976

US: Capitol SWCO 11593, 11 December 1976

Reissued: Capitol B000007638, 19 February 1990/HRM-34338-02 May
2013

Venus And Mars/Rock Show/Jet/Let Me Roll It/Spirits Of Ancient Egypt/
Medicine Jar/Maybe I'm Amazed/Call Me Back Again/Lady Madonna/The
Long And Winding Road/Live And Let Die/Picasso's Last Words (Drink To
Me)/Richard Cory/Bluebird/I've Just Seen A Face/Blackbird/Yesterday/You
Gave Me The Answer/Magneto And Titanium Man/Go Now/My Love/
Listen To What The Man Said/Let 'Em In/Time To Hide/Silly Love Songs/
Beware My Love/Letting Go/Band On The Run/Hi Hi Hi/Soily

London Town

UK: Parlophone PAS 10012, 31 March 1978

US: Capitol SW11777, 31 March 1978

Reissued: Parlophone B000007221I, 7 June 1993

London Town/Café On The Left Bank/I'm Carrying/Backwards Traveller-
Cuff Link/Children Children/Girlfriend/I've Had Enough/With A Little
Luck/Famous Groupies/Deliver Your Children/Name And Address/Don't
Let It Bring You Down/Morse Moose And The Grey Goose

Wings Greatest
UK: Parlophone PCTC256, 2 November 1978
US: Capitol SOO11905, 13 November 1978
Reissued: Parlophone B000002U8M, 7 June 1993
Another Day/Silly Love Songs/Live And Let Die/Junior's Farm/With A
    Little Luck/Band On The Run/Uncle Albert-Admiral Halsey/Hi Hi Hi/
    Let 'Em In/My Love/Jet/Mull Of Kintyre

Back To The Egg
UK: Parlophone PCTC257, 11 June 1979
US: Columbia 3-11020, 8 June 1979
Reissued: Parlophone B000000721D 9 August 1993
Reception/Getting Closer/We're Open Tonight/Spin It On/Again And Again
    And Again/Old Siam, Sir/Arrow Through Me/Rockestra Theme/To You/
    After The Ball/Million Miles/Winter Rose/Love Awake/The Broadcast/So
    Glad To See You Here/Baby's Request

SINGLES

PAUL McCARTNEY
Another Day/Oh Woman Oh Why
UK: Apple R 5889, 19 February 1971
US: Apple 1829, 22 February 1971

Wonderful Christmastime/Rudolph The Red-Nosed Reggae
UK: Parlophone R6029, 16 November 1979
US: Columbia 1-111162, 20 November 1979

Coming Up/Coming Up (Live – Paul McCartney And Wings)
UK: Parlophone R6035, 11 April 1980
US: Columbia 1-11263, 15 April 1980

Waterfalls/Check My Machine
UK: Parlophone R6037, 14 June 1980
US: Columbia 1-11335, 22 July 1980

Temporary Secretary/Secret Friend (Ltd. Edition Twelve Inch)
UK: Parlophone 12R6039, 15 September 1980

(With Stevie Wonder)
Ebony And Ivory/Rainclouds
UK: Parlophone R6054, 29 March 1982
US: Columbia 18-02860, 2 April 1982

Take It Away/I'll Give You A Ring
UK: Parlophone R6056, 21 June 1982
US: Columbia 18-03018, 29 June 1982

Tug Of War/Get It (with Carl Perkins)
UK: Parlophone R6057, 20 September 1982
US: Columbia 38-03235, 14 September 1982

PAUL AND LINDA McCARTNEY
The Back Seat Of My Car/Heart Of The Country
UK: Apple R 5914, 13 August 1971

Uncle Albert-Admiral Halsey/Too Many People
US: Apple 1837, 2 August 1971

PAUL McCARTNEY AND WINGS
My Love/The Mess
UK: Apple R5985, 23 March 1973
US: Apple 1861, 9 April 1973
Live And Let Die/I Lie Around
UK: Apple R5987, 1 June 1973
US: Apple 1863, 18 June 1973

Helen Wheels/Country Dreamer
UK: Apple R5993, 26 October 1973
US: Apple 1869, 12 November 1973

Jet/Let Me Roll It
UK: Apple R5996, 18 February 1974
US: Apple 1871, 28 January 1974

Band On The Run/Zoo Gang
UK: Apple R5997, 28 June 1974
Band On The Run Nineteen Hundred And Eighty-Five
US: Apple 1873, 8 April 1974

Junior's Farm/Sally G
UK: Apple R5999, 25 October 1974

WINGS

Give Ireland Back To The Irish/Give Ireland Back to The Irish
  (Instrumental)
UK: Apple R 5936, 25 February 1972
US: Apple 1847, 28 February 1972

Mary Had A Little Lamb/Little Woman Love
UK: Apple R5949, 5 May 1972
US: Apple 1851, 29 May 1972

Hi Hi Hi/C Moon
UK: Apple R5973, 1 December 1972
US: Apple 1857, 4 December 1972

Listen To What The Man Said/Love In Song
UK: Capitol R6006, 16 May 1975
US: Capitol 4091, 23 May 1975

Letting Go/You Gave Me The Answer
UK: Capitol R6008, 18 October 1975
US: Capitol 4145, 4 October 1975

Venus And Mars-Rock Show/Magneto And Titanium Man
UK: Capitol R6010, 28 November 1975
US: Capitol 4175, 27 October 1975

Silly Love Songs/Cook Of The House
UK: Parlophone R6014, 30 April 1976
US: Capitol 4293, 1 April 1976

Maybe I'm Amazed/Soily
UK: Parlophone R6017, 4 February 1977
US: Capitol 4385, 7 February 1977

Mull Of Kintyre/Girls School
UK: Capitol R6018, 11 November 1977
US: Capitol 4505, 14 November 1977

With A Little Luck/Backwards Traveller-Cuff Link
UK: Parlophone R6019, 23 March 1978
US: Capitol 4559, 20 March 1978

I've Had Enough/Deliver Your Children
UK: Parlophone R6020, 15 September 1978
US: Capitol 4594, 12 June 1978

London Town/I'm Carrying
UK: Parlophone R6021, 15 September 1978
US: Capitol 4625, 21 August 1978

Goodnight Tonight/Daytime Nighttime Suffering
UK: Parlophone 12YR6023, 23 March 1979
US: Columbia 3-10939, 15 March 1979
Old Siam, Sir/Spin It On
UK: Parlophone R6026, 1 June 1979

Arrow Through Me/Old Siam, Sir
US: Columbia 1-11070, 14 August 1979

Getting Closer/Baby's Request
UK: Parlophone R6027, 10 August 1979

Getting Closer/Spin It On
US: Columbia 3-11020, 5 June 1979

MISCELLANEOUS RELEASES

The Country Hams
Walking In The Park With Eloise/Bridge Over The River Suite
UK: EMI 2220, 18 October 1974
US: EMI 3977, 2 December 1974

Percy 'Thrills' Thrillington
Uncle Albert-Admiral Halsey/Eat At Home
UK: Regal Zonophone EMI 2594, 22 April 1977

Percy 'Thrills' Thrillington
Thrillington
UK: Regal Zonophone EMC3175, 29 April 1977
Too Many People/3 Legs/Ram On/Dear Boy/Uncle Albert-Admiral Halsey/
    Smile Away/Heart Of The Country/Monkberry Moon Delight/Eat At
    Home/Long Haired Lady/The Back Seat Of My Car

Suzy And The Red Stripes
Seaside Woman/B Side To Seaside
UK: A&M AASP7461, 10 August 1979/A&M AMS 7458, 18 July 1980
US: EPIC 8-504403, 31 May 1977

Selected Gigography

1972

9 February – Nottingham University, Nottingham, UK
10 February – Goodricke College Dining Room, University of York, York, UK
11 February – Hull University, Hull, UK
13 February – Newcastle University, Newcastle, UK
14 February – Lancaster University, Lancaster, UK
16 February – Leeds Town Hall, Leeds, UK
17 February – Sheffield University, Sheffield, UK
21 February – Birmingham University, Birmingham, UK
22 February – Swansea University, Swansea, UK
23 February – Oxford University, Oxford, UK
9 July – Centre Culturel, Châteauvallon, France
12 July – Juan-les-Pins, Juan-les-Pins, France
13 July – Théatre Antique, Arles, France
16 July – Olympia Théatre, Paris, France
18 July – Zirkus-Krone-Bau, Munich, Germany
19 July – Offenbach-Halle, Frankfurt, Germany
21 July – Kongresshaus, Zurich, Switzerland
22 July – Pavilion, Montreux, Switzerland
1 August – KB Hallen, Copenhagen, Denmark
4 August – Messuhalli, Helsinki, Finland
5 August – Kupittaan Urheiluhalli, Turku, Finland
7 August – Kungliga Tennishallen, Stockholm, Sweden
8 August – Idretshalle, Örebro, Sweden

9 August – Njaardhallen, Oslo, Norway

10 August – Scandinavium Halle, Gothenburg, Sweden

11 August – Olympen, Lund, Sweden

12 August – Fyns Forum, Odense, Denmark

14 August – Vejiby-Risskov Hallen, Aarhus, Denmark

16 August – Rhinehalle, Düsseldorf, West Germany

17 August – De Doelen, Rotterdam, The Netherlands

19 August – Evenementenhal, Groningen, The Netherlands

20 August – Concertgebouw, Amsterdam, The Netherlands

21 August – Concertgebouw, Amsterdam, The Netherlands

22 August – Ciné Roma, Antwerp, Belgium

24 August – Deutschlandhalle, West Berlin, West Germany

1973

18 March – Hard Rock Café, London, UK (Benefit concert for the charity Release)

11 May – Hippodrome, Bristol, UK

12 May – New Theatre, Oxford, UK

13 May – Capitol Cinema, Cardiff, UK

15 May – Winter Gardens, Bournemouth, UK

16 May – Hard Rock, Manchester, UK

17 May – Hard Rock, Manchester, UK

18 May – Empire Theatre, Liverpool, UK (two performances)

19 May – Leeds University, Leeds, UK

21 May – Guildhall, Preston, UK

22 May – Odeon Cinema, Newcastle, UK

23 May – Odeon Cinema, Edinburgh, UK (two performances)

24 May – Green's Playhouse, Glasgow, UK

25 May – Odeon Cinema, Hammersmith, London, UK

26 May – Odeon Cinema, Hammersmith, London, UK

27 May – Odeon Cinema, Hammersmith, London, UK

4 July – City Hall, Sheffield, UK

6 July – Odeon Cinema, Birmingham, UK

9 July – Odeon Cinema, Leicester, UK

10 July – City Hall, Newcastle, UK

1975

6 September – Elstree Film Studios, UK (warm-up)

9 September – Gaumont Cinema, Southampton, UK

10 September – Hippodrome, Bristol, UK

11 September – Capitol Cinema, Cardiff, UK

12 September – Free Trade Hall, Manchester, UK

13 September – Hippodrome, Birmingham, UK

15 September – Empire Theatre, Liverpool, UK

16 September – City Hall, Newcastle, UK

17 September – Odeon Cinema, Hammersmith, London, UK

18 September – Odeon Cinema, Hammersmith, London, UK

20 September – Usher Hall, Edinburgh, UK

21 September – Apollo Theatre, Glasgow, UK

22 September – Capitol Cinema, Aberdeen, UK

23 September – Caird Hall, Dundee, UK

1 November – Entertainment Centre, Perth, Australia

4 November – Apollo Stadium, Adelaide, Australia

5 November – Apollo Stadium, Adelaide, Australia

7 November – Hordern Pavilion, Sydney, Australia

8 November – Hordern Pavilion, Sydney, Australia

10 November – Festival Hall, Brisbane, Australia

11 November – Festival Hall, Brisbane, Australia

13 November – Sidney Myer Music Bowl, Melbourne, Australia

14 November – Sidney Myer Music Bowl, Melbourne, Australia

1976

20 March – Falkoner Theatre, Copenhagen, Denmark

21 March – Falkoner Theatre, Copenhagen, Denmark

23 March – Deutschlandhalle, West Berlin, West Germany

25 March – Ahoy Sportpaleis, Rotterdam, The Netherlands

26 March – Pavillon de Paris, Paris, France

3 May – Tarrant County Convention Center, Fort Worth, Texas, USA

4 May – The Summit, Houston, Texas, USA

7 May – Olympia Stadium, Detroit, Michigan, USA

8 May – Olympia Stadium, Detroit, Michigan, USA

9 May – Maple Leaf Gardens, Toronto, Canada
10 May – Richfield Coliseum, Richfield, Ohio, USA
12 May – The Spectrum, Philadelphia, Pennsylvania, USA
14 May – The Spectrum, Philadelphia, Pennsylvania, USA
15 May – Capital Center, Landover, Maryland, USA
16 May – Capital Center, Landover, Maryland, USA
18 May – Omni Coliseum, Atlanta, Georgia, USA
19 May – Omni Coliseum, Atlanta, USA
21 May – Nassau Coliseum, Uniondale, New York, USA
22 May – Boston Garden, Boston, Massachusetts, USA
24 May – Madison Square Garden, New York City, USA
25 May – Madison Square Garden, New York City, USA
27 May – Riverfront Coliseum, Cincinnati, Ohio, USA
29 May – Kemper Arena, Kansas City, Missouri, USA
31 May – Chicago Stadium, Chicago, Illinois, USA
1 June – Chicago Stadium, Chicago, Illinois, USA
2 June – Chicago Stadium, Chicago, Illinois, USA
4 June – Civic Center, St Paul, Minnesota, USA
7 June – McNichols Sports Arena, Denver, Colorado, USA
10 June – Kingdome, Seattle, Washington, USA
13 June – Cow Palace, San Francisco, California, USA
14 June – Cow Palace, San Francisco, California, USA
16 June – Sports Arena, San Diego, California, USA
18 June – Community Center Music Hall, Tucson, Arizona, USA
21 June – Forum, Los Angeles, California, USA
22 June – Forum, Los Angeles, California, USA
23 June – Forum, Los Angeles, California, USA
19 September – Stadthalle, Vienna, Austria
21 September – Dom Sportova, Zagreb, Yugoslavia
25 September – St Mark's Square, Venice, Italy (Benefit concert for Unesco/ Venice in Peril)
27 September – Olympiahalle, Munich, West Germany
19 October – Empire Pool, Wembley, London, UK
20 October – Empire Pool, Wembley, London, UK
21 October – Empire Pool, Wembley, London, UK

1979

23 November – Royal Court Theatre, Liverpool, UK
24 November – Royal Court Theatre, Liverpool, UK
25 November – Royal Court Theatre, Liverpool, UK
26 November – Royal Court Theatre, Liverpool, UK
28 November – Apollo Theatre, Manchester, UK
29 November – Apollo Theatre, Manchester, UK
 1 December – Gaumont Cinema, Southampton, UK
 2 December – Brighton Centre, Brighton, UK
 3 December – Odeon Cinema, Lewisham, London, UK
 5 December – Rainbow Theatre, Finsbury Park, London, UK
 7 December – Empire Pool, Wembley, London, UK
 8 December – Empire Pool, Wembley, London, UK
 9 December – Empire Pool, Wembley, London, UK
10 December – Empire Pool, Wembley, London, UK
12 December – Odeon Cinema, Birmingham, UK
14 December – City Hall, Newcastle, UK
15 December – Odeon Cinema, Edinburgh, UK
16 December – Apollo Theatre, Glasgow, UK
17 December – Apollo Theatre, Glasgow, UK
29 December – Odeon Cinema, Hammersmith, London, UK (Benefit performance for Concerts for the People of Kampuchea)

Bibliography

Badman, Keith, *The Beatles after the Break-Up 1970–2000: A Day-by-Day Diary* (London, Omnibus, 1999)

Baker, Ginger, with Ginette Baker, *Ginger Baker – Hellraiser* (London, John Blake, 2009)

Beatles, The, *The Beatles Anthology* (London, Weidenfeld & Nicolson, 2000)

Blaney, John, *Lennon and McCartney, Together Alone: A Critical Discography of the Solo Work* (New York/London, Jawbone Press, 2007)

Blaney, John, *Paul McCartney: The Songs He Was Singing, Vol.1 The Seventies* (Paper Jukebox, 2010)

Carlin, Peter Ames, *Paul McCartney: A Life* (New York: JR Books Ltd, 2009)

Clayson, Alan, *Paul McCartney* (London, Sanctuary, 2003)

Coleman, Ray: *McCartney – Yesterday . . . and Today* (London, Boxtree, 1995)

Connolly, Ray, *The Ray Connolly Beatles Archive* (London, Plumray, 2011)

Davies, Hunter, *The Beatles: The Authorised Biography* (London, Ebury Press, 2009)

Doggett, Peter, *You Never Give Me Your Money: The Battle for the Soul of The Beatles* (London, Vintage, 2010)

Emerick, Geoff & Massey, Howard *Here, There And Everywhere: My Life Recording the Music of The Beatles* (New York, Gotham Books, 2006)

Fields, Danny, *Linda McCartney: The Biography* (London, Little, Brown & Co., 2000)

Fletcher, Tony, *Dear Boy: The Life of Keith Moon* (London, Omnibus Press, 1998)

Flippo, Chet, *McCartney: The Biography* (London, Sidgwick & Jackson, 1988)

Gambaccini, Paul, *Paul McCartney: In His Own Words* (New York/London, Omnibus Press, 1976)

Gambaccini, Paul, *The McCartney Interviews: After the Break-up* (London, Omnibus Press, 1996)

Gelly, David, *The Facts About a Pop Group* (London, André Deutsch, 1976)

Giuliano, Geoffrey, *Blackbird: The Life and Times of Paul McCartney* (London, Penguin Books, 1991)

Harry, Bill, *The Encyclopaedia of Beatles People* (London, Cassell Illustrated, 1997)

Jackson, Michael: *Moonwalk* (New York, Doubleday, 1988)

MacDonald, Ian, *Revolution in the Head: The Beatles' Records and the Sixties* (London, Henry Holt & Co., 1994)

McCartney, Paul, *Wingspan: Paul McCartney's Band on the Run* (London, Little, Brown & Co., 2002)

McGee, Garry, *Band on the Run: A History of Paul McCartney and Wings* (New York, Taylor Trade Publishing, 2003)

McNab, Ken, *The Beatles in Scotland* (Edinburgh, Polygon, 2008)

Martin, George, *All You Need Is Ears* (New York, St Martin's Press, 1995)

Miles, Barry, *Paul McCartney: Many Years from Now* (London, Secker & Warburg, 1997)

Moore, Carlos, *Fela – This Bitch of a Life* (London, Allison and Busby, 1982)

Norman, Philip: *Shout! The True Story of The Beatles* (New York, Simon & Schuster, 1981)

Norman, Philip, *John Lennon: The Life* (London, HarperCollins, 2008)

Pascall, Jeremy, *Paul McCartney and Wings* (London, Littlehampton Book Services Ltd, 1977)

Sandford, Christopher, *McCartney* (London, Century, 2006)

Seaman, Frederic, *John Lennon: Living on Borrowed Time* (London, Xanadu, 1993)

Sounes, Howard, *Fab: An Intimate Life of Paul McCartney* (London, HarperCollins, 2010)

Tremlett, George, *The Paul McCartney Story* (London, White Lion Publishers, 1976)

Welch, Chris, *Paul McCartney: The Definitive Biography* (New York, Proteus Books, 1984)

Index

Acknowledgements

For their generous interview time and for quotes that made their way into this book, thanks to Paul McCartney, Ringo Starr, Yoko Ono, Michael Parkinson, May Pang, Denny Laine, Denny Seiwell, Henry McCullough, Clive Arrowsmith, Laurence Juber, Steve Holley, Robert Ellis, Dave Clarke, Bob Gruen, Robin Black, Alan Parsons, Howie Casey, Jimmy McGeachy and Jimmy Iovine. For allowing me to use additional transcripts of interviews with Denny Laine and Denny Seiwell, thanks to Tom O'Dell and Elio Espana of Prism Films.

Thanks also to Phil Alexander and Paul Rees, under whose editorships the original McCartney interviews were conducted for *Mojo* and *Q*. For continuing to employ me and putting up with me in general, not to mention indulging my frequent disappearing acts while writing this book, I'd like to thank: Danny Eccleston (and his idea for the interstitial quotes), Ian Harrison, Andrew Male, Jenny Bulley, Ross Bennett, Mark Wagstaff, Andrew Harrison, Ted Kessler, Chris Catchpole, Niall Doherty, Matt Mason, James Mannion, Gordon Thomson and Sam Inglis. To my writerly comrades – keep the faith, people: Sylvia Patterson (the big sister I never wanted), John Aizlewood, Craig McLean, Mark Blake, Andy Fyfe, Dave Everley, Mark Ellen, John Harris, Gareth Grundy, Helena Drakakis, Louise Millar, Allan Brown and Daryl Easlea.

Very special thanks to Simon Goddard for his Staropramen-induced, lightbulb-above-the-head notion that gave this book its title, and to Dorian Lynskey, who also came up with the same title, only just a bit later.

To all at Polygon: Neville Moir, Sarah Morrison, Vikki Reilly, Jan Rutherford and especially my utterly ace editor, Alison Rae, who calmly extended my deadline more than once with a reassuring 'Oh, don't *worry*.' To my unflappable agent Kevin Pocklington at Jenny Brown Associates, for 'getting' this book and getting it off the ground.

Additional thanks to Stuart Bell at DawBell and to Claudia Schmid at MPL.

For allowing me to bore them senseless in the pub about Paul McCartney for an entire year: Anth Brown, Mike Brown, Steve Aungle, Derek Hood, Steve Wilkins, Dave Black, Dave Scott, Nick Roberts, Paul Esposito, Sophie Mayerhoeffer, Robbie and Parm Gunn-Hamilton, Alan Shaw (who's still wrong about 'Smile Away'), Allan Shanks, Aidan Rose, Kieran Leonard, Martin Low, Steve Hands, Dave Tomlinson, Jon Bennett, Steve Donoghue, Kris O'Mahoney, Nick Holywell-Walker, Jon Mills and Gary Clark. For simply just encouraging me or sorting stuff or helping with research: the McCombies, Paul Salley, Lorraine Wilson, Roddy Isles, Linda Barclay Isles, Rosha Kasravi, Richard and Ben at Audio Gold, Nick de Grunwald at Isis Productions.

To my family up in Scotland, for understanding why I didn't phone so often: Dad and Heather, Brian, Caroline and Ryan. And to the all-knowing, all-suffering, saintly patient love of my life, Karen, and to Milly, who manages to get bigger and cheekier and funnier and cleverer and more beautiful with every day.

T.D.